UNCA[…] AVENGERS

D1289087

AXIS PRELUDE

CANNY AVENGERS #23
WRITER
ICK REMENDER
ARTIST
NFORD GREENE
COLOR ARTIST
DEAN WHITE
COVER ART
AGUSTIN ALESSIO

MAGNETO #9-10
WRITER
CULLEN BUNN
ARTISTS
GABRIEL HERNANDEZ WALTA
WITH JAVIER FERNANDEZ (#10)
COLOR ARTISTS
JORDIE BELLAIRE WITH DAN BROWN (#10)
COVER ART
DAVID YARDIN

UNCANNY AVENGERS #24
WRITER
RICK REMENDER
ARTIST
SALVADOR LARROCA
COLOR ARTIST
DEAN WHITE
COVER ART
PAUL RENAUD

CANNY AVENGERS #25
WRITER
RICK REMENDER
ARTIST
DANIEL ACUÑA
COVER ART
PAUL RENAUD

UNCANNY AVENGERS ANNUAL #1
WRITER
RICK REMENDER
ARTIST
PAUL RENAUD
COVER ART
ARTHUR ADAMS & JASON KEITH

LETTERERS
VC'S CLAYTON COWLES
(UNCANNY AVENGERS)
& VC'S CORY PETIT (MAGNETO)
ASSISTANT EDITOR
XANDER JAROWEY
EDITORS
TOM BREVOORT
& DANIEL KETCHUM

AVENGERS CREATED BY STAN LEE & JACK KIRBY

EVIOUSLY: UNABLE TO COME TOGETHER AS A COHESIVE TEAM, THE AVENGERS UNITY SQUAD FAILED TO STOP TIME-TRAVELING ERMIND KANG THE CONQUEROR FROM OBLITERATING THE EARTH. AFTER ENDURING YEARS ON PLANET X, THE AVENGERS RETURNED TO THE PAST AND, WITH THE HELP OF IMMORTUS AND HIS INFINITY WATCH, THEY DEFEATED KANG AND SAVED EARTH.

THE VICTORY WAS NOT WITHOUT COST: IN THE FINAL BATTLE WITH KANG, SUNFIRE'S BODY WAS DESTROYED, LEAVING HIM A BEING NSTITUTED ENTIRELY OF COSMIC FIRE. AND CAUGHT IN THE BLAST OF SUNFIRE'S DETONATION, HAVOK'S FACE WAS BURNED AND GURED. MEANWHILE, ROGUE USED THE COMBINED POWERS OF EARTH'S HEROES TO DEFEND THE PLANET. BUT WHILE SHE WAS ABLE UCCESSFULLY RETURN MOST OF THE BORROWED POWERS, WONDER MAN WAS TRAPPED INSIDE ROGUE'S PSYCHE. AND HOPING TO OVER THE DAUGHTER THEY RAISED ON PLANET X, HAVOK AND WASP WERE HEARTBROKEN WHEN KANG AND HIS CHRONOS CORPS ESCAPED BACK INTO THE TIMESTREAM, TAKING ANY HOPE OF BEING REUNITED WITH THEIR DAUGHTER WITH THEM.

COLLECTION EDITOR: **JENNIFER GRÜNWALD** ASSISTANT EDITOR: **SARAH BRUNSTAD**
ASSOCIATE MANAGING EDITOR: **ALEX STARBUCK** EDITOR, SPECIAL PROJECTS: **MARK D. BEAZLEY**
SENIOR EDITOR, SPECIAL PROJECTS: **JEFF YOUNGQUIST** SVP PRINT, SALES & MARKETING: **DAVID GABRIEL**

EDITOR IN CHIEF: **AXEL ALONSO** CHIEF CREATIVE OFFICER: **JOE QUESADA**
PUBLISHER: **DAN BUCKLEY** EXECUTIVE PRODUCER: **ALAN FINE**

VENGERS VOL. 5: AXIS PRELUDE. Contains material originally published in magazine form as UNCANNY AVENGERS #23-25, MAGNETO #9-10 and UNCANNY AVENGERS ANNUAL #1. First printing 2015. ISBN# 978-0-7851-5426-6. MARVEL WORLDWIDE, INC., a subsidiary of MARVEL ENTERTAINMENT, LLC. OFFICE OF PUBLICATION: 135 West 50th Street, New York, NY 10020. **Printed in the U.S.A.** ALAN FINE, President, Marvel Entertainment; Y, President, TV, Publishing and Brand Management; JOE QUESADA, Chief Creative Officer; TOM BREVOORT, SVP of Publishing; DAVID BOGART, SVP of Operations & Procurement, Publishing; C.B. CEBULSKI, VP of International & Brand Management; DAVID GABRIEL, SVP Print, Sales & Marketing; JIM O'KEEFE, VP of Operations & Logistics; DAN CARR, Executive Director of Publishing Technology; SUSAN CRESPI, Editorial Operations Manager; ALEX ublishing Operations Manager; STAN LEE, Chairman Emeritus. For information regarding advertising in Marvel Comics or on Marvel.com, please contact Jonathan Rheingold, VP of Custom Solutions & Ad Sales, at jrheingold@ For Marvel subscription inquiries, please call 800-217-9158. **Manufactured between 6/5/2015 and 7/13/2015 by R.R. DONNELLEY, INC., SALEM, VA, USA.**

4321

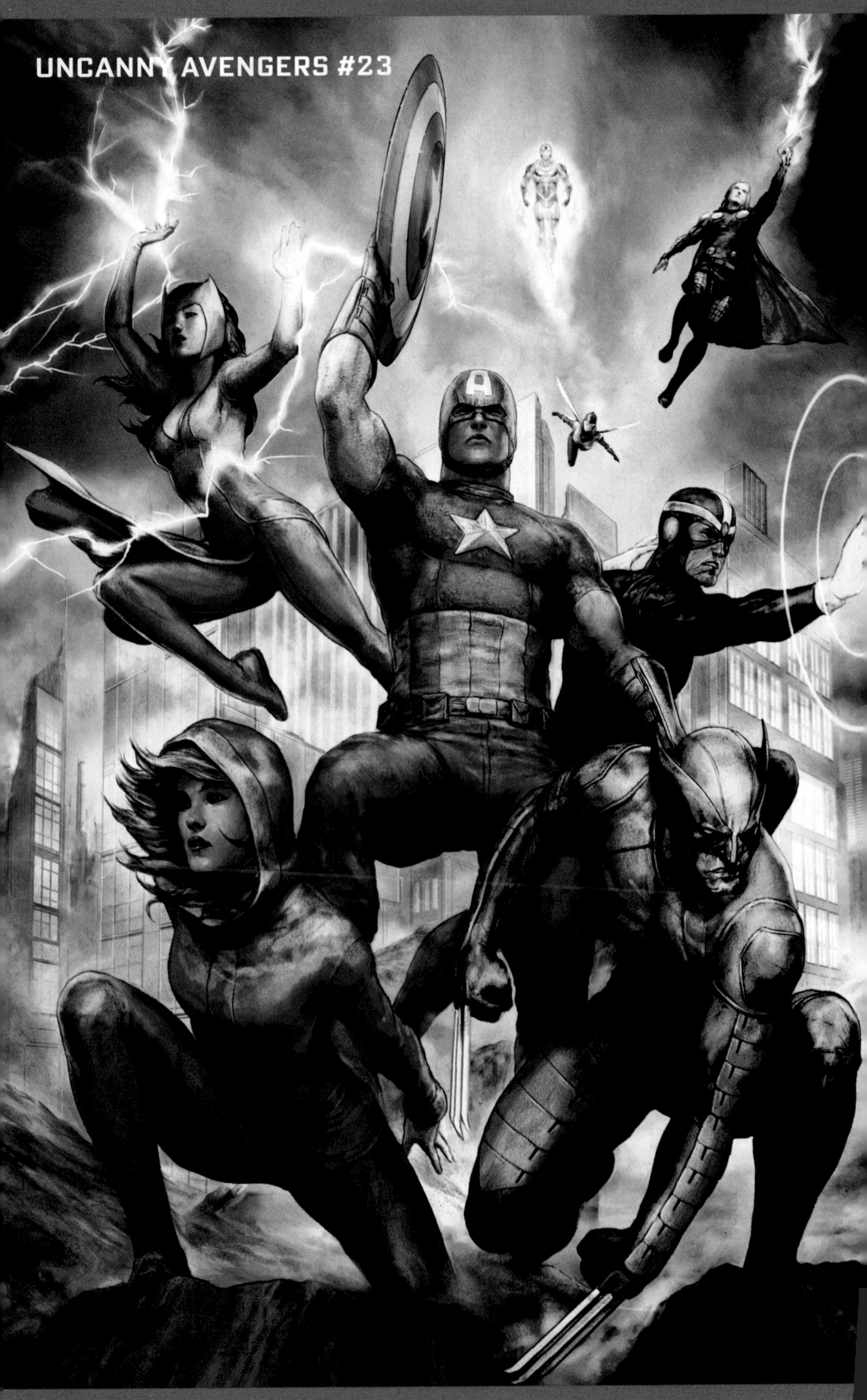
UNCANNY AVENGERS #23

AFTER SO MANY WEEKS AWAY, THE SIGHT OF MANHATTAN *SHOULD* BRING JOY. NOT JUST TO BE HOME, BUT THE COMING REUNION AS WELL.

BUT INSTEAD I FEEL *ANXIOUS.*

I SHOULD BE HAPPY, AND THE FACT I'M *NOT...*

...ONLY MAKES EVERYTHING ELSE FEEL THAT MUCH *WORSE.*

WE *COULD* TURN AROUND, JANET. GO BACK TO YOUR FATHER'S CABIN, HIDE OUT FOREVER.

A *BEAUTIFUL* FANTASY, WANDA.

IT'S BEEN A MUCH-NEEDED SABBATICAL, BUT IT'S TIME TO COME HOME.

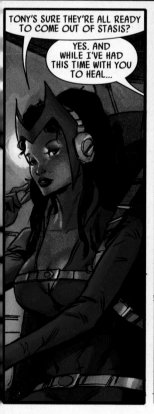

TONY'S SURE THEY'RE ALL READY TO COME OUT OF STASIS?

YES. AND WHILE I'VE HAD THIS TIME WITH YOU TO HEAL...

...ALEX WON'T HAVE HAD ANY TIME TO PROCESS THE LOSS OF...

I CAN'T EVEN SAY HER NAME.

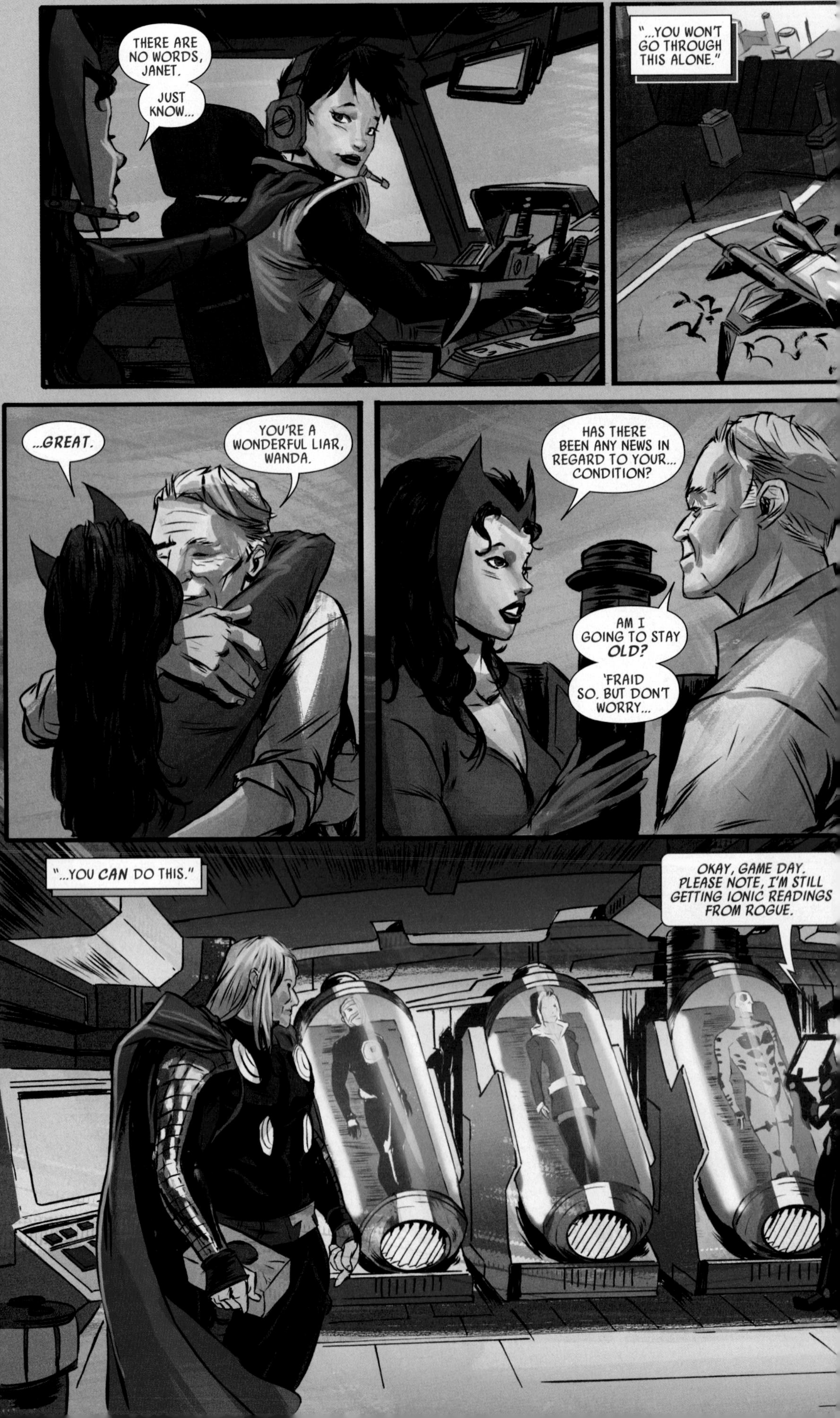
THERE ARE NO WORDS, JANET.
JUST KNOW...
"...YOU WON'T GO THROUGH THIS ALONE."
...GREAT.
YOU'RE A WONDERFUL LIAR, WANDA.
HAS THERE BEEN ANY NEWS IN REGARD TO YOUR... CONDITION?
AM I GOING TO STAY OLD?
'FRAID SO. BUT DON'T WORRY...
"...YOU CAN DO THIS."
OKAY, GAME DAY. PLEASE NOTE, I'M STILL GETTING IONIC READINGS FROM ROGUE.

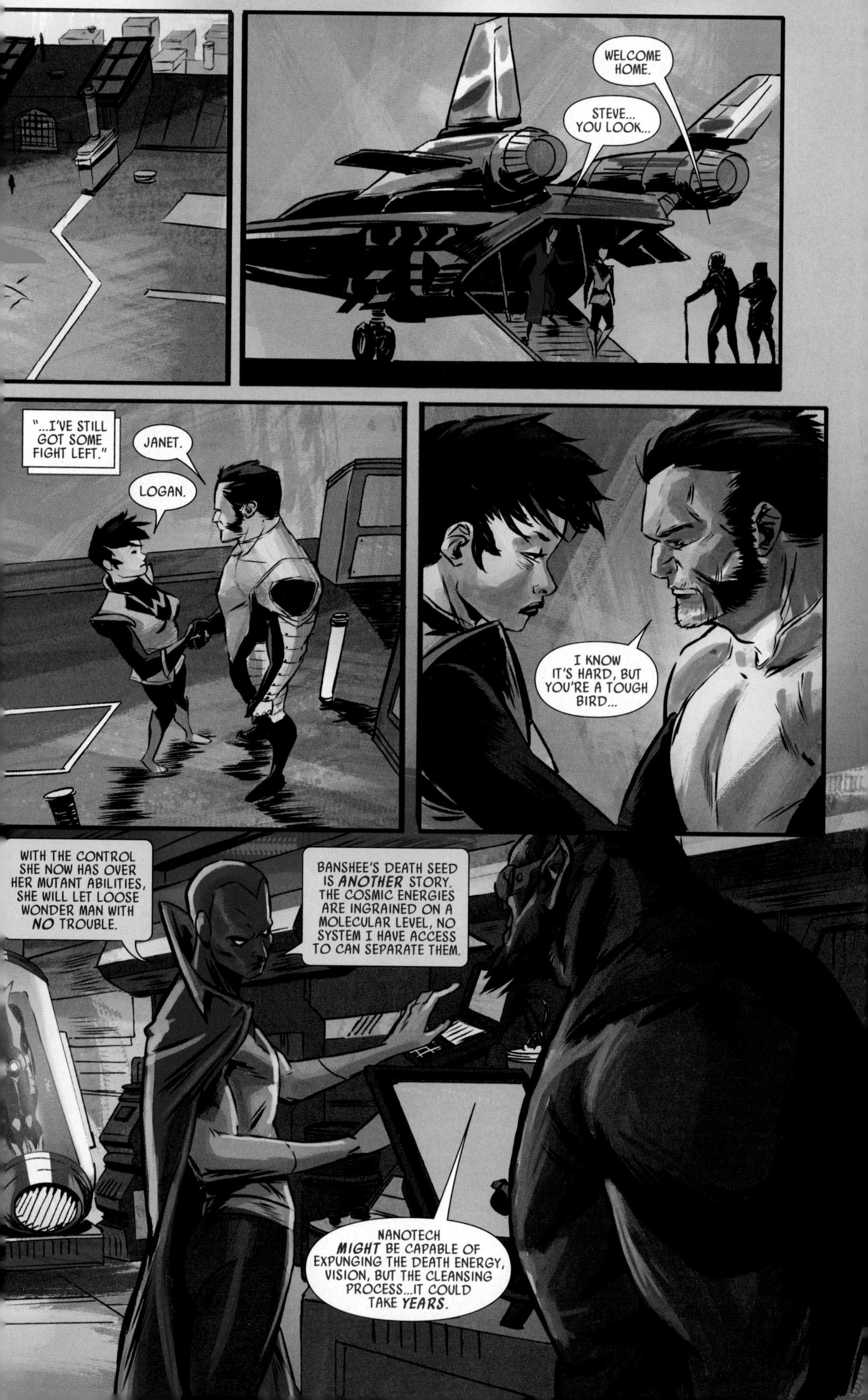

WELCOME HOME.
STEVE... YOU LOOK...
"...I'VE STILL GOT SOME FIGHT LEFT."
JANET.
LOGAN.
I KNOW IT'S HARD, BUT YOU'RE A TOUGH BIRD...
WITH THE CONTROL SHE NOW HAS OVER HER MUTANT ABILITIES, SHE WILL LET LOOSE WONDER MAN WITH NO TROUBLE.
BANSHEE'S DEATH SEED IS ANOTHER STORY. THE COSMIC ENERGIES ARE INGRAINED ON A MOLECULAR LEVEL, NO SYSTEM I HAVE ACCESS TO CAN SEPARATE THEM.
NANOTECH MIGHT BE CAPABLE OF EXPUNGING THE DEATH ENERGY, VISION, BUT THE CLEANSING PROCESS...IT COULD TAKE YEARS.

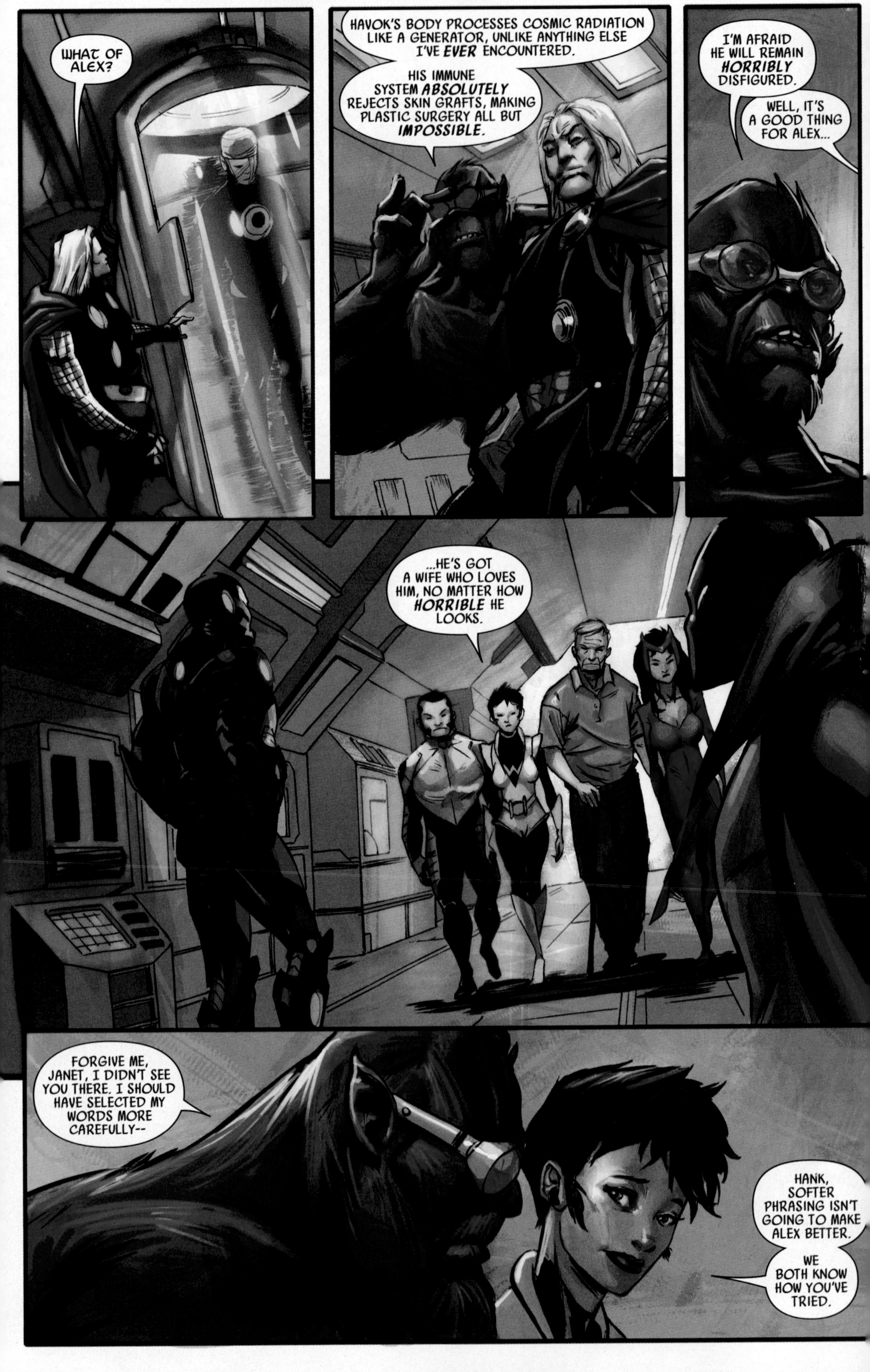
WHAT OF ALEX?
HAVOK'S BODY PROCESSES COSMIC RADIATION LIKE A GENERATOR, UNLIKE ANYTHING ELSE I'VE EVER ENCOUNTERED.
HIS IMMUNE SYSTEM ABSOLUTELY REJECTS SKIN GRAFTS, MAKING PLASTIC SURGERY ALL BUT IMPOSSIBLE.
I'M AFRAID HE WILL REMAIN HORRIBLY DISFIGURED.
WELL, IT'S A GOOD THING FOR ALEX...
...HE'S GOT A WIFE WHO LOVES HIM, NO MATTER HOW HORRIBLE HE LOOKS.
FORGIVE ME, JANET, I DIDN'T SEE YOU THERE. I SHOULD HAVE SELECTED MY WORDS MORE CAREFULLY--
HANK, SOFTER PHRASING ISN'T GOING TO MAKE ALEX BETTER.
WE BOTH KNOW HOW YOU'VE TRIED.

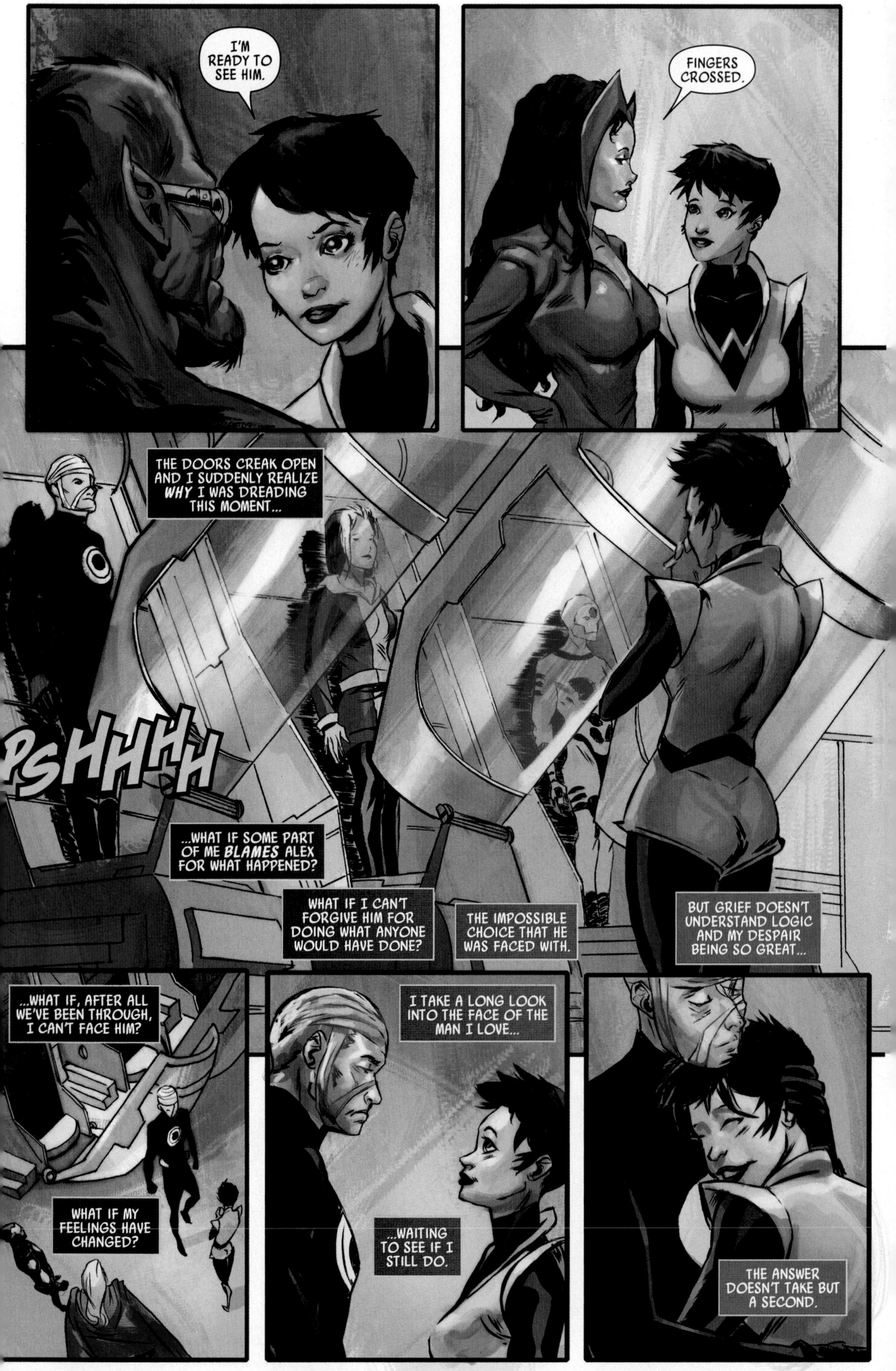
I'M READY TO SEE HIM.
FINGERS CROSSED.
THE DOORS CREAK OPEN AND I SUDDENLY REALIZE WHY I WAS DREADING THIS MOMENT...
PSHHHH
...WHAT IF SOME PART OF ME BLAMES ALEX FOR WHAT HAPPENED?
WHAT IF I CAN'T FORGIVE HIM FOR DOING WHAT ANYONE WOULD HAVE DONE?
THE IMPOSSIBLE CHOICE THAT HE WAS FACED WITH.
BUT GRIEF DOESN'T UNDERSTAND LOGIC AND MY DESPAIR BEING SO GREAT...
...WHAT IF, AFTER ALL WE'VE BEEN THROUGH, I CAN'T FACE HIM?
WHAT IF MY FEELINGS HAVE CHANGED?
I TAKE A LONG LOOK INTO THE FACE OF THE MAN I LOVE...
...WAITING TO SEE IF I STILL DO.
THE ANSWER DOESN'T TAKE BUT A SECOND.

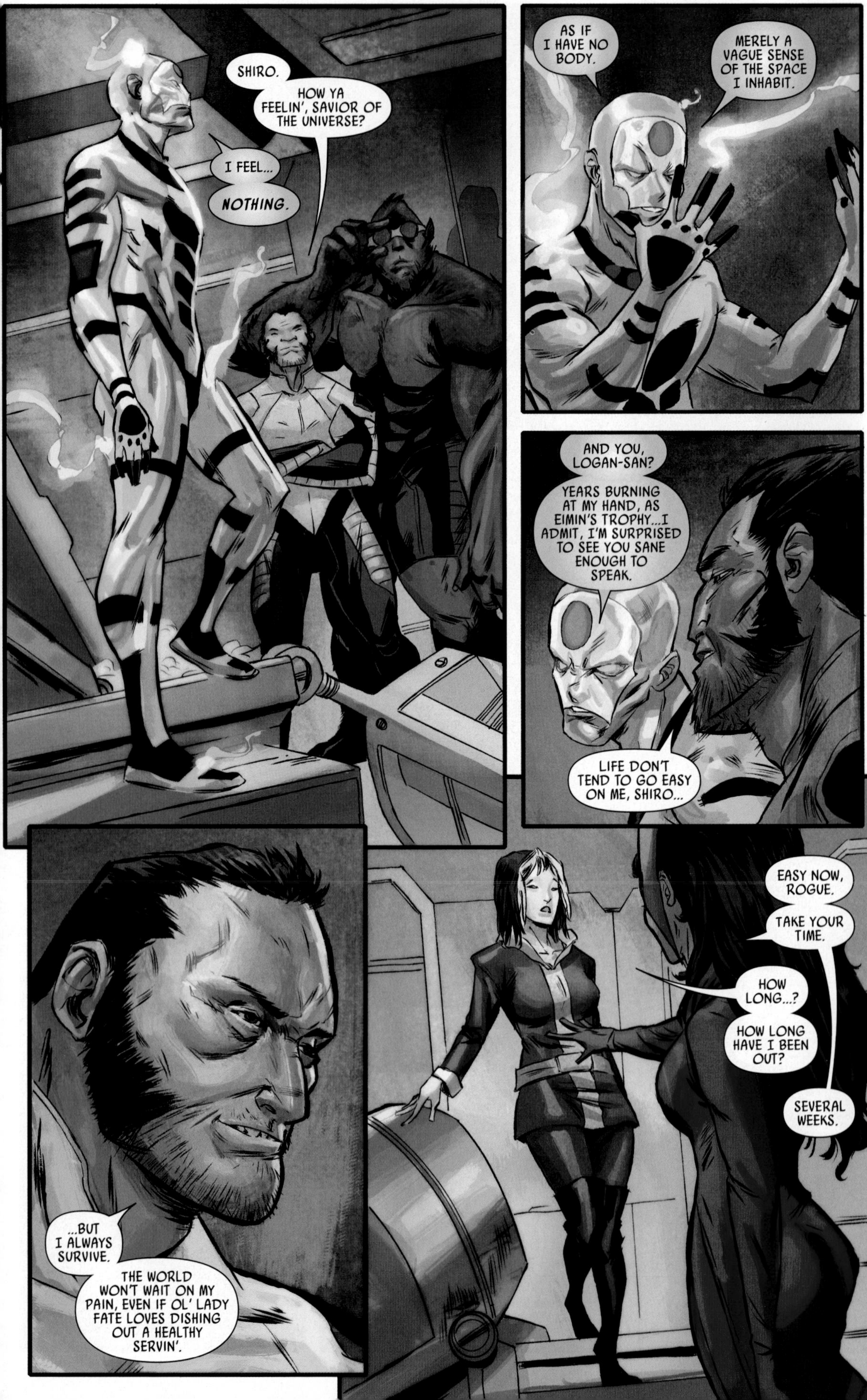
SHIRO.
HOW YA FEELIN', SAVIOR OF THE UNIVERSE?
I FEEL...
NOTHING.
AS IF I HAVE NO BODY.
MERELY A VAGUE SENSE OF THE SPACE I INHABIT.
AND YOU, LOGAN-SAN?
YEARS BURNING AT MY HAND, AS EIMIN'S TROPHY...I ADMIT, I'M SURPRISED TO SEE YOU SANE ENOUGH TO SPEAK.
LIFE DON'T TEND TO GO EASY ON ME, SHIRO...
...BUT I ALWAYS SURVIVE.
THE WORLD WON'T WAIT ON MY PAIN, EVEN IF OL' LADY FATE LOVES DISHING OUT A HEALTHY SERVIN'.
EASY NOW, ROGUE.
TAKE YOUR TIME.
HOW LONG...?
HOW LONG HAVE I BEEN OUT?
SEVERAL WEEKS.

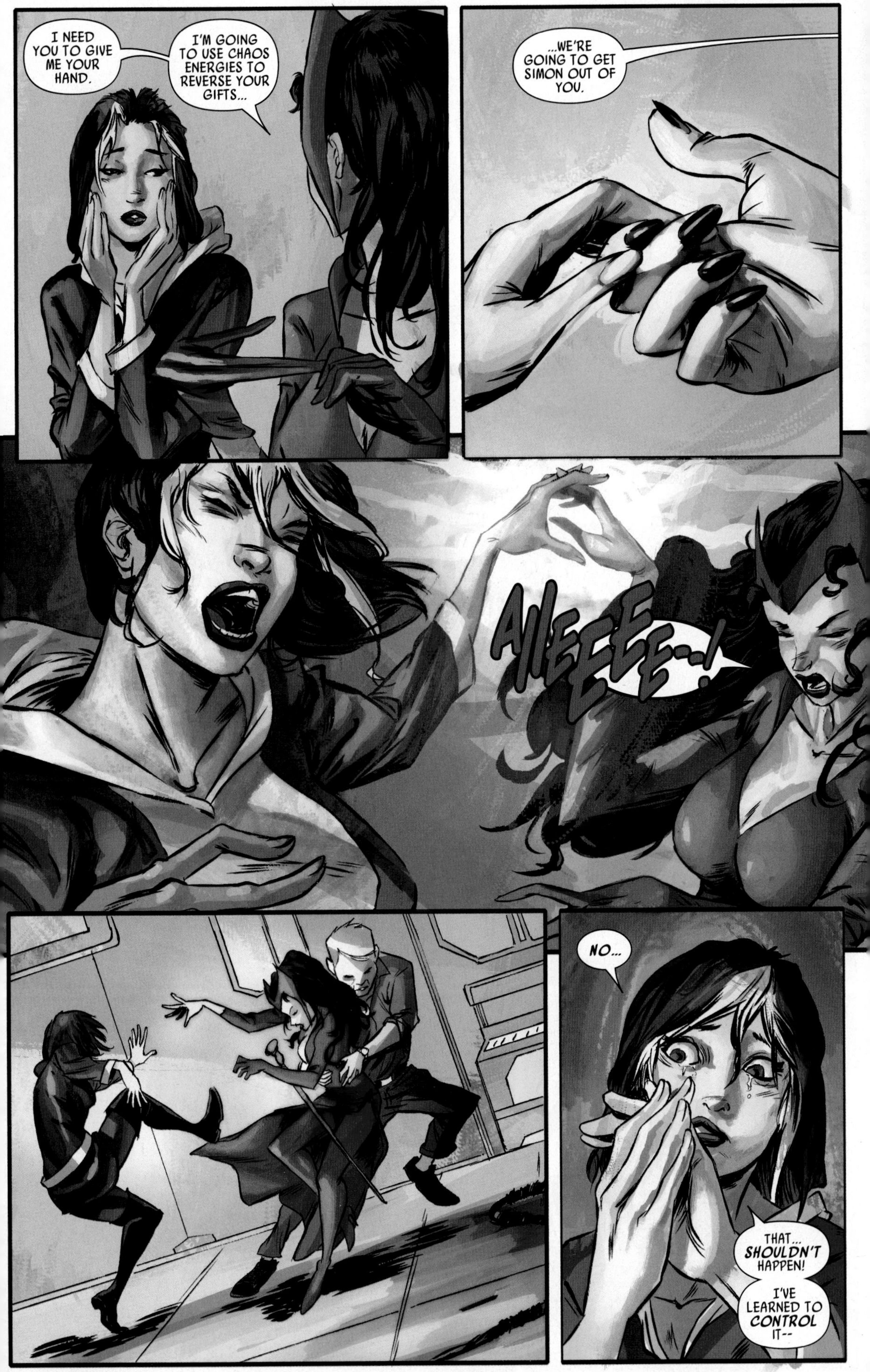
I NEED YOU TO GIVE ME YOUR HAND.
I'M GOING TO USE CHAOS ENERGIES TO REVERSE YOUR GIFTS...
...WE'RE GOING TO GET SIMON OUT OF YOU.
AIIEEEE--!
NO...
THAT... SHOULDN'T HAPPEN!
I'VE LEARNED TO CONTROL IT--

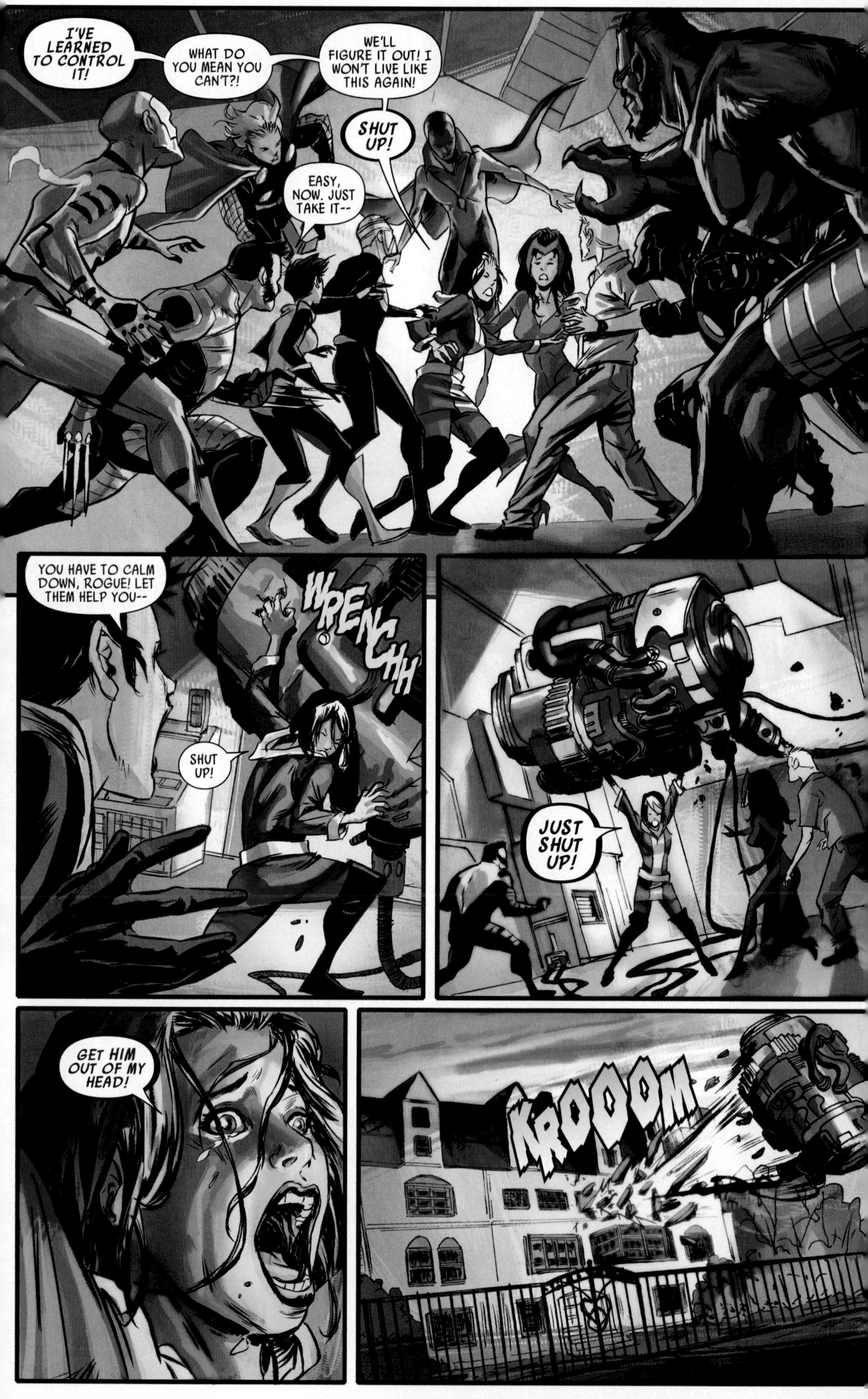
I'VE LEARNED TO CONTROL IT!
WHAT DO YOU MEAN YOU CAN'T?!
WE'LL FIGURE IT OUT! I WON'T LIVE LIKE THIS AGAIN!
SHUT UP!
EASY, NOW. JUST TAKE IT--
YOU HAVE TO CALM DOWN, ROGUE! LET THEM HELP YOU--
WRENCHH
SHUT UP!
JUST SHUT UP!
GET HIM OUT OF MY HEAD!
KROOOM

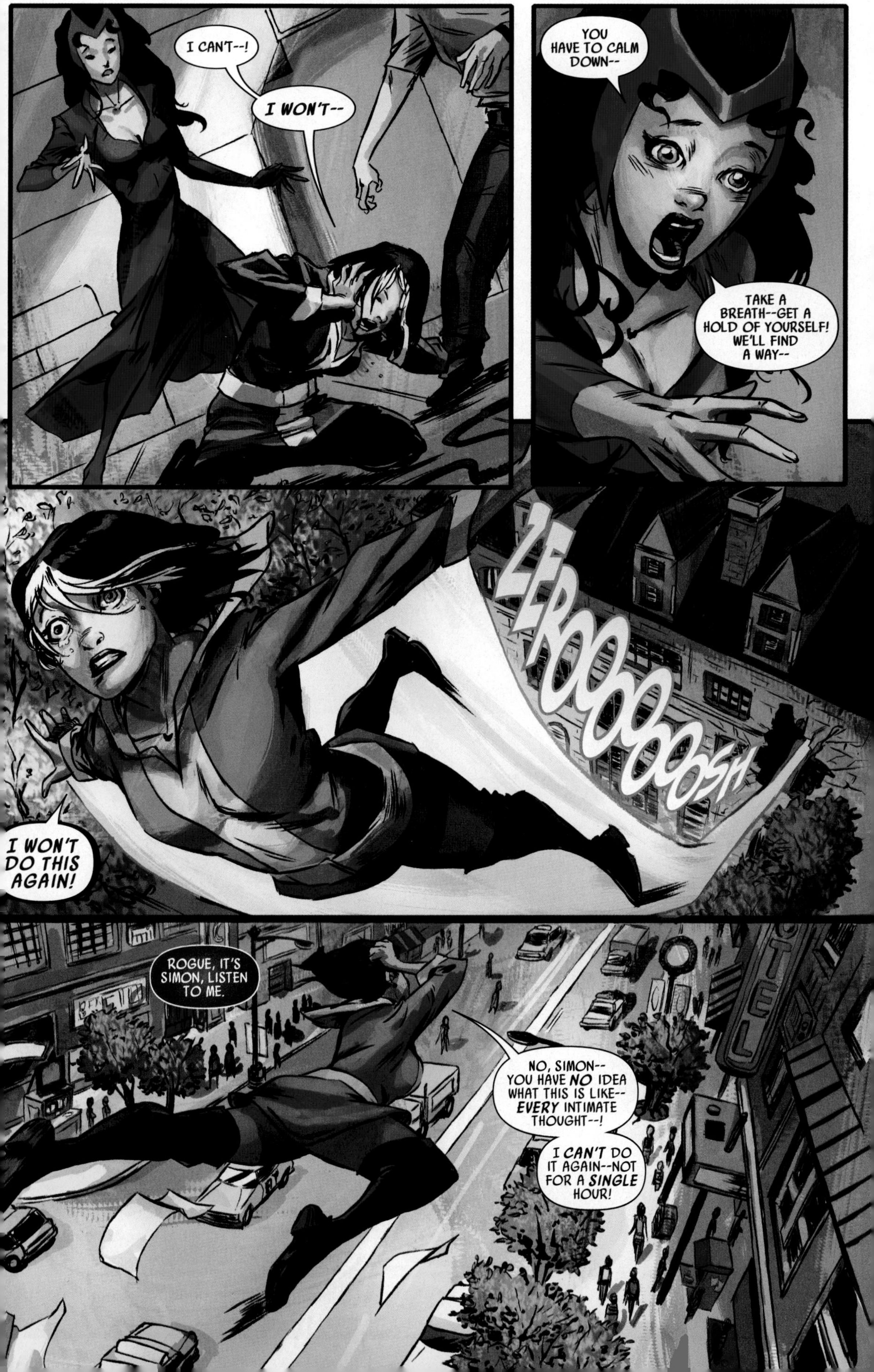
I CAN'T--!
I WON'T--
YOU HAVE TO CALM DOWN--
TAKE A BREATH--GET A HOLD OF YOURSELF! WE'LL FIND A WAY--
ZEROOOOOOOSH
I WON'T DO THIS AGAIN!
ROGUE, IT'S SIMON, LISTEN TO ME.
NO, SIMON-- YOU HAVE NO IDEA WHAT THIS IS LIKE-- EVERY INTIMATE THOUGHT--!
I CAN'T DO IT AGAIN--NOT FOR A SINGLE HOUR!

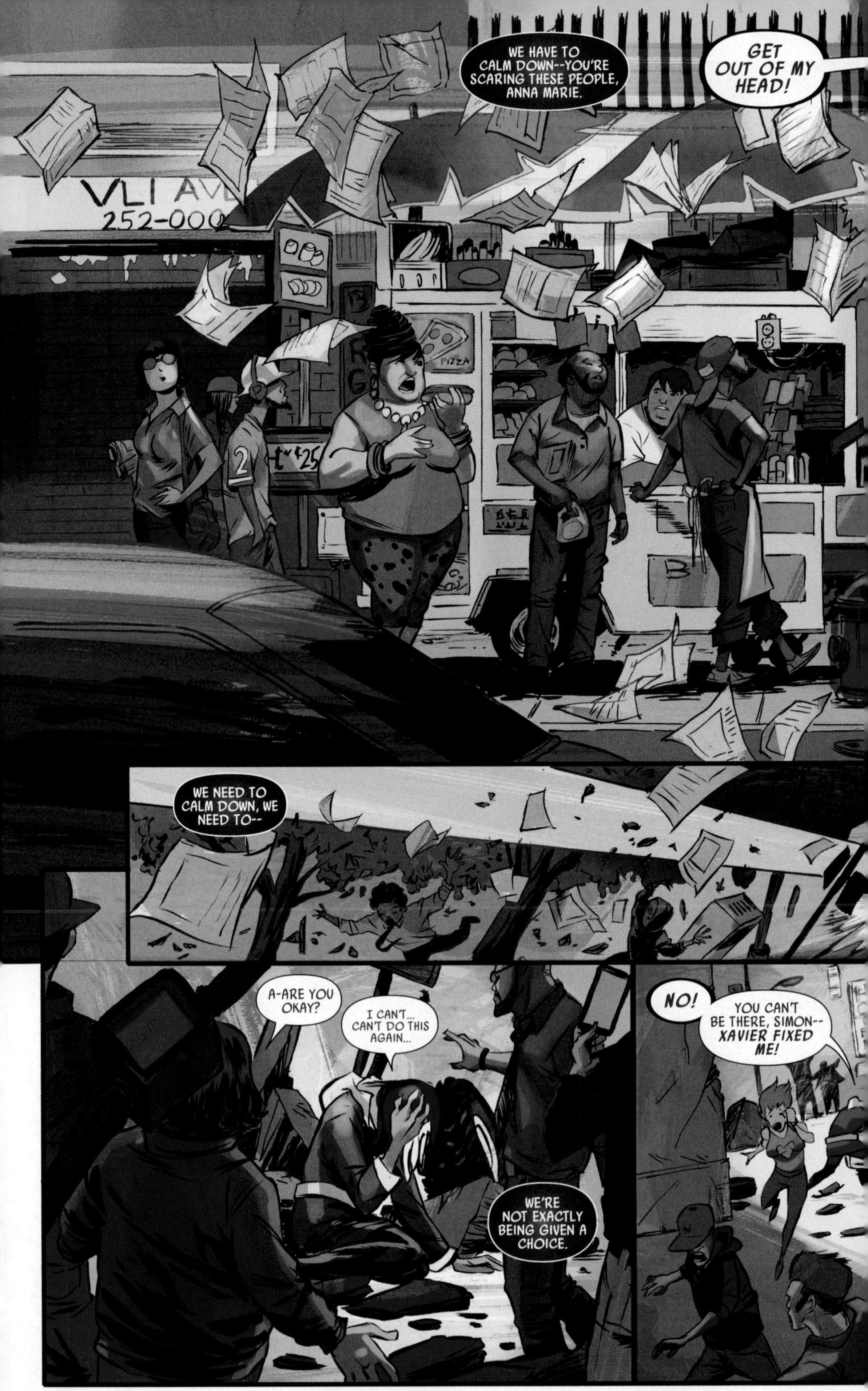

WE HAVE TO CALM DOWN--YOU'RE SCARING THESE PEOPLE, ANNA MARIE.
GET OUT OF MY HEAD!
VLI AVE
252-000
PIZZA
WE NEED TO CALM DOWN, WE NEED TO--
A-ARE YOU OKAY?
I CAN'T... CAN'T DO THIS AGAIN...
WE'RE NOT EXACTLY BEING GIVEN A CHOICE.
NO!
YOU CAN'T BE THERE, SIMON--XAVIER FIXED ME!

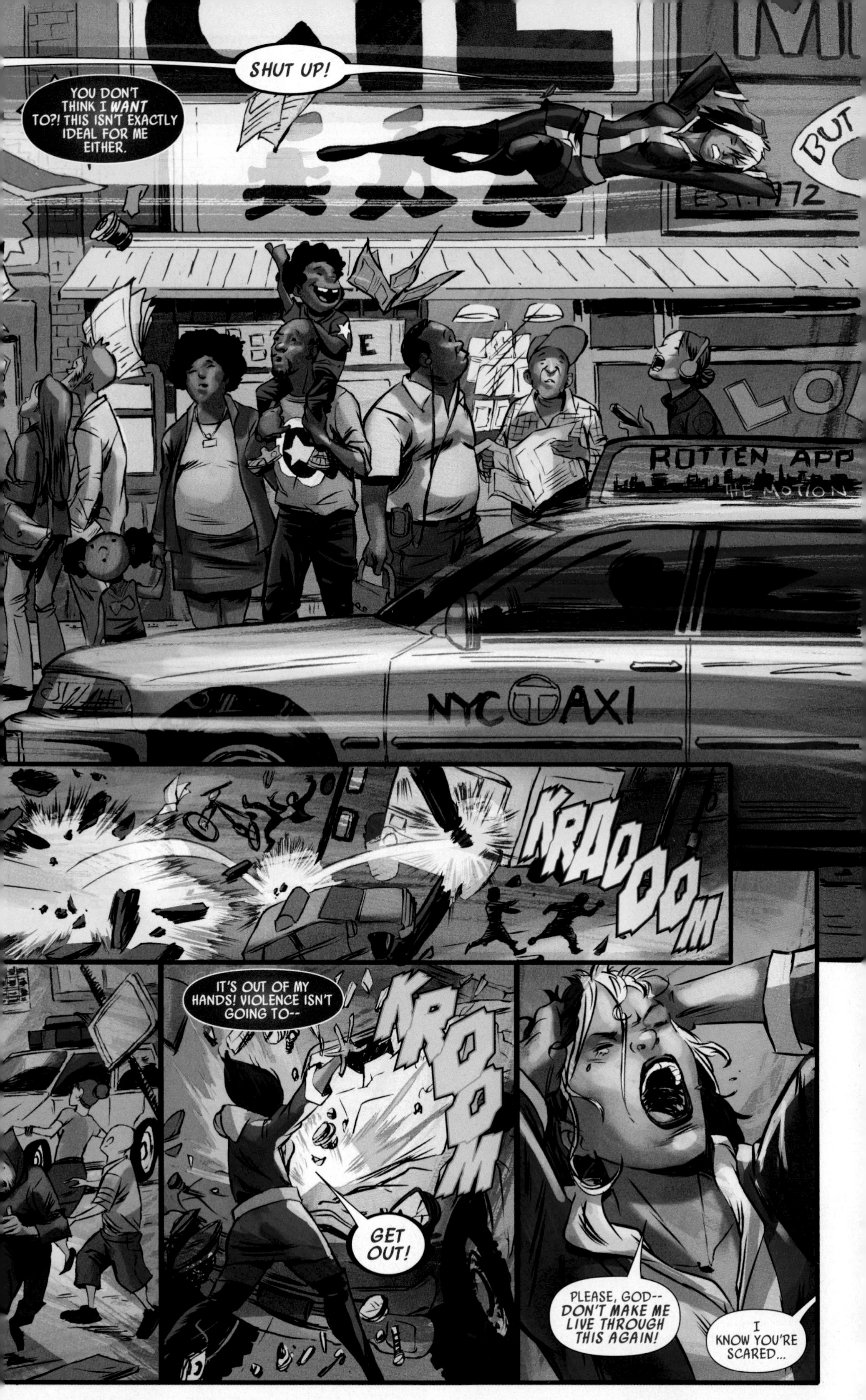
SHUT UP!
YOU DON'T THINK I *WANT* TO?! THIS ISN'T EXACTLY IDEAL FOR ME EITHER.
BUT
EST. 1972
ROTTEN APP
THE MOTION
NYC TAXI
KRADOOOM
IT'S OUT OF MY HANDS! VIOLENCE ISN'T GOING TO--
KROOOM
GET OUT!
PLEASE, GOD-- *DON'T MAKE ME LIVE THROUGH THIS AGAIN!*
I KNOW YOU'RE SCARED...

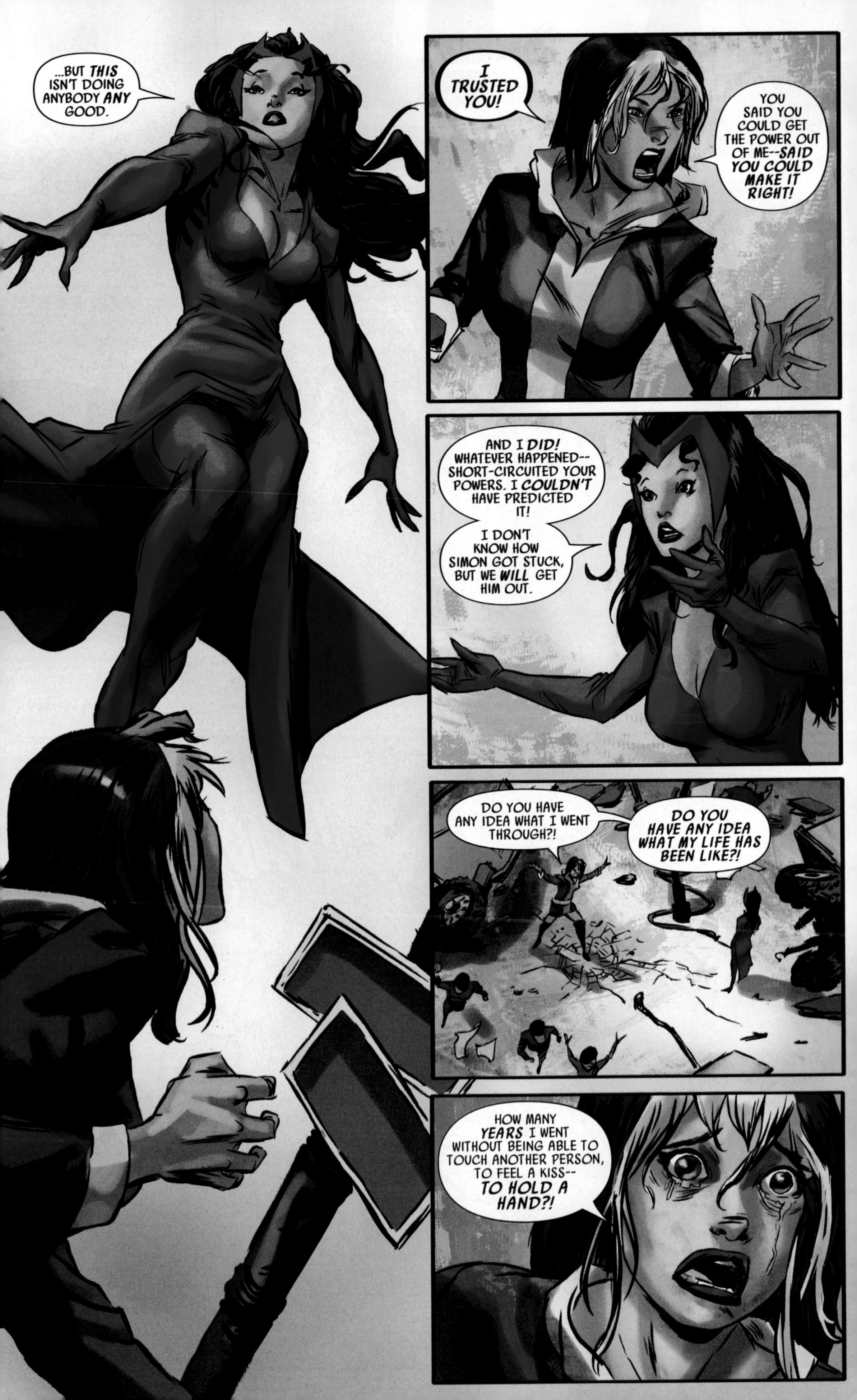
...BUT THIS ISN'T DOING ANYBODY ANY GOOD.
I TRUSTED YOU!
YOU SAID YOU COULD GET THE POWER OUT OF ME--SAID YOU COULD MAKE IT RIGHT!
AND I DID! WHATEVER HAPPENED-- SHORT-CIRCUITED YOUR POWERS. I COULDN'T HAVE PREDICTED IT!
I DON'T KNOW HOW SIMON GOT STUCK, BUT WE WILL GET HIM OUT.
DO YOU HAVE ANY IDEA WHAT I WENT THROUGH?!
DO YOU HAVE ANY IDEA WHAT MY LIFE HAS BEEN LIKE?!
HOW MANY YEARS I WENT WITHOUT BEING ABLE TO TOUCH ANOTHER PERSON, TO FEEL A KISS-- TO HOLD A HAND?!

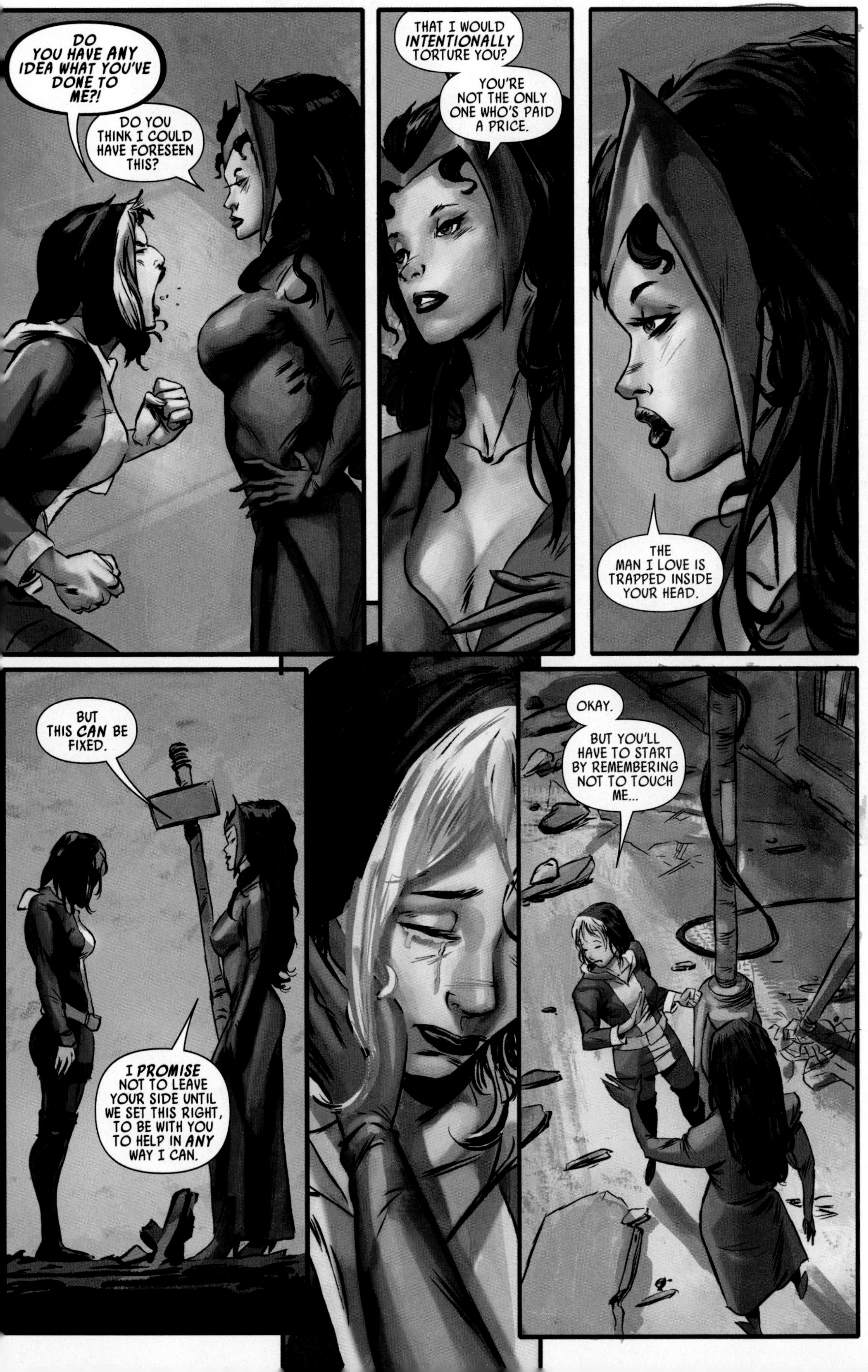
DO YOU HAVE ANY IDEA WHAT YOU'VE DONE TO ME?!
DO YOU THINK I COULD HAVE FORESEEN THIS?
THAT I WOULD INTENTIONALLY TORTURE YOU?
YOU'RE NOT THE ONLY ONE WHO'S PAID A PRICE.
THE MAN I LOVE IS TRAPPED INSIDE YOUR HEAD.
BUT THIS CAN BE FIXED.
I PROMISE NOT TO LEAVE YOUR SIDE UNTIL WE SET THIS RIGHT, TO BE WITH YOU TO HELP IN ANY WAY I CAN.
OKAY.
BUT YOU'LL HAVE TO START BY REMEMBERING NOT TO TOUCH ME...

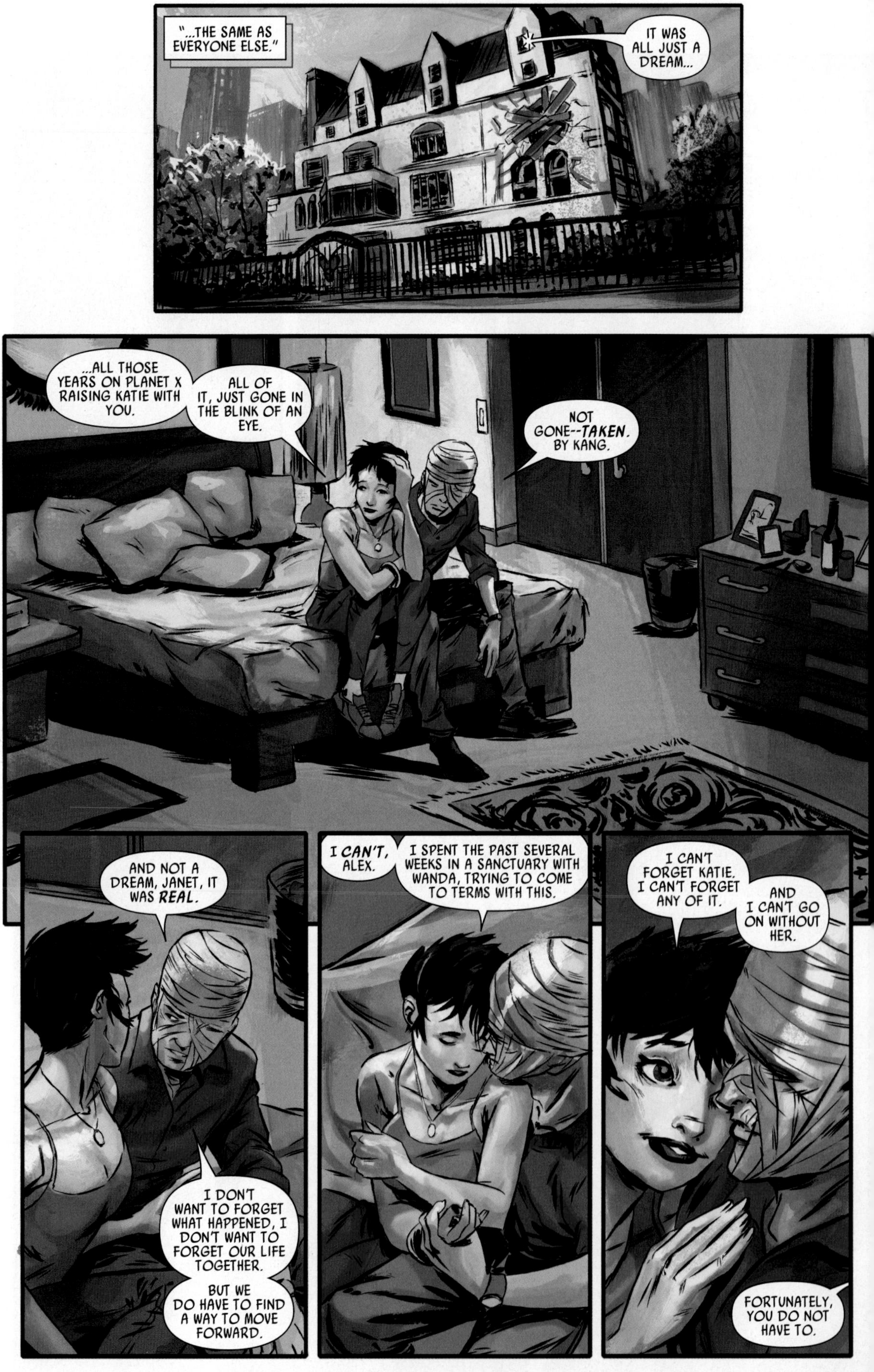
"...THE SAME AS EVERYONE ELSE."
IT WAS ALL JUST A DREAM...
...ALL THOSE YEARS ON PLANET X RAISING KATIE WITH YOU.
ALL OF IT, JUST GONE IN THE BLINK OF AN EYE.
NOT GONE--TAKEN. BY KANG.
AND NOT A DREAM, JANET, IT WAS REAL.
I DON'T WANT TO FORGET WHAT HAPPENED, I DON'T WANT TO FORGET OUR LIFE TOGETHER.
BUT WE DO HAVE TO FIND A WAY TO MOVE FORWARD.
I CAN'T, ALEX.
I SPENT THE PAST SEVERAL WEEKS IN A SANCTUARY WITH WANDA, TRYING TO COME TO TERMS WITH THIS.
I CAN'T FORGET KATIE. I CAN'T FORGET ANY OF IT.
AND I CAN'T GO ON WITHOUT HER.
FORTUNATELY, YOU DO NOT HAVE TO.

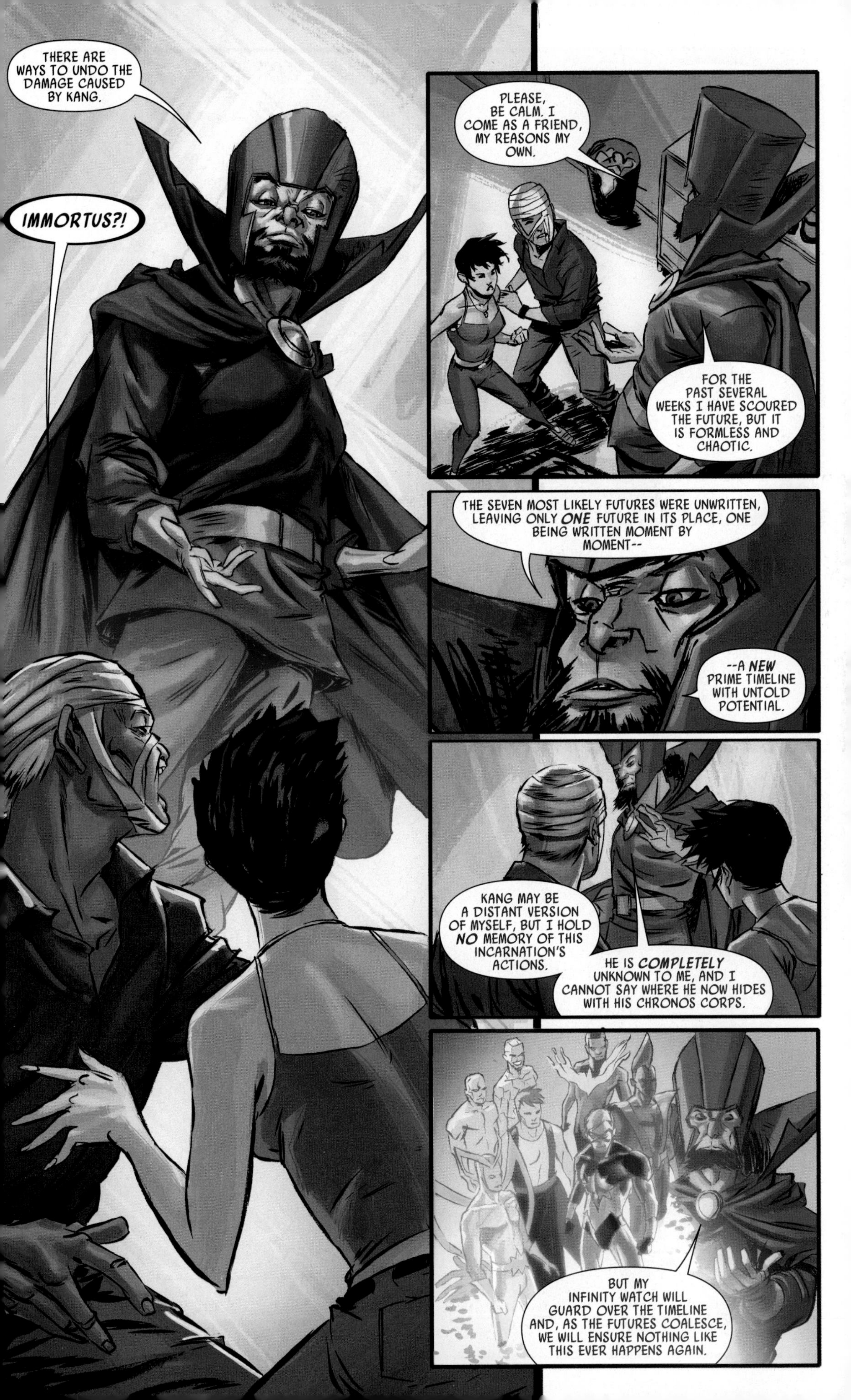
THERE ARE WAYS TO UNDO THE DAMAGE CAUSED BY KANG.
IMMORTUS?!
PLEASE, BE CALM. I COME AS A FRIEND, MY REASONS MY OWN.
FOR THE PAST SEVERAL WEEKS I HAVE SCOURED THE FUTURE, BUT IT IS FORMLESS AND CHAOTIC.
THE SEVEN MOST LIKELY FUTURES WERE UNWRITTEN, LEAVING ONLY ONE FUTURE IN ITS PLACE, ONE BEING WRITTEN MOMENT BY MOMENT--
--A NEW PRIME TIMELINE WITH UNTOLD POTENTIAL.
KANG MAY BE A DISTANT VERSION OF MYSELF, BUT I HOLD NO MEMORY OF THIS INCARNATION'S ACTIONS.
HE IS COMPLETELY UNKNOWN TO ME, AND I CANNOT SAY WHERE HE NOW HIDES WITH HIS CHRONOS CORPS.
BUT MY INFINITY WATCH WILL GUARD OVER THE TIMELINE AND, AS THE FUTURES COALESCE, WE WILL ENSURE NOTHING LIKE THIS EVER HAPPENS AGAIN.

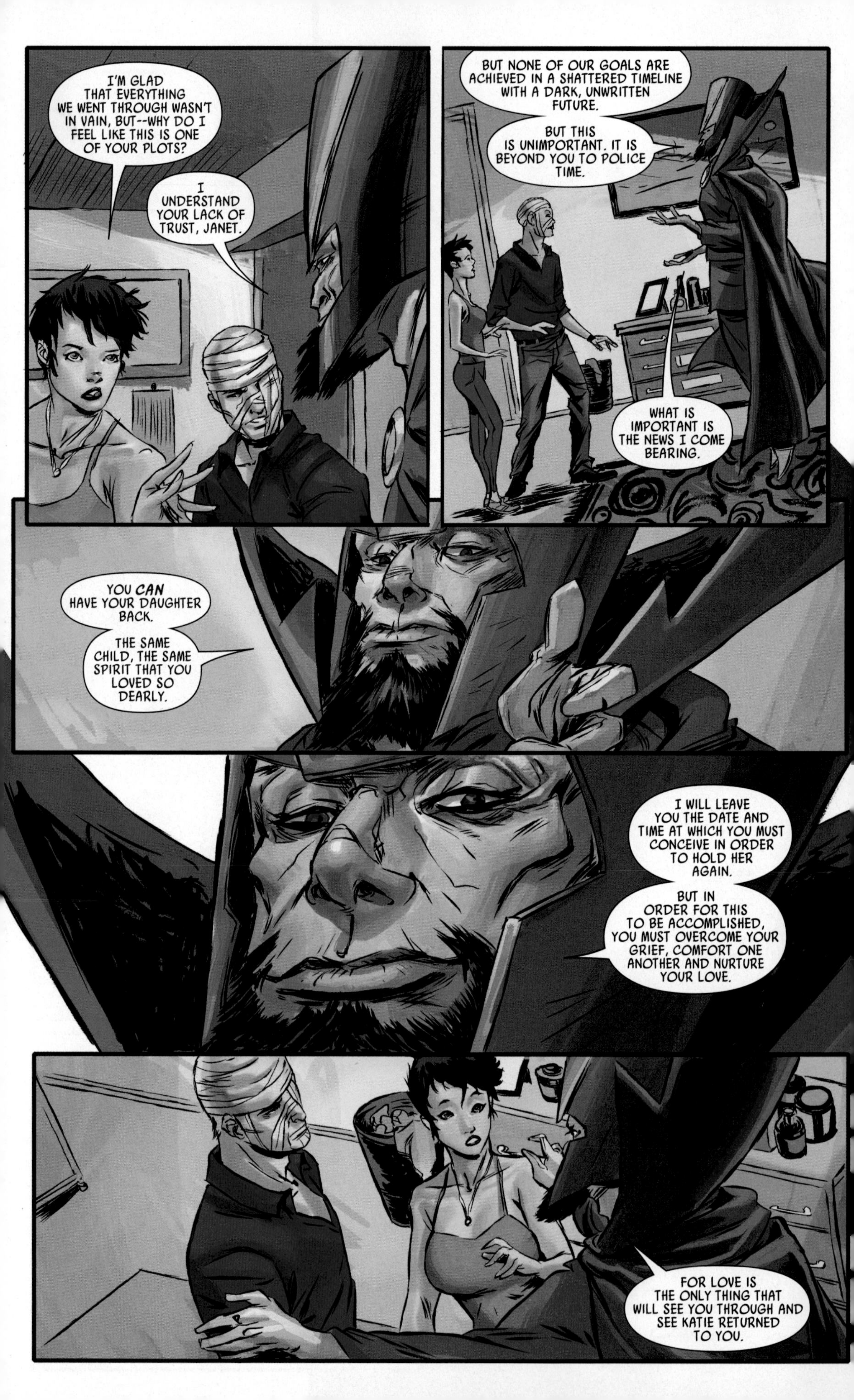

I'M GLAD THAT EVERYTHING WE WENT THROUGH WASN'T IN VAIN, BUT--WHY DO I FEEL LIKE THIS IS ONE OF YOUR PLOTS?
I UNDERSTAND YOUR LACK OF TRUST, JANET.
BUT NONE OF OUR GOALS ARE ACHIEVED IN A SHATTERED TIMELINE WITH A DARK, UNWRITTEN FUTURE.
BUT THIS IS UNIMPORTANT. IT IS BEYOND YOU TO POLICE TIME.
WHAT IS IMPORTANT IS THE NEWS I COME BEARING.
YOU *CAN* HAVE YOUR DAUGHTER BACK.
THE SAME CHILD, THE SAME SPIRIT THAT YOU LOVED SO DEARLY.
I WILL LEAVE YOU THE DATE AND TIME AT WHICH YOU MUST CONCEIVE IN ORDER TO HOLD HER AGAIN.
BUT IN ORDER FOR THIS TO BE ACCOMPLISHED, YOU MUST OVERCOME YOUR GRIEF, COMFORT ONE ANOTHER AND NURTURE YOUR LOVE.
FOR LOVE IS THE ONLY THING THAT WILL SEE YOU THROUGH AND SEE KATIE RETURNED TO YOU.

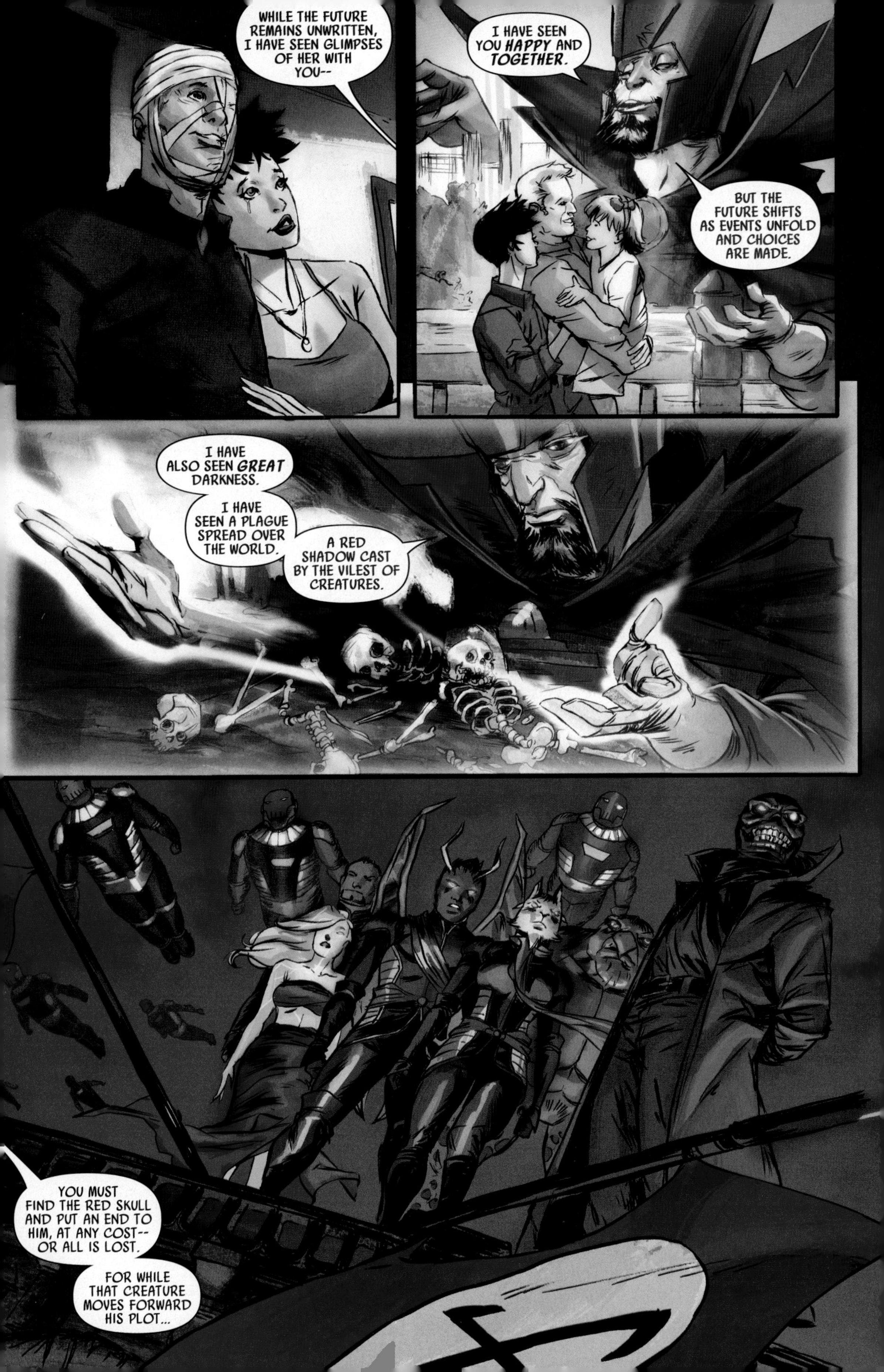
WHILE THE FUTURE REMAINS UNWRITTEN, I HAVE SEEN GLIMPSES OF HER WITH YOU--
I HAVE SEEN YOU HAPPY AND TOGETHER.
BUT THE FUTURE SHIFTS AS EVENTS UNFOLD AND CHOICES ARE MADE.
I HAVE ALSO SEEN GREAT DARKNESS.
I HAVE SEEN A PLAGUE SPREAD OVER THE WORLD.
A RED SHADOW CAST BY THE VILEST OF CREATURES.
YOU MUST FIND THE RED SKULL AND PUT AN END TO HIM, AT ANY COST-- OR ALL IS LOST.
FOR WHILE THAT CREATURE MOVES FORWARD HIS PLOT...

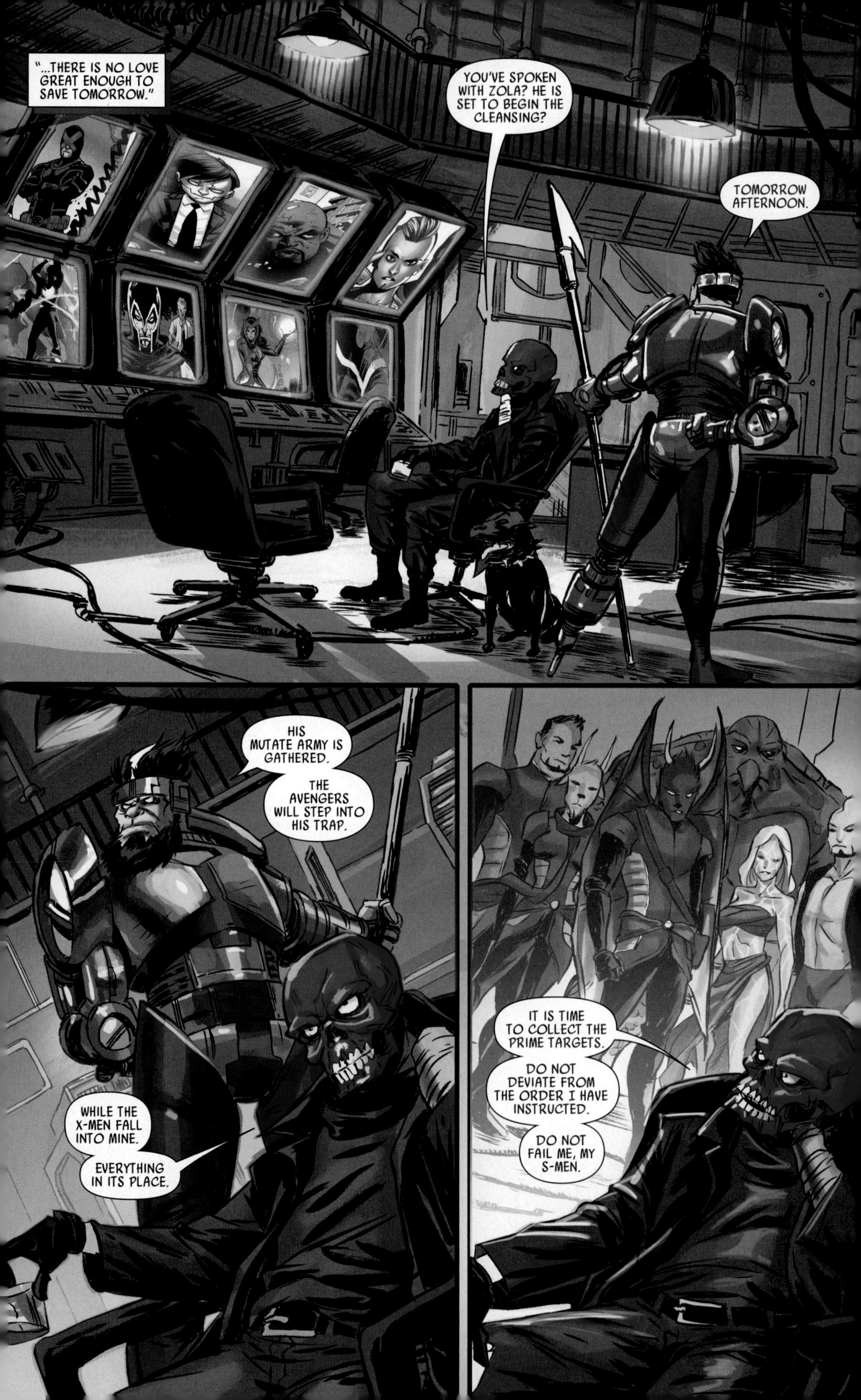
"...THERE IS NO LOVE GREAT ENOUGH TO SAVE TOMORROW."
YOU'VE SPOKEN WITH ZOLA? HE IS SET TO BEGIN THE CLEANSING?
TOMORROW AFTERNOON.
HIS MUTATE ARMY IS GATHERED.
THE AVENGERS WILL STEP INTO HIS TRAP.
WHILE THE X-MEN FALL INTO MINE.
EVERYTHING IN ITS PLACE.
IT IS TIME TO COLLECT THE PRIME TARGETS.
DO NOT DEVIATE FROM THE ORDER I HAVE INSTRUCTED.
DO NOT FAIL ME, MY S-MEN.

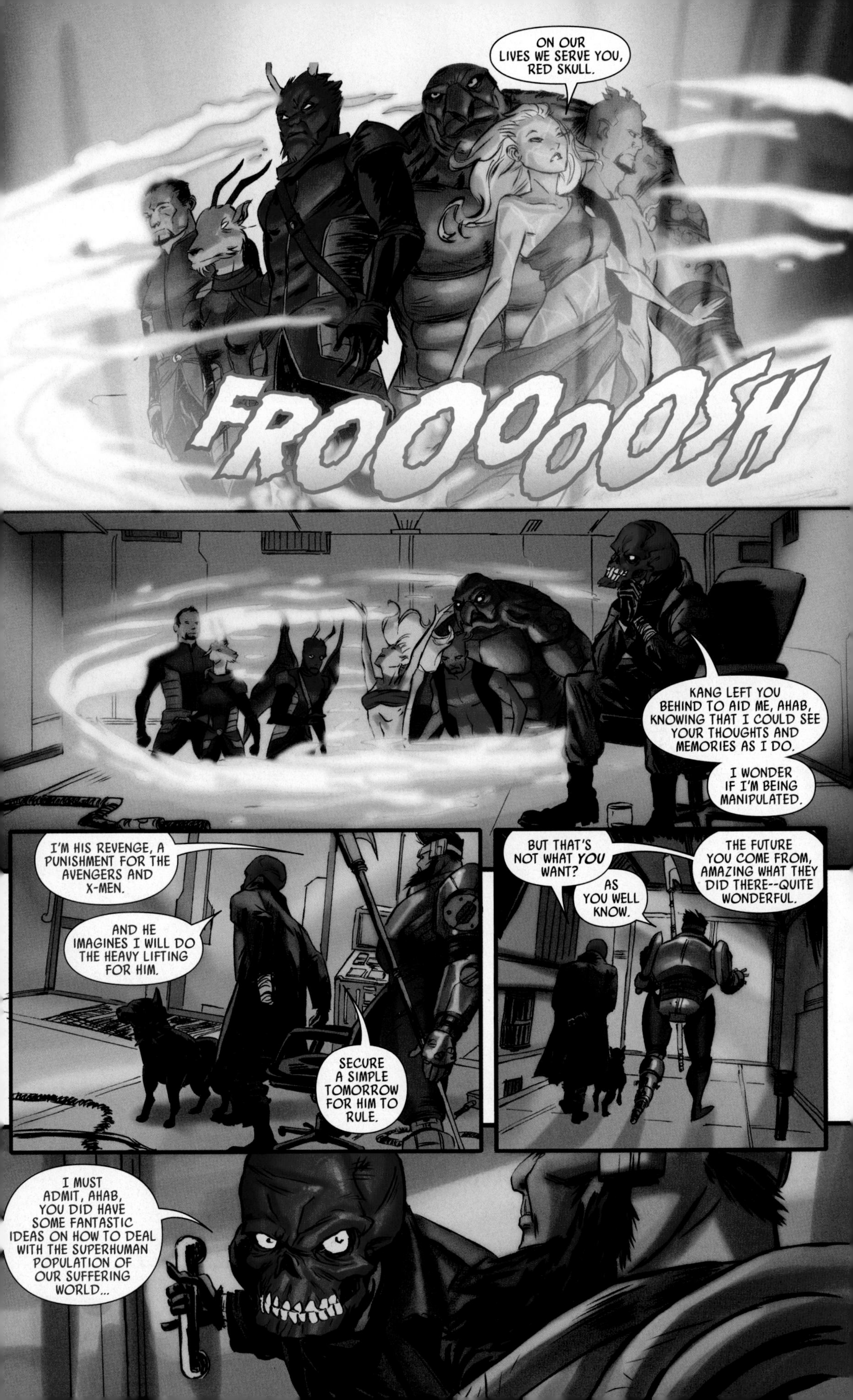
ON OUR LIVES WE SERVE YOU, RED SKULL.
FROOOOOSH
KANG LEFT YOU BEHIND TO AID ME, AHAB, KNOWING THAT I COULD SEE YOUR THOUGHTS AND MEMORIES AS I DO.
I WONDER IF I'M BEING MANIPULATED.
I'M HIS REVENGE, A PUNISHMENT FOR THE AVENGERS AND X-MEN.
AND HE IMAGINES I WILL DO THE HEAVY LIFTING FOR HIM.
SECURE A SIMPLE TOMORROW FOR HIM TO RULE.
BUT THAT'S NOT WHAT YOU WANT?
AS YOU WELL KNOW.
THE FUTURE YOU COME FROM, AMAZING WHAT THEY DID THERE--QUITE WONDERFUL.
I MUST ADMIT, AHAB, YOU DID HAVE SOME FANTASTIC IDEAS ON HOW TO DEAL WITH THE SUPERHUMAN POPULATION OF OUR SUFFERING WORLD...

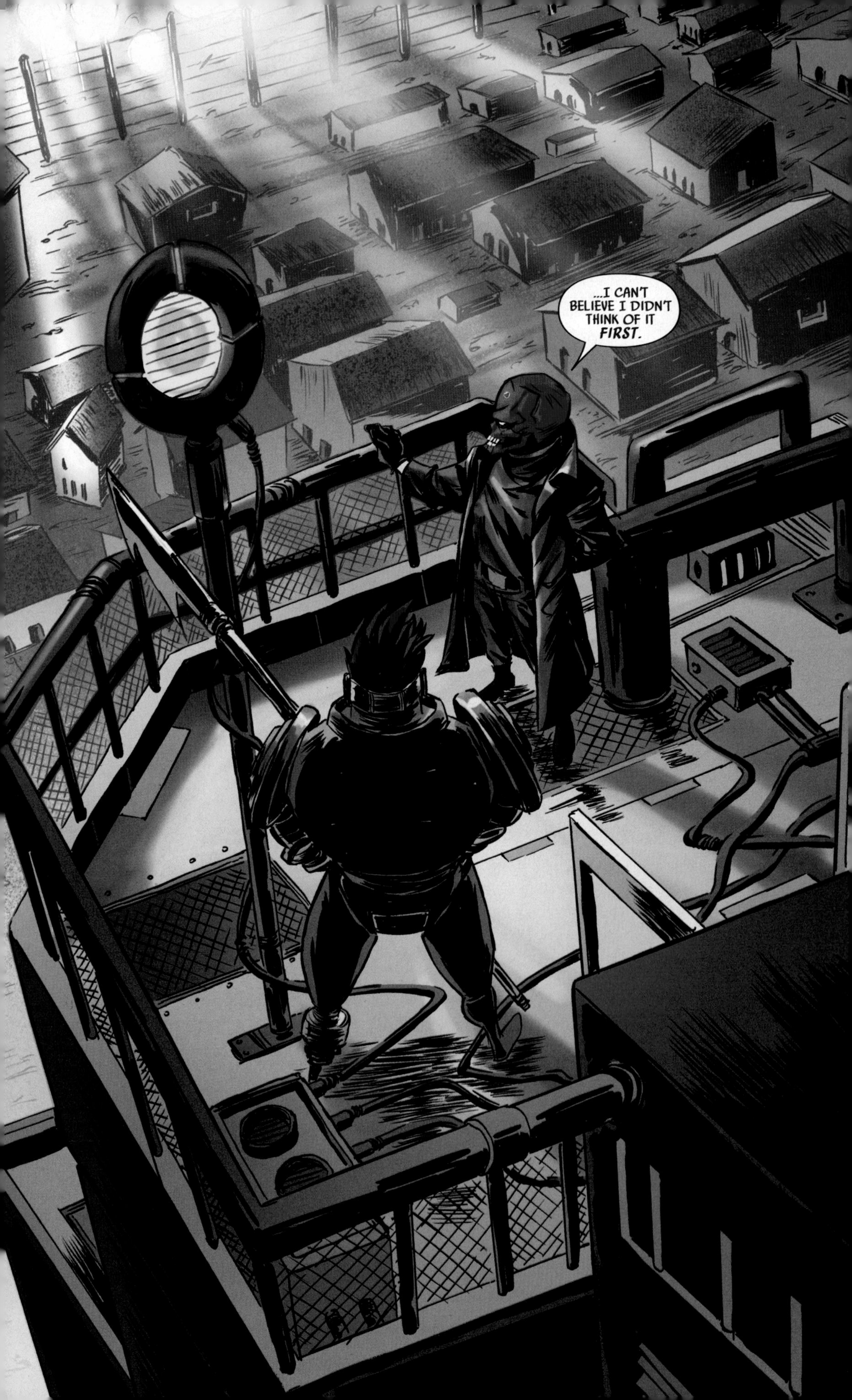
...I CAN'T BELIEVE I DIDN'T THINK OF IT *FIRST*.

MAGNETO #9

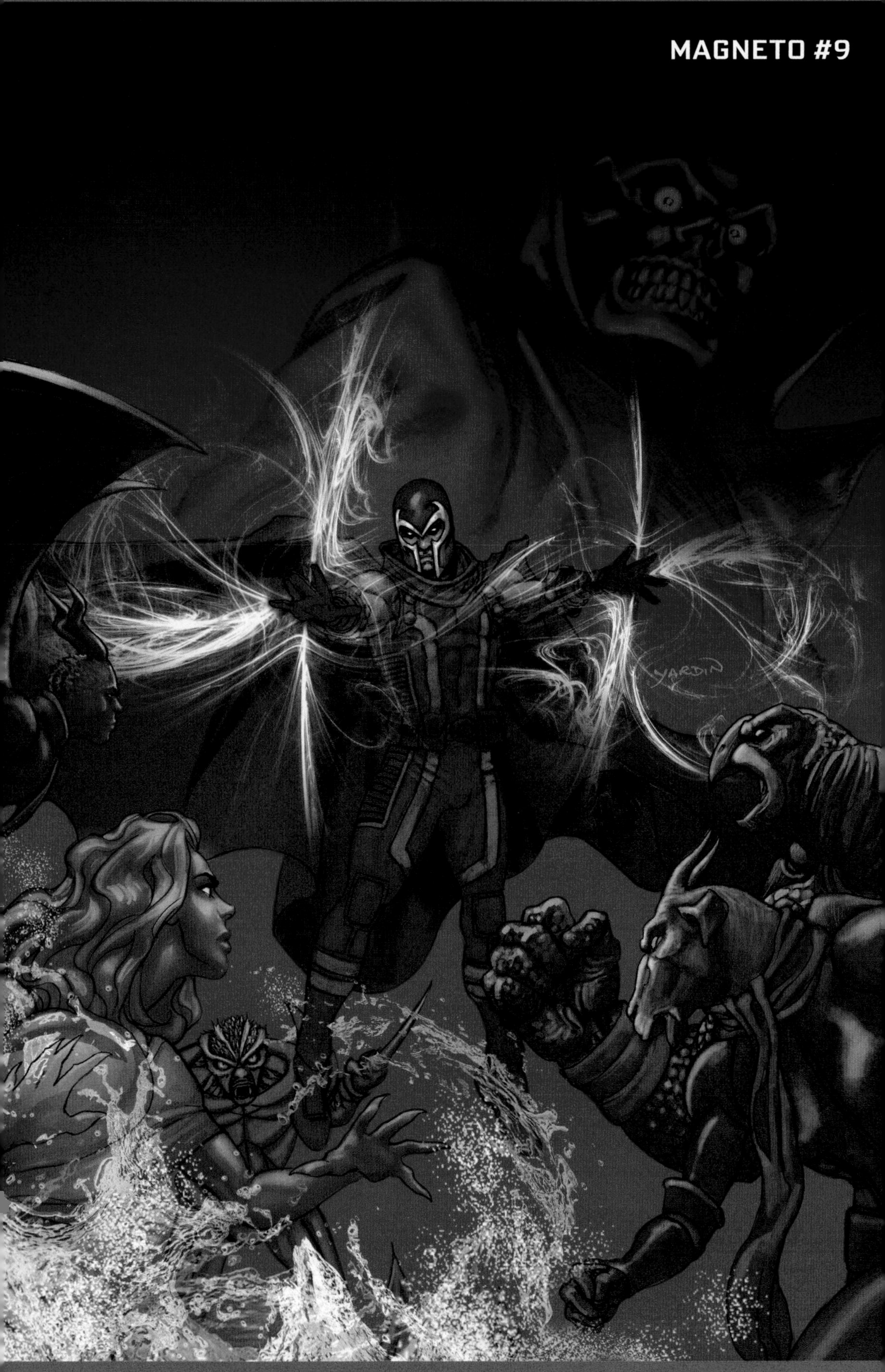
YARDIN

MAGNETO

ASSUMING THE MANTLE OF "PROTECTOR OF MUTANTKIND" ONCE MORE, MAGNETO HAS
TAKEN TO WORKING AS A LONE VIGILANTE, EXACTING REVENGE ON THE PERPETRATORS
OF ANTI-MUTANT CRIMES.

AFTER DISCOVERING MUTANT GROWTH HORMONE IN A HONG KONG BASED
MUTANT-MURDER ARENA, MAGNETO TRACED ITS SOURCE BACK TO A MAKESHIFT
LABORATORY. BUT HIS CONFRONTATION WITH THE MEN RESPONSIBLE WAS INTERRUPTED
AS S.H.I.E.L.D. BURST THROUGH THE CEILING. FINALLY FACE-TO-FACE WITH THE AGENTS
WHO HAD BEEN TRACKING HIM, MAGNETO MANAGED TO ESCAPE, TAKING WITH HIM THE
MAN WHO HAD DEVELOPED THE FORMULA FOR THE MGH. THOUGH THE CHEMIST THOUGHT
HIMSELF DEAD TO RIGHTS, MAGNETO HAD A DIFFERENT PLAN FOR HIM--TO PRODUCE A
VERSION OF MGH THAT WOULD RESTORE HIS MAGNETIC POWERS TO THEIR FULL
STRENGTH.

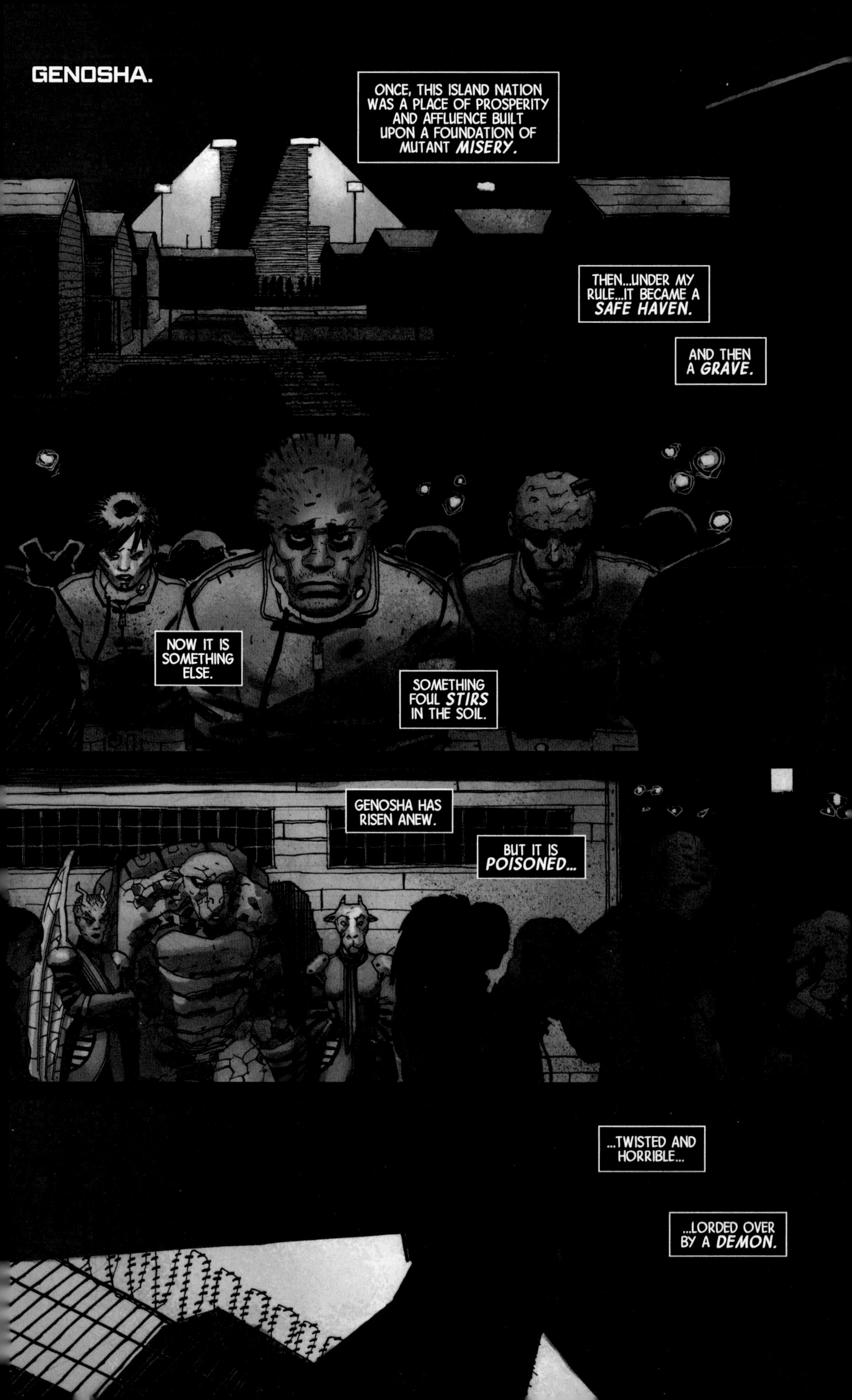
GENOSHA.
ONCE, THIS ISLAND NATION WAS A PLACE OF PROSPERITY AND AFFLUENCE BUILT UPON A FOUNDATION OF MUTANT MISERY.
THEN...UNDER MY RULE...IT BECAME A SAFE HAVEN.
AND THEN A GRAVE.
NOW IT IS SOMETHING ELSE.
SOMETHING FOUL STIRS IN THE SOIL.
GENOSHA HAS RISEN ANEW.
BUT IT IS POISONED...
...TWISTED AND HORRIBLE...
...LORDED OVER BY A DEMON.

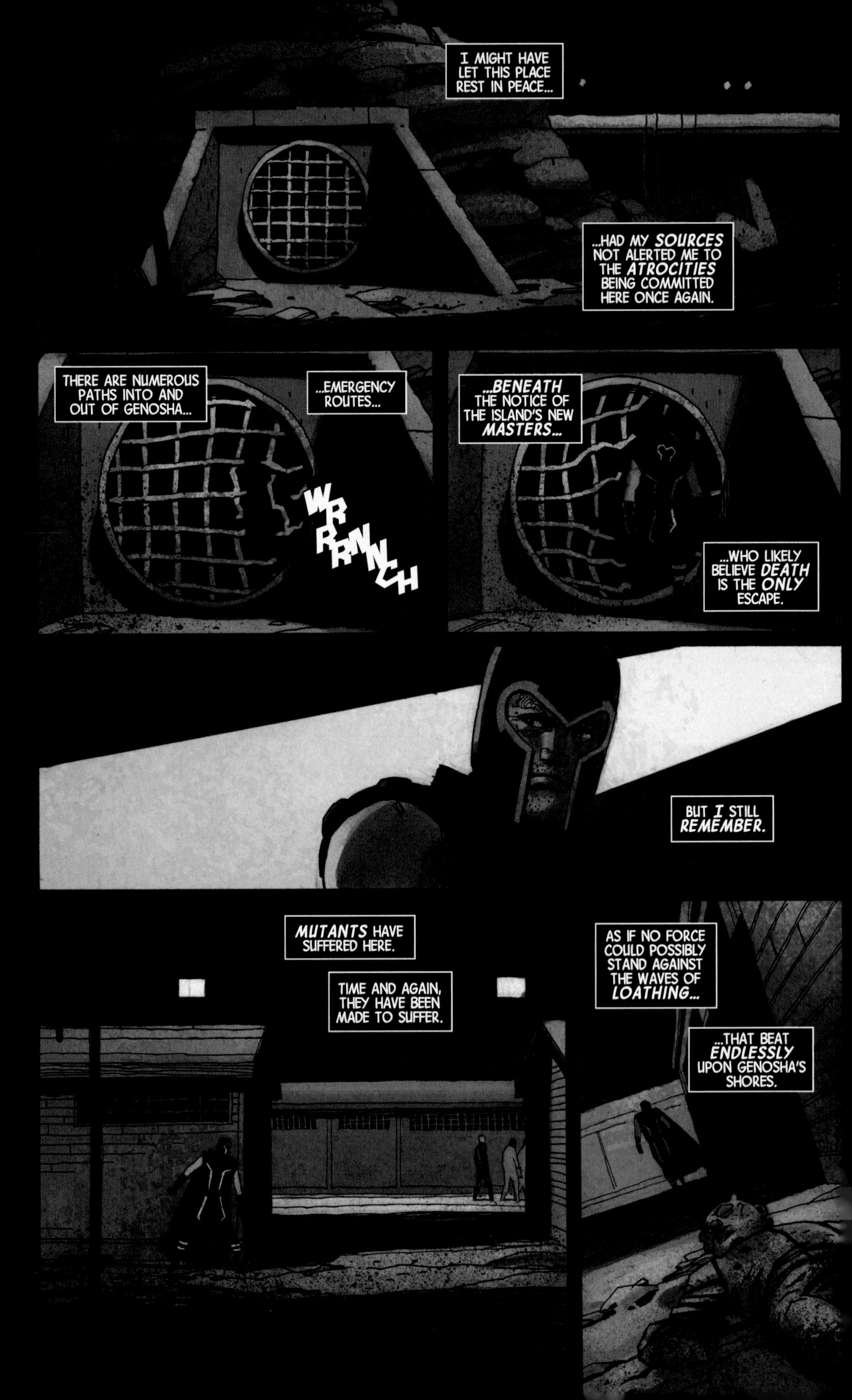
I MIGHT HAVE LET THIS PLACE REST IN PEACE...
...HAD MY SOURCES NOT ALERTED ME TO THE ATROCITIES BEING COMMITTED HERE ONCE AGAIN.
THERE ARE NUMEROUS PATHS INTO AND OUT OF GENOSHA...
...EMERGENCY ROUTES...
WRRNNCH
...BENEATH THE NOTICE OF THE ISLAND'S NEW MASTERS...
...WHO LIKELY BELIEVE DEATH IS THE ONLY ESCAPE.
BUT I STILL REMEMBER.
MUTANTS HAVE SUFFERED HERE.
TIME AND AGAIN, THEY HAVE BEEN MADE TO SUFFER.
AS IF NO FORCE COULD POSSIBLY STAND AGAINST THE WAVES OF LOATHING...
...THAT BEAT ENDLESSLY UPON GENOSHA'S SHORES.

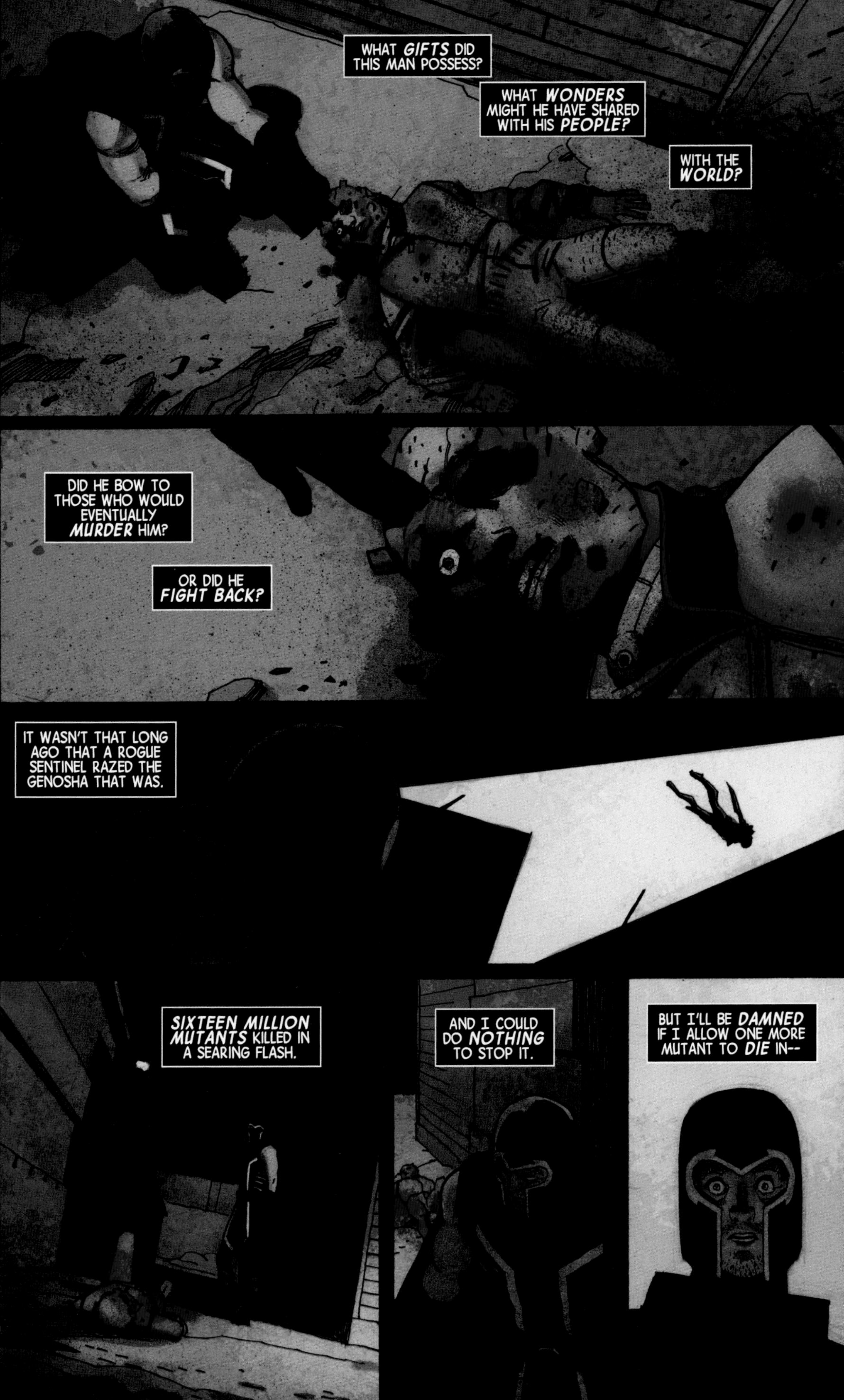
WHAT GIFTS DID THIS MAN POSSESS?
WHAT WONDERS MIGHT HE HAVE SHARED WITH HIS PEOPLE?
WITH THE WORLD?
DID HE BOW TO THOSE WHO WOULD EVENTUALLY MURDER HIM?
OR DID HE FIGHT BACK?
IT WASN'T THAT LONG AGO THAT A ROGUE SENTINEL RAZED THE GENOSHA THAT WAS.
SIXTEEN MILLION MUTANTS KILLED IN A SEARING FLASH.
AND I COULD DO NOTHING TO STOP IT.
BUT I'LL BE DAMNED IF I ALLOW ONE MORE MUTANT TO DIE IN--

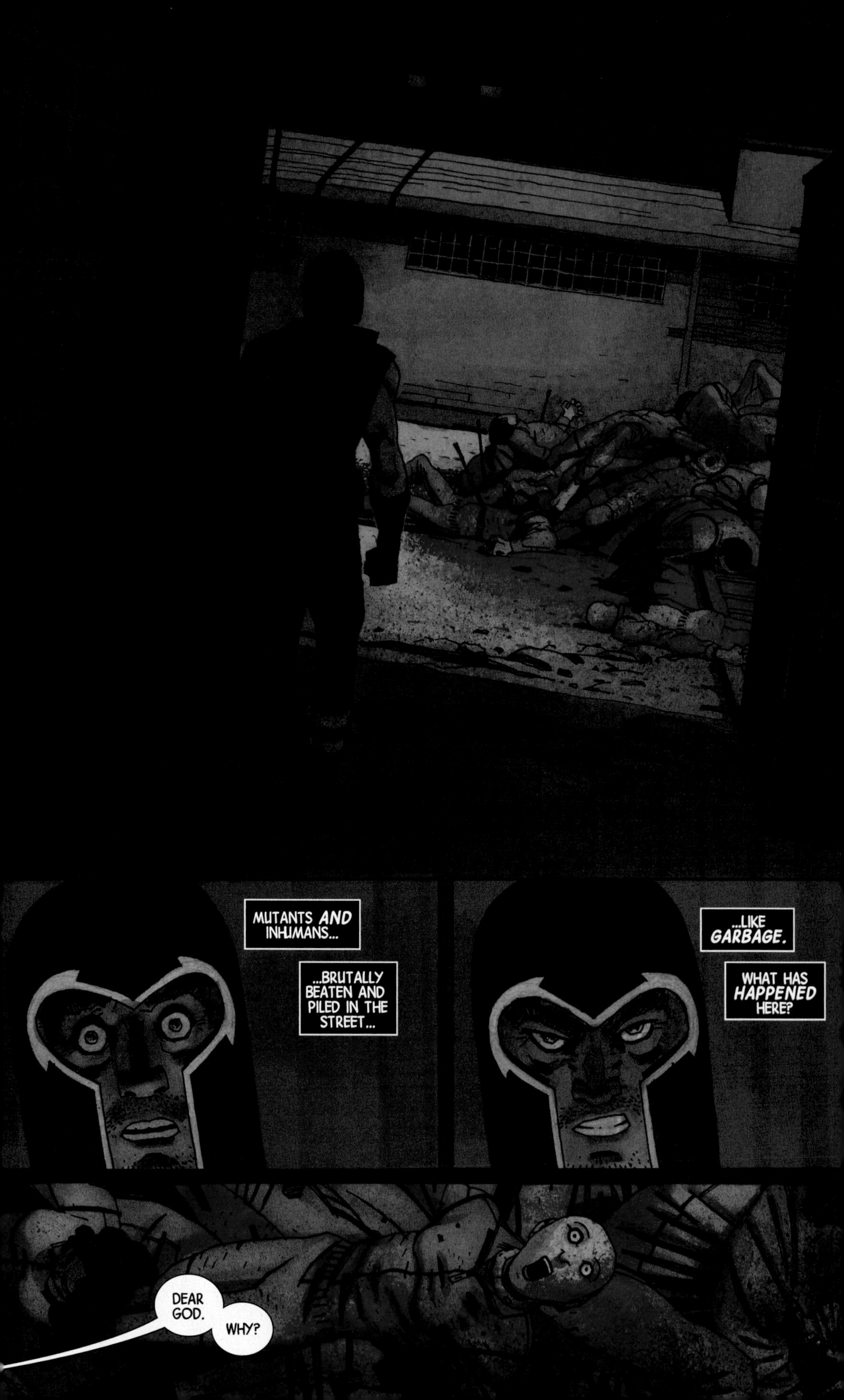
MUTANTS AND INHUMANS...
...BRUTALLY BEATEN AND PILED IN THE STREET...
...LIKE GARBAGE.
WHAT HAS HAPPENED HERE?
DEAR GOD.
WHY?

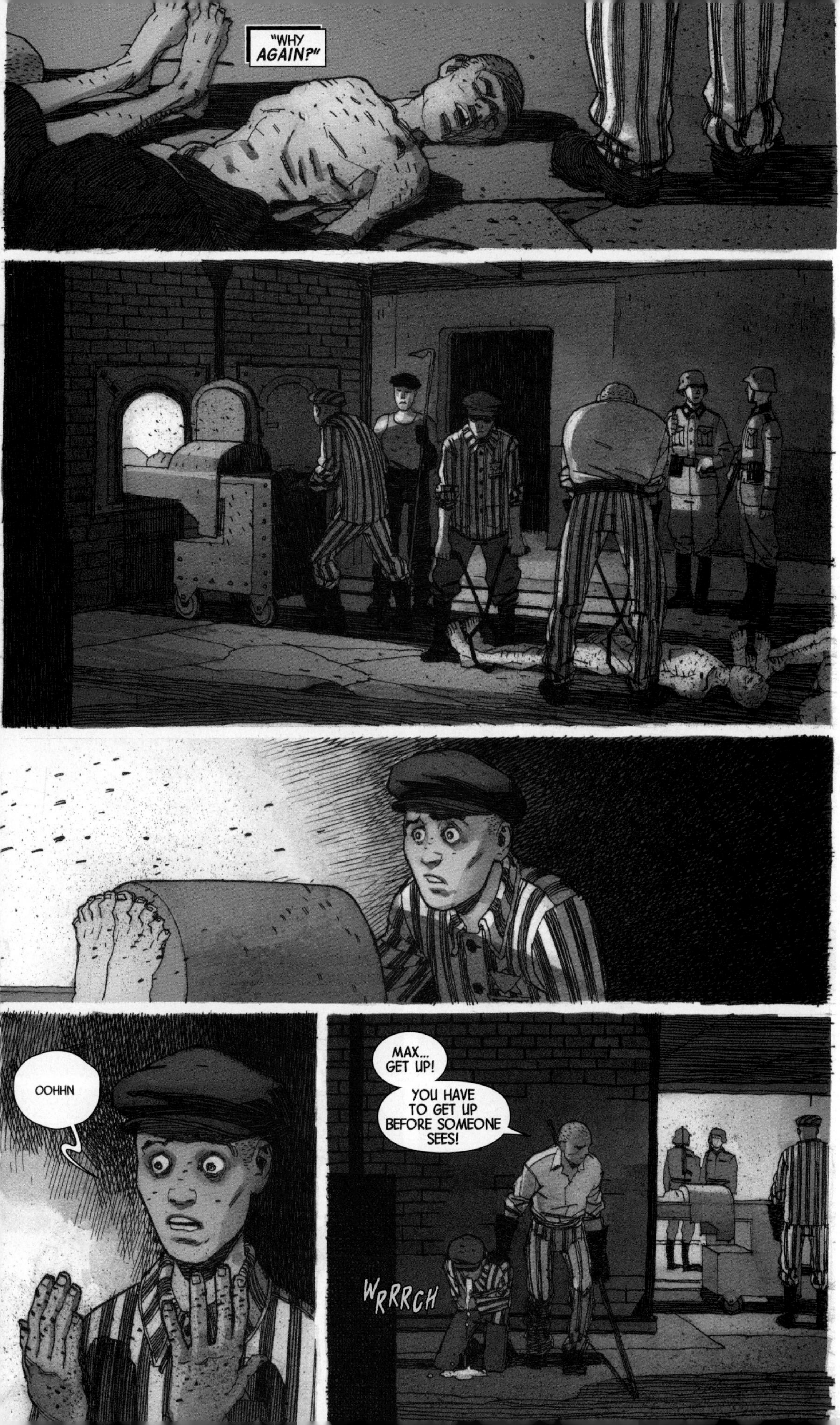
"WHY AGAIN?"
OOHHN
MAX... GET UP!
YOU HAVE TO GET UP BEFORE SOMEONE SEES!
WRRRCH

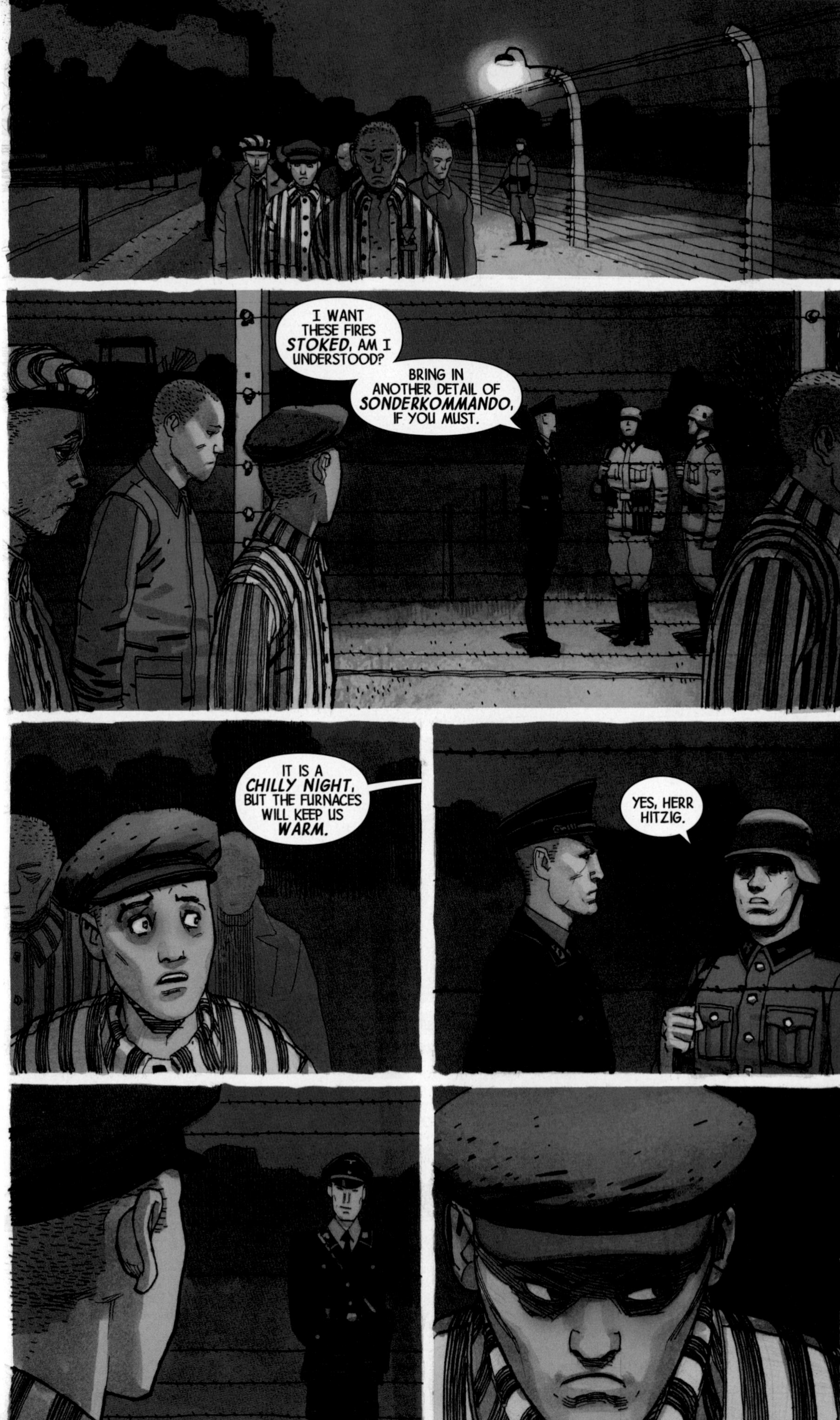
I WANT THESE FIRES STOKED, AM I UNDERSTOOD?
BRING IN ANOTHER DETAIL OF SONDERKOMMANDO, IF YOU MUST.
IT IS A CHILLY NIGHT, BUT THE FURNACES WILL KEEP US WARM.
YES, HERR HITZIG.

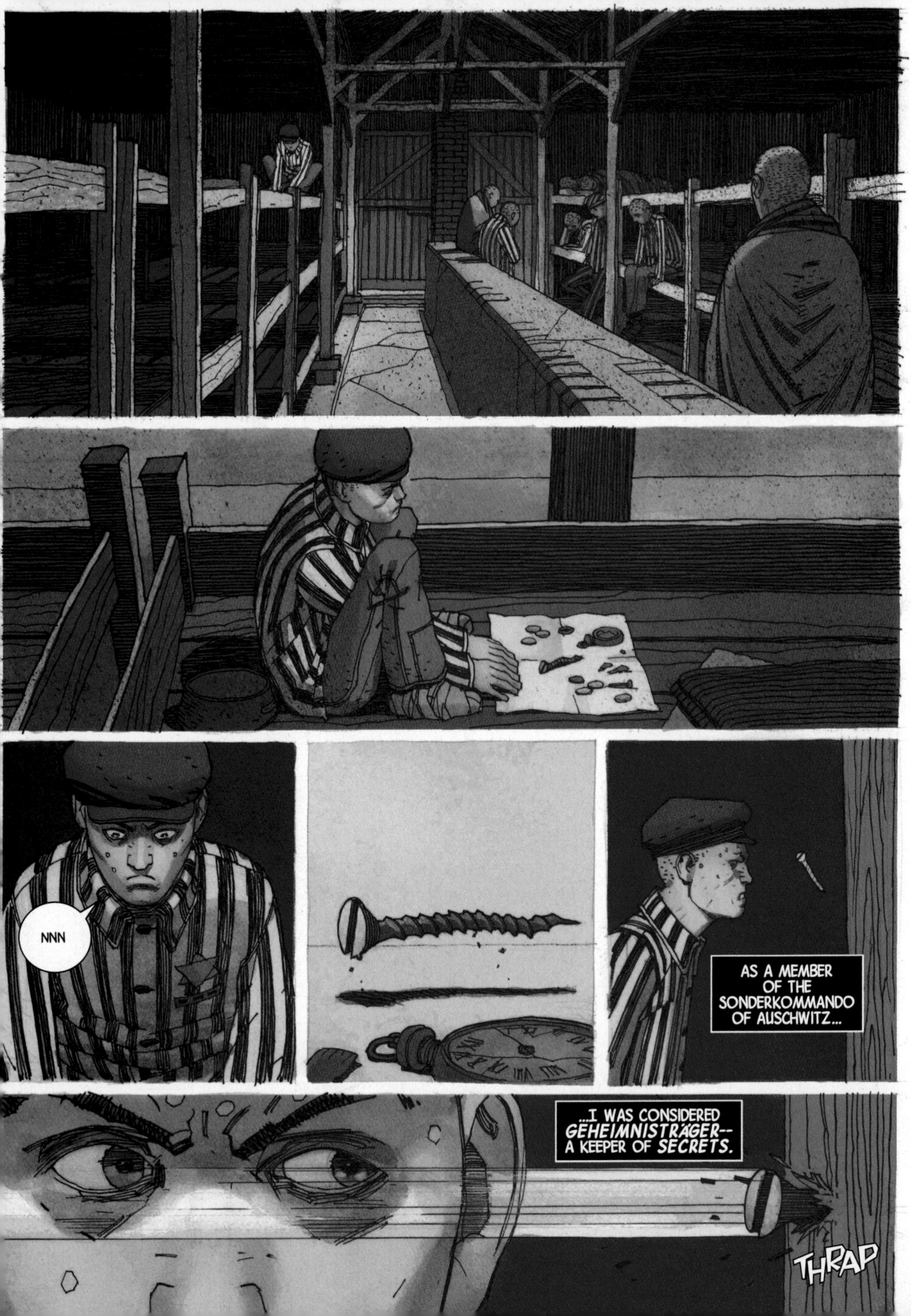
NNN
AS A MEMBER OF THE SONDERKOMMANDO OF AUSCHWITZ...
...I WAS CONSIDERED GEHEIMNISTRÄGER-- A KEEPER OF SECRETS.
THRAP

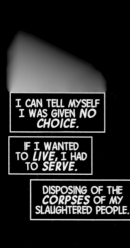

I CAN TELL MYSELF I WAS GIVEN *NO CHOICE.*

IF I WANTED TO *LIVE,* I HAD TO *SERVE.*

DISPOSING OF THE *CORPSES* OF MY SLAUGHTERED PEOPLE.

I CAN TELL MYSELF THAT I *ENDURED* SUCH DISGRACE IN ORDER TO *POSITION* MYSELF FOR *REVENGE...*

...TO STRIKE BACK AGAINST *HITZIG.*

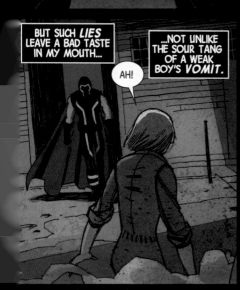

BUT SUCH *LIES* LEAVE A BAD TASTE IN MY MOUTH...

AH!

...NOT UNLIKE THE SOUR TANG OF A WEAK BOY'S *VOMIT.*

IT'S ALL RIGHT.

I AM HERE TO *HELP* YOU.

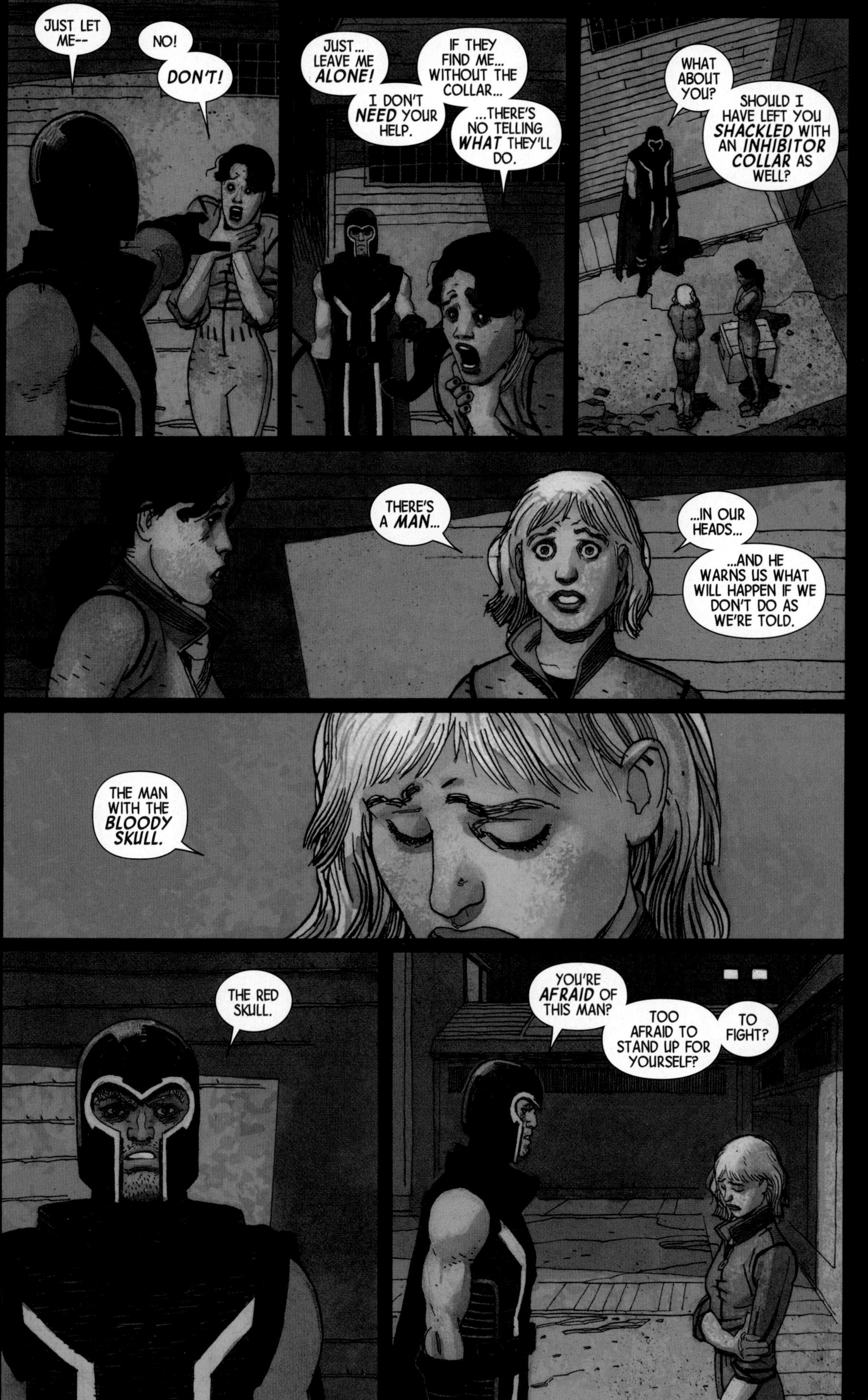
JUST LET ME--
NO! DON'T!
JUST... LEAVE ME ALONE!
I DON'T NEED YOUR HELP.
IF THEY FIND ME... WITHOUT THE COLLAR...
...THERE'S NO TELLING WHAT THEY'LL DO.
WHAT ABOUT YOU?
SHOULD I HAVE LEFT YOU SHACKLED WITH AN INHIBITOR COLLAR AS WELL?
THERE'S A MAN...
...IN OUR HEADS...
...AND HE WARNS US WHAT WILL HAPPEN IF WE DON'T DO AS WE'RE TOLD.
THE MAN WITH THE BLOODY SKULL.
THE RED SKULL.
YOU'RE AFRAID OF THIS MAN?
TOO AFRAID TO STAND UP FOR YOURSELF?
TO FIGHT?

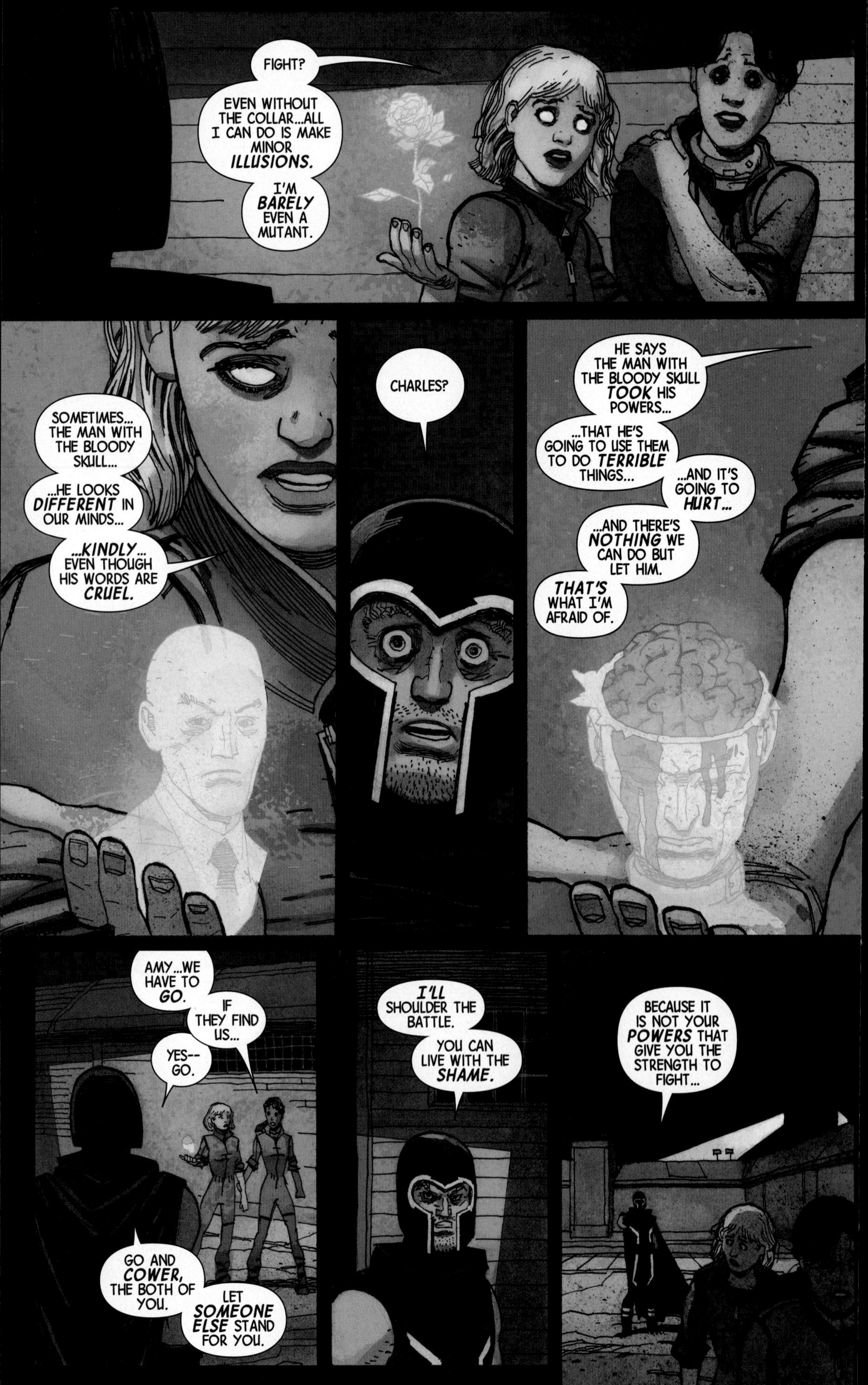
FIGHT?
EVEN WITHOUT THE COLLAR...ALL I CAN DO IS MAKE MINOR ILLUSIONS.
I'M BARELY EVEN A MUTANT.
SOMETIMES... THE MAN WITH THE BLOODY SKULL...
...HE LOOKS DIFFERENT IN OUR MINDS...
...KINDLY... EVEN THOUGH HIS WORDS ARE CRUEL.
CHARLES?
HE SAYS THE MAN WITH THE BLOODY SKULL TOOK HIS POWERS...
...THAT HE'S GOING TO USE THEM TO DO TERRIBLE THINGS...
...AND IT'S GOING TO HURT...
...AND THERE'S NOTHING WE CAN DO BUT LET HIM.
THAT'S WHAT I'M AFRAID OF.
AMY...WE HAVE TO GO.
IF THEY FIND US...
YES--GO.
GO AND COWER, THE BOTH OF YOU.
LET SOMEONE ELSE STAND FOR YOU.
I'LL SHOULDER THE BATTLE.
YOU CAN LIVE WITH THE SHAME.
BECAUSE IT IS NOT YOUR POWERS THAT GIVE YOU THE STRENGTH TO FIGHT...

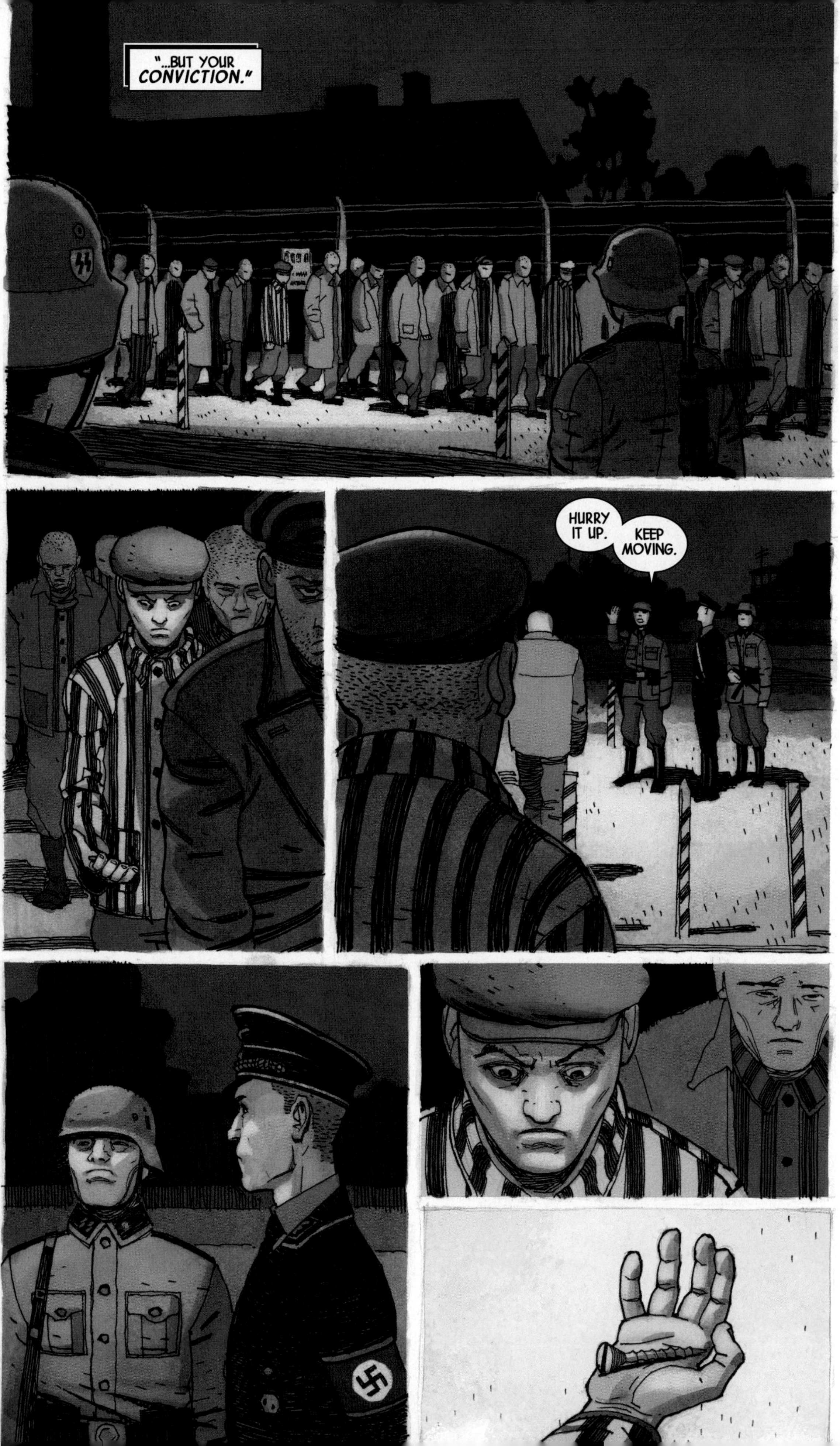
"...BUT YOUR CONVICTION."
HURRY IT UP.
KEEP MOVING.

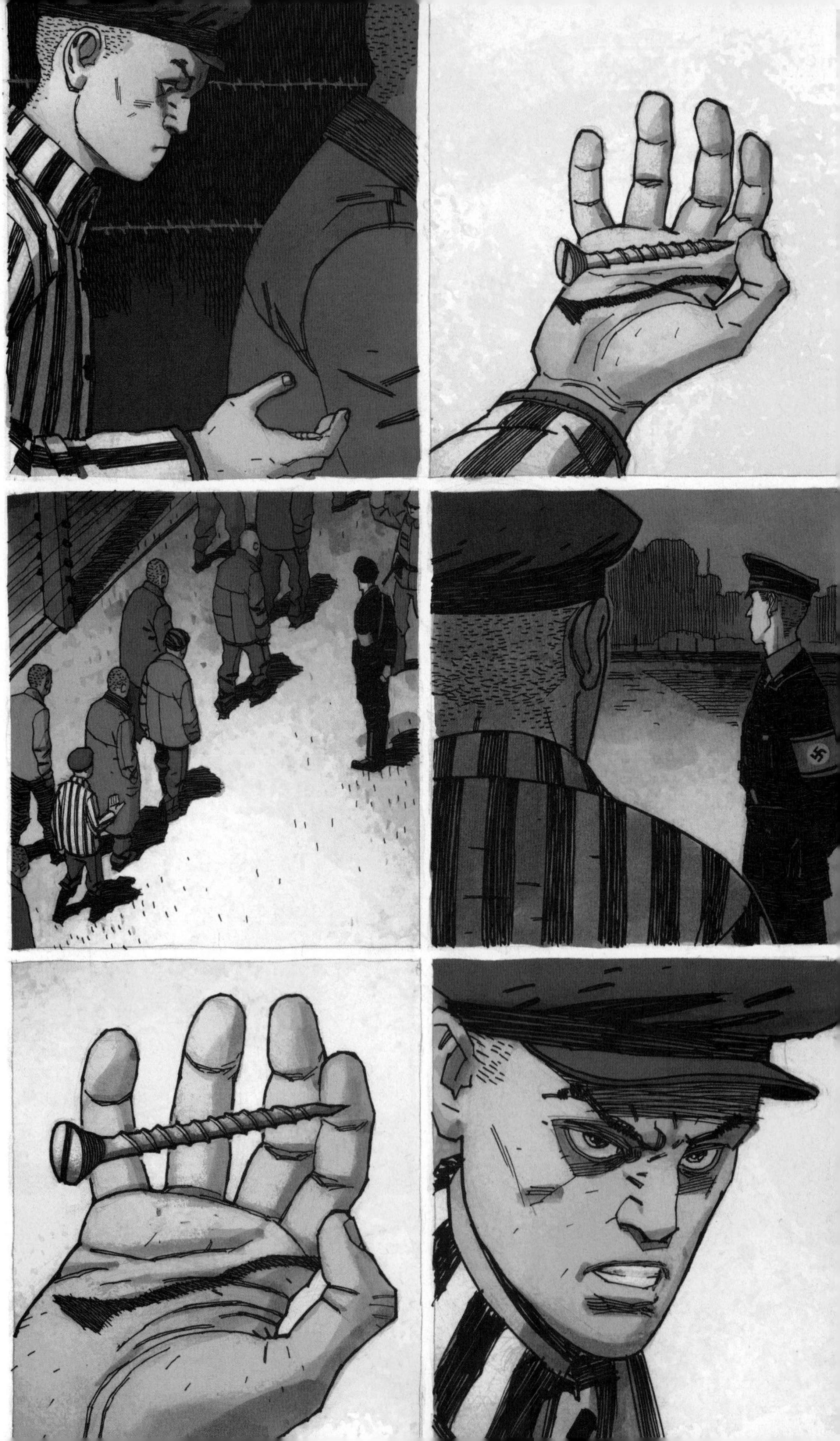

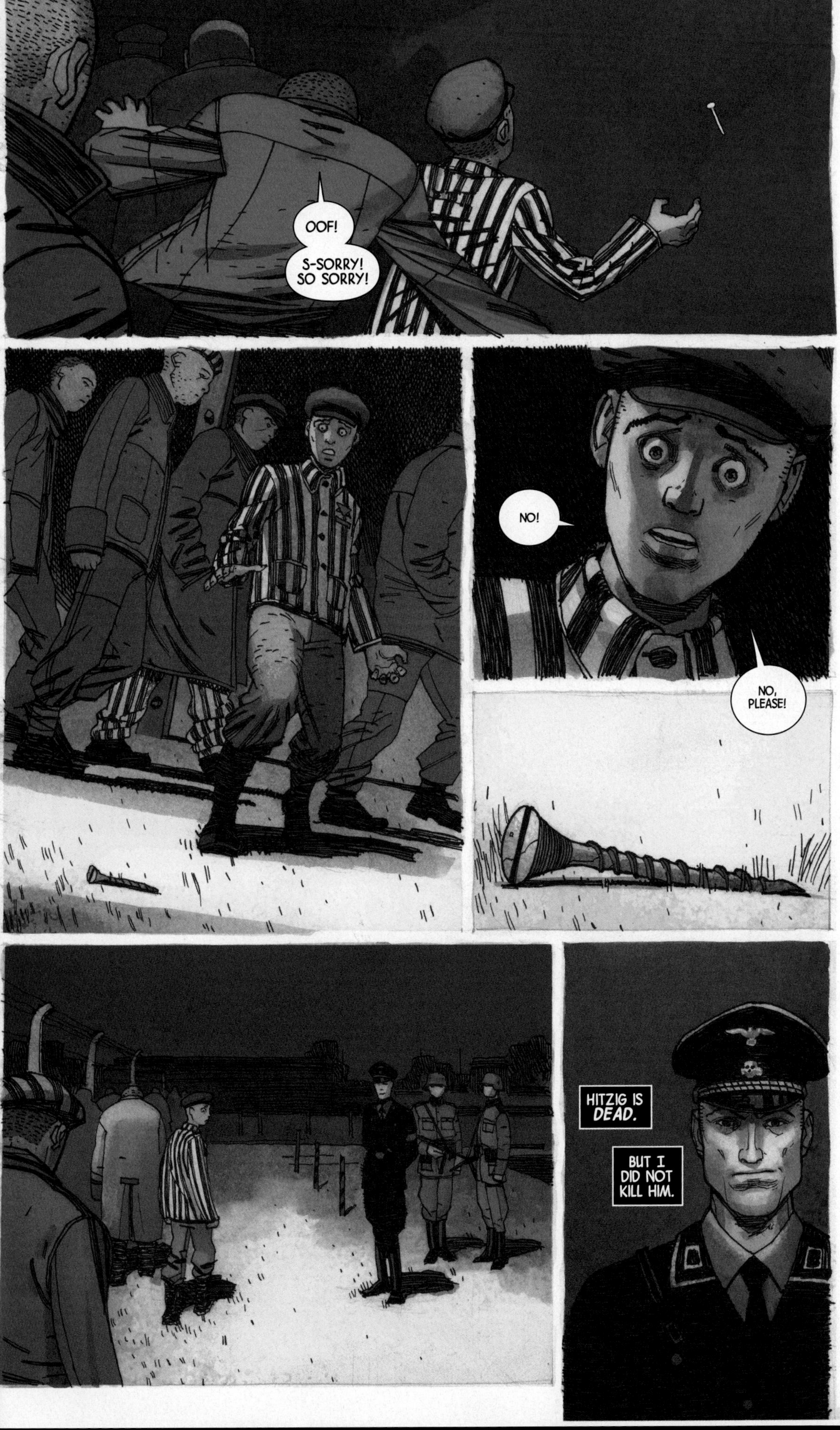
OOF!
S-SORRY! SO SORRY!
NO!
NO, PLEASE!
HITZIG IS DEAD.
BUT I DID NOT KILL HIM.

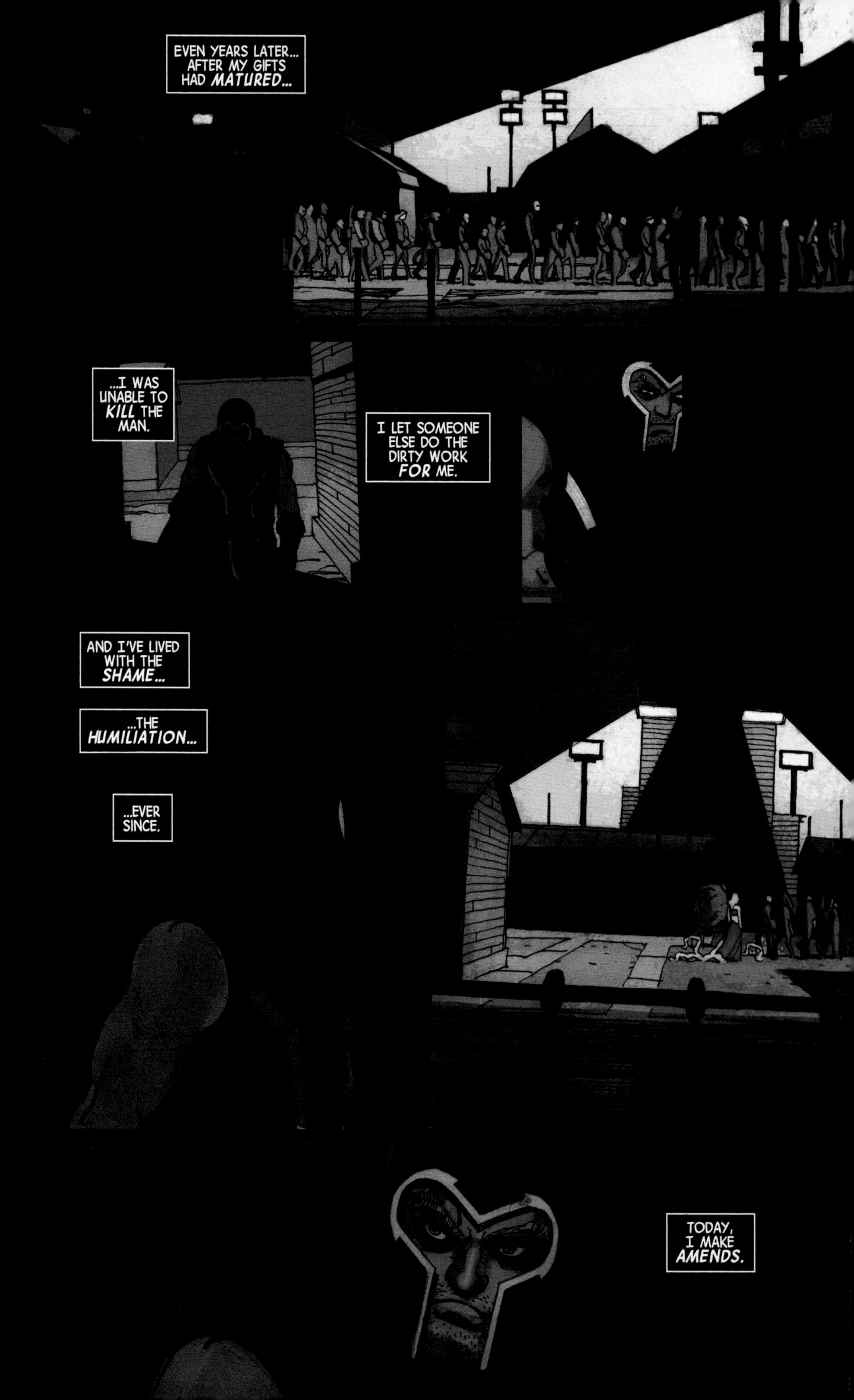
EVEN YEARS LATER... AFTER MY GIFTS HAD MATURED...
...I WAS UNABLE TO KILL THE MAN.
I LET SOMEONE ELSE DO THE DIRTY WORK FOR ME.
AND I'VE LIVED WITH THE SHAME...
...THE HUMILIATION...
...EVER SINCE.
TODAY, I MAKE AMENDS.

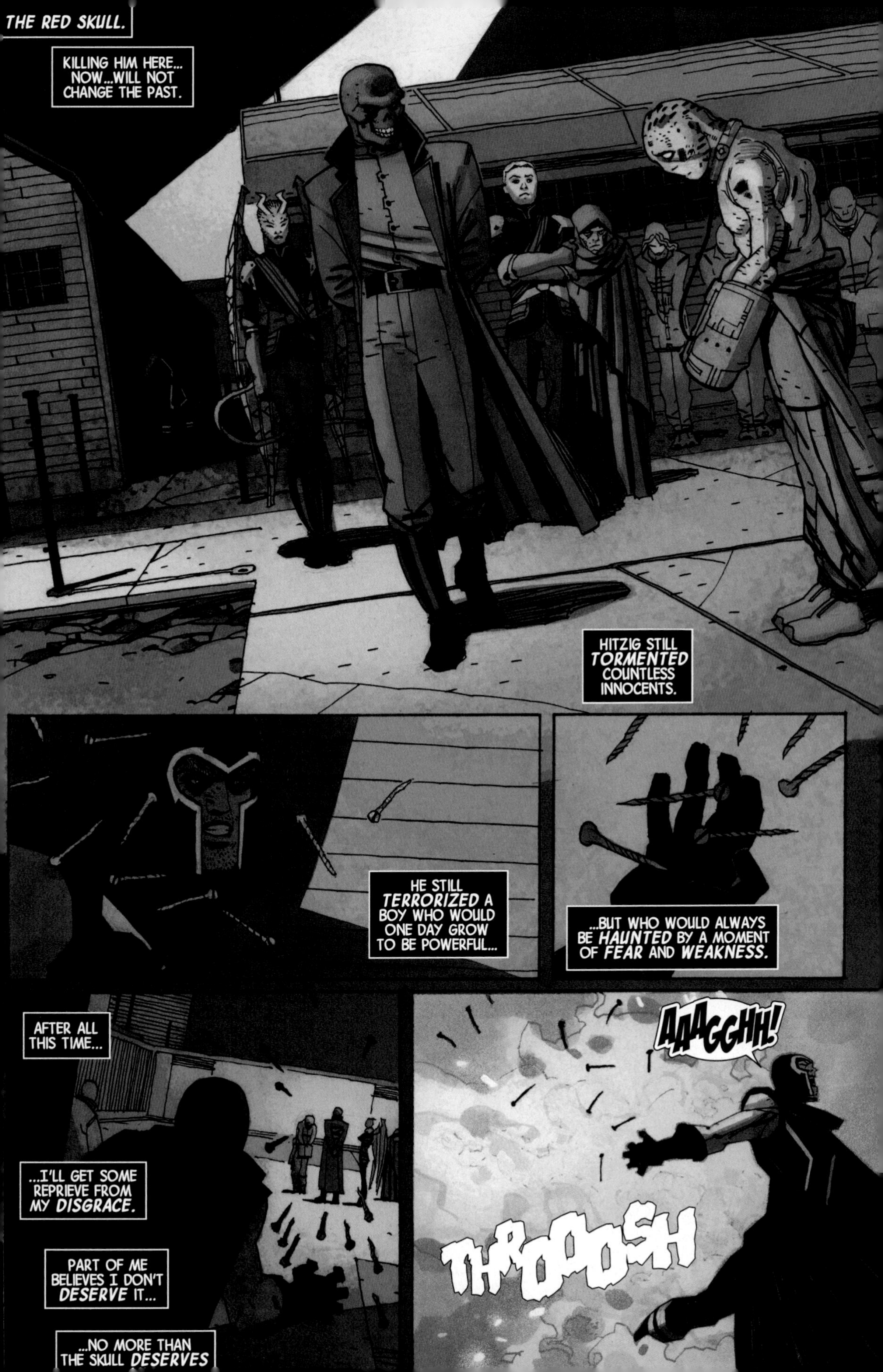
THE RED SKULL.
KILLING HIM HERE... NOW...WILL NOT CHANGE THE PAST.
HITZIG STILL TORMENTED COUNTLESS INNOCENTS.
HE STILL TERRORIZED A BOY WHO WOULD ONE DAY GROW TO BE POWERFUL...
...BUT WHO WOULD ALWAYS BE HAUNTED BY A MOMENT OF FEAR AND WEAKNESS.
AFTER ALL THIS TIME...
...I'LL GET SOME REPRIEVE FROM MY DISGRACE.
PART OF ME BELIEVES I DON'T DESERVE IT...
...NO MORE THAN THE SKULL DESERVES
AAAGGHH!
THROOOSH

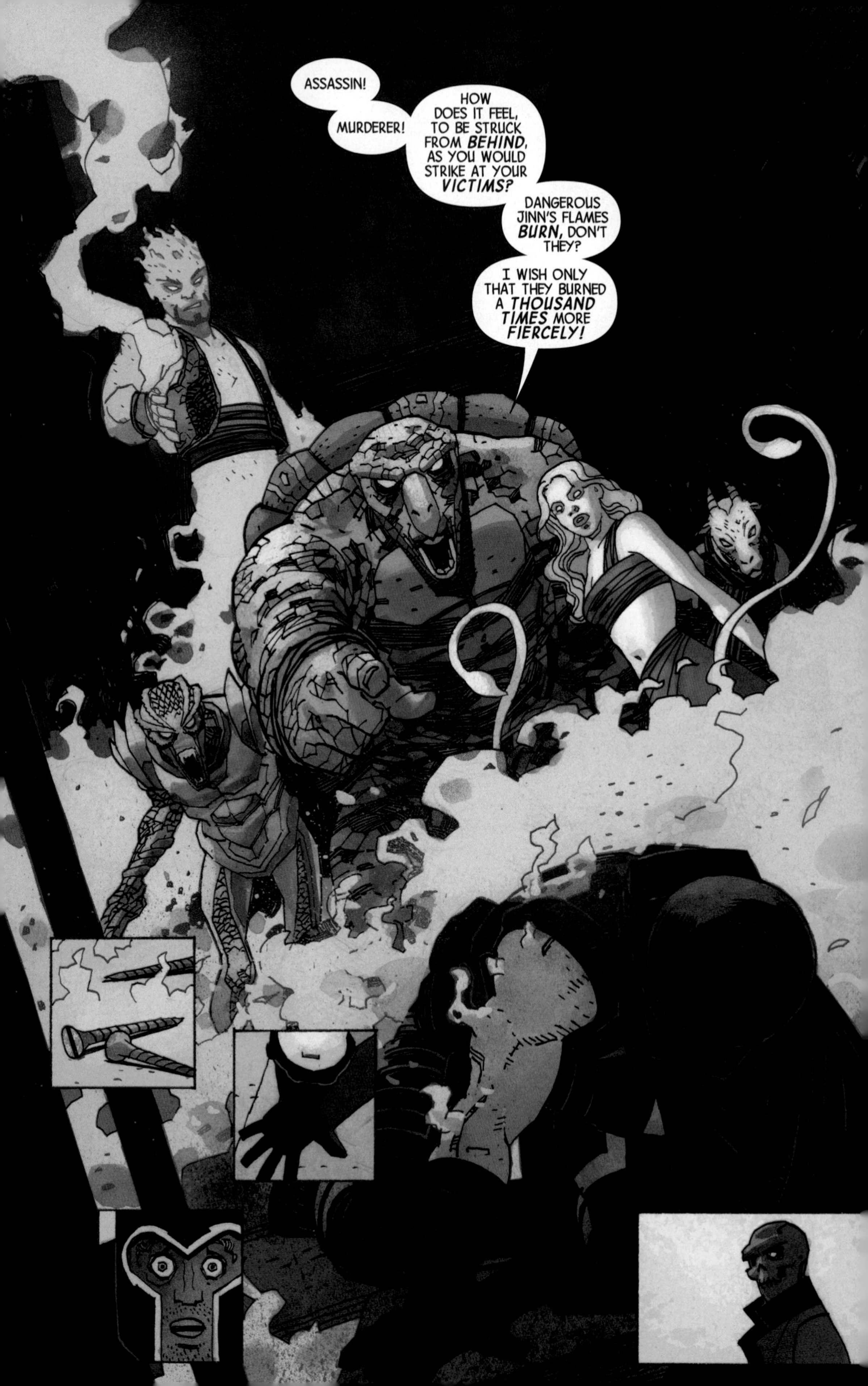
ASSASSIN!
MURDERER!
HOW DOES IT FEEL, TO BE STRUCK FROM BEHIND, AS YOU WOULD STRIKE AT YOUR VICTIMS?
DANGEROUS JINN'S FLAMES BURN, DON'T THEY?
I WISH ONLY THAT THEY BURNED A THOUSAND TIMES MORE FIERCELY!

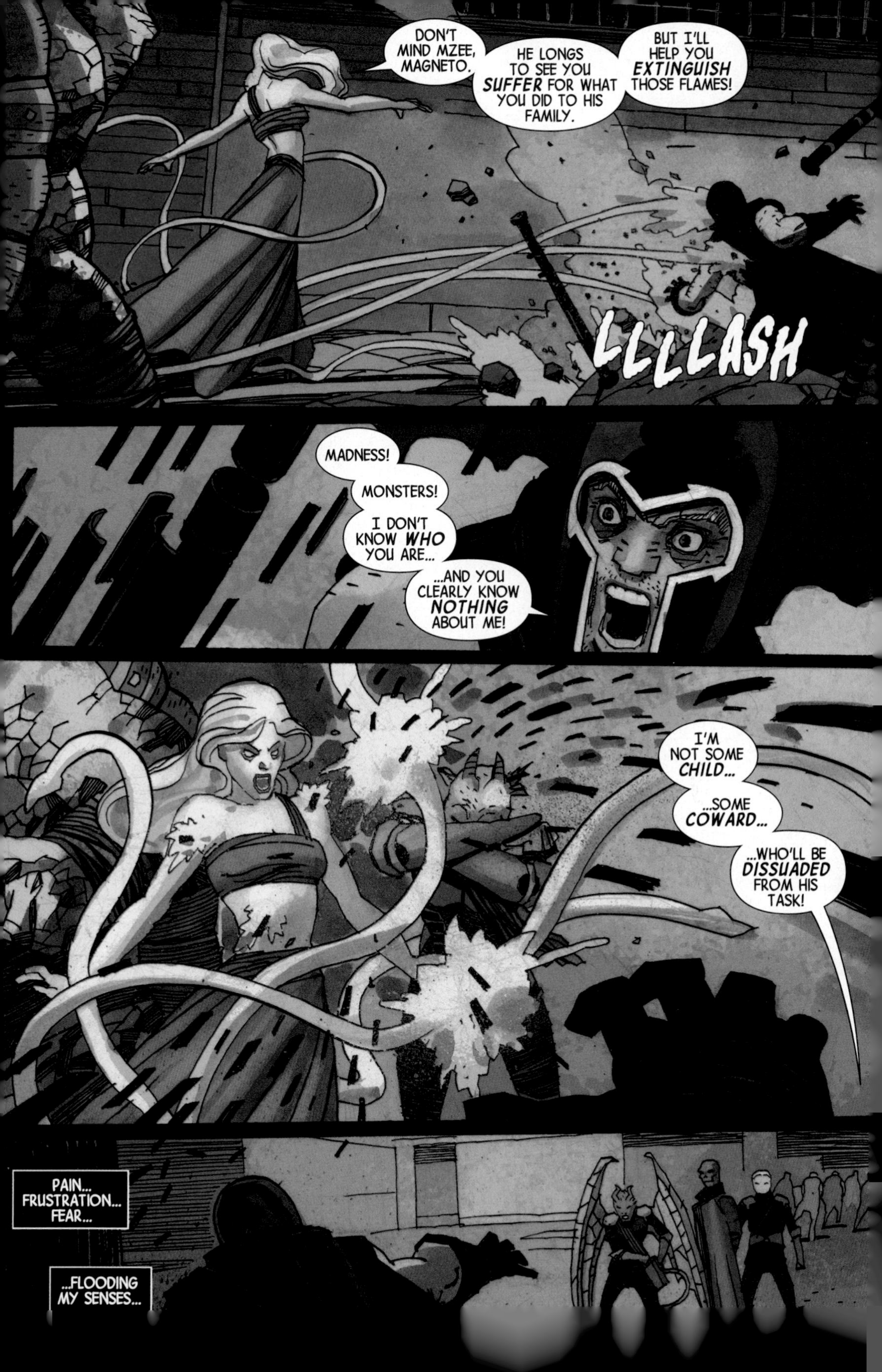
DON'T MIND MZEE, MAGNETO.
HE LONGS TO SEE YOU SUFFER FOR WHAT YOU DID TO HIS FAMILY.
BUT I'LL HELP YOU EXTINGUISH THOSE FLAMES!
LLLLASH
MADNESS!
MONSTERS!
I DON'T KNOW WHO YOU ARE...
...AND YOU CLEARLY KNOW NOTHING ABOUT ME!
I'M NOT SOME CHILD...
...SOME COWARD...
...WHO'LL BE DISSUADED FROM HIS TASK!
PAIN... FRUSTRATION... FEAR...
...FLOODING MY SENSES...

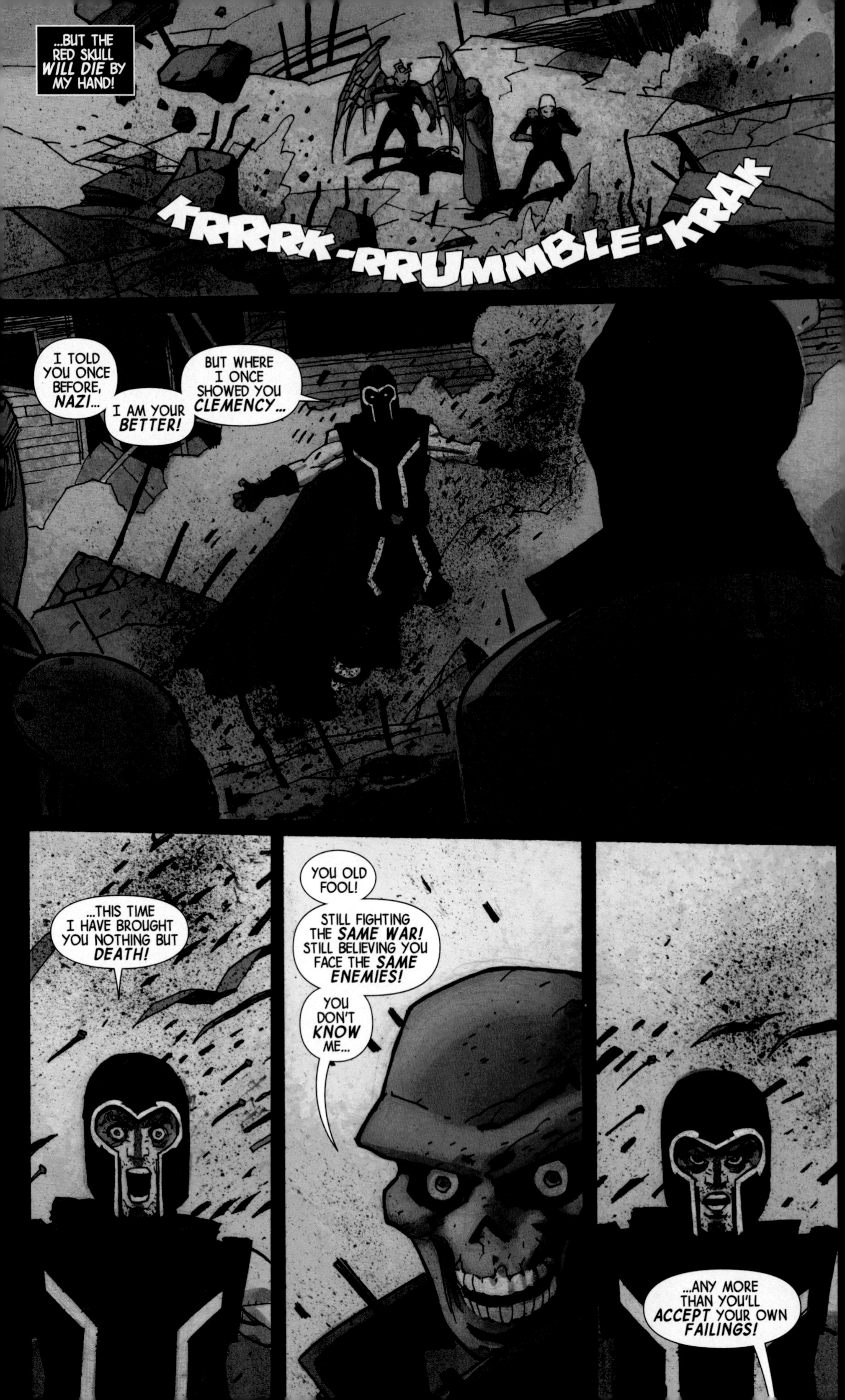
...BUT THE RED SKULL WILL DIE BY MY HAND!
KRRRK-RRUMMBLE-KRAK
I TOLD YOU ONCE BEFORE, NAZI...
I AM YOUR BETTER!
BUT WHERE I ONCE SHOWED YOU CLEMENCY...
...THIS TIME I HAVE BROUGHT YOU NOTHING BUT DEATH!
YOU OLD FOOL!
STILL FIGHTING THE SAME WAR! STILL BELIEVING YOU FACE THE SAME ENEMIES!
YOU DON'T KNOW ME...
...ANY MORE THAN YOU'LL ACCEPT YOUR OWN FAILINGS!

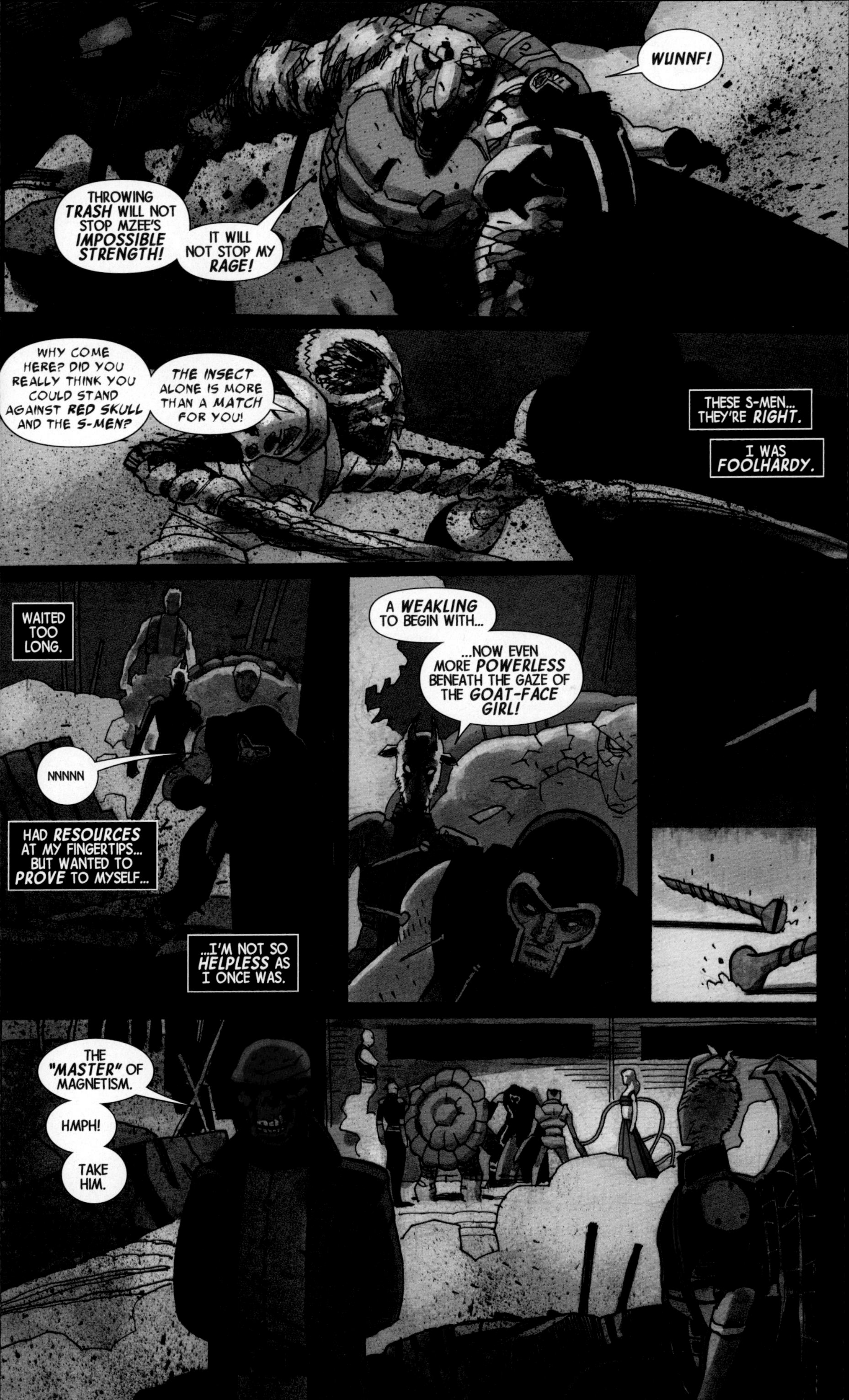
WUNNF!
THROWING TRASH WILL NOT STOP MZEE'S IMPOSSIBLE STRENGTH!
IT WILL NOT STOP MY RAGE!
WHY COME HERE? DID YOU REALLY THINK YOU COULD STAND AGAINST RED SKULL AND THE S-MEN?
THE INSECT ALONE IS MORE THAN A MATCH FOR YOU!
THESE S-MEN... THEY'RE RIGHT.
I WAS FOOLHARDY.
WAITED TOO LONG.
NNNNN
HAD RESOURCES AT MY FINGERTIPS... BUT WANTED TO PROVE TO MYSELF...
...I'M NOT SO HELPLESS AS I ONCE WAS.
A WEAKLING TO BEGIN WITH...
...NOW EVEN MORE POWERLESS BENEATH THE GAZE OF THE GOAT-FACE GIRL!
THE "MASTER" OF MAGNETISM.
HMPH!
TAKE HIM.

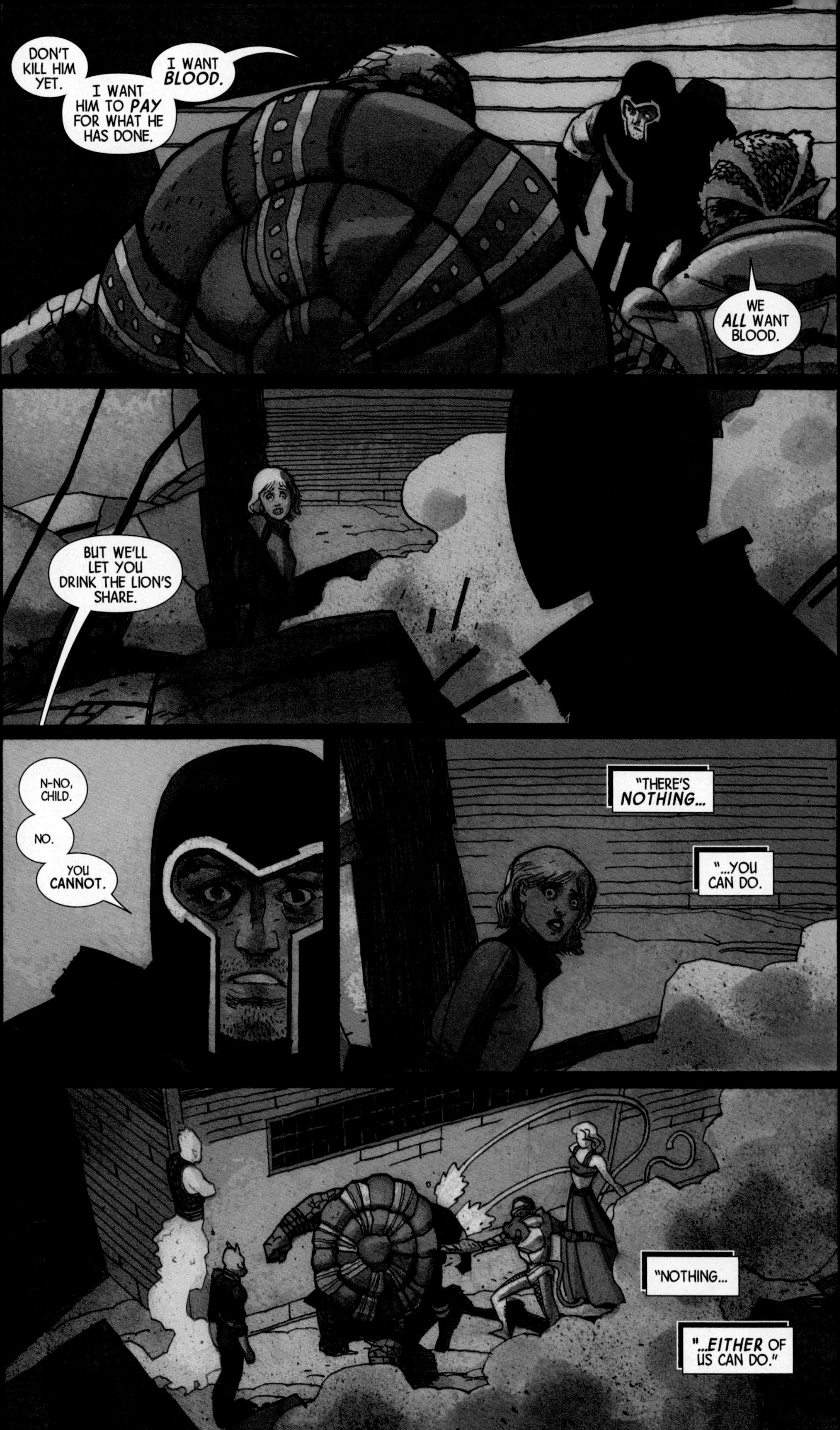
DON'T KILL HIM YET.
I WANT HIM TO PAY FOR WHAT HE HAS DONE.
I WANT BLOOD.
WE ALL WANT BLOOD.
BUT WE'LL LET YOU DRINK THE LION'S SHARE.
N-NO, CHILD.
NO.
YOU CANNOT.
"THERE'S NOTHING...
"...YOU CAN DO.
"NOTHING...
"...EITHER OF US CAN DO."

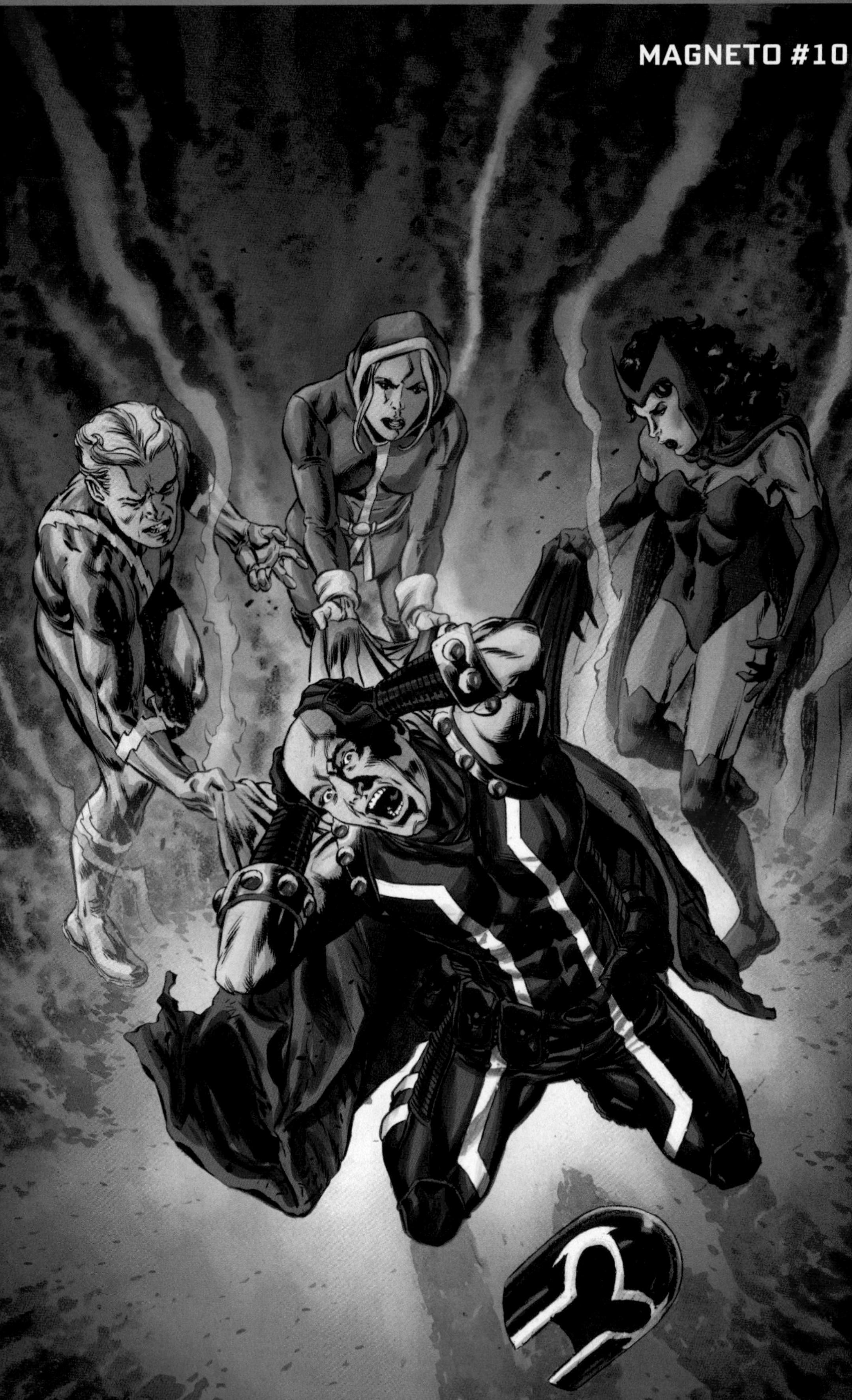
MAGNETO #10

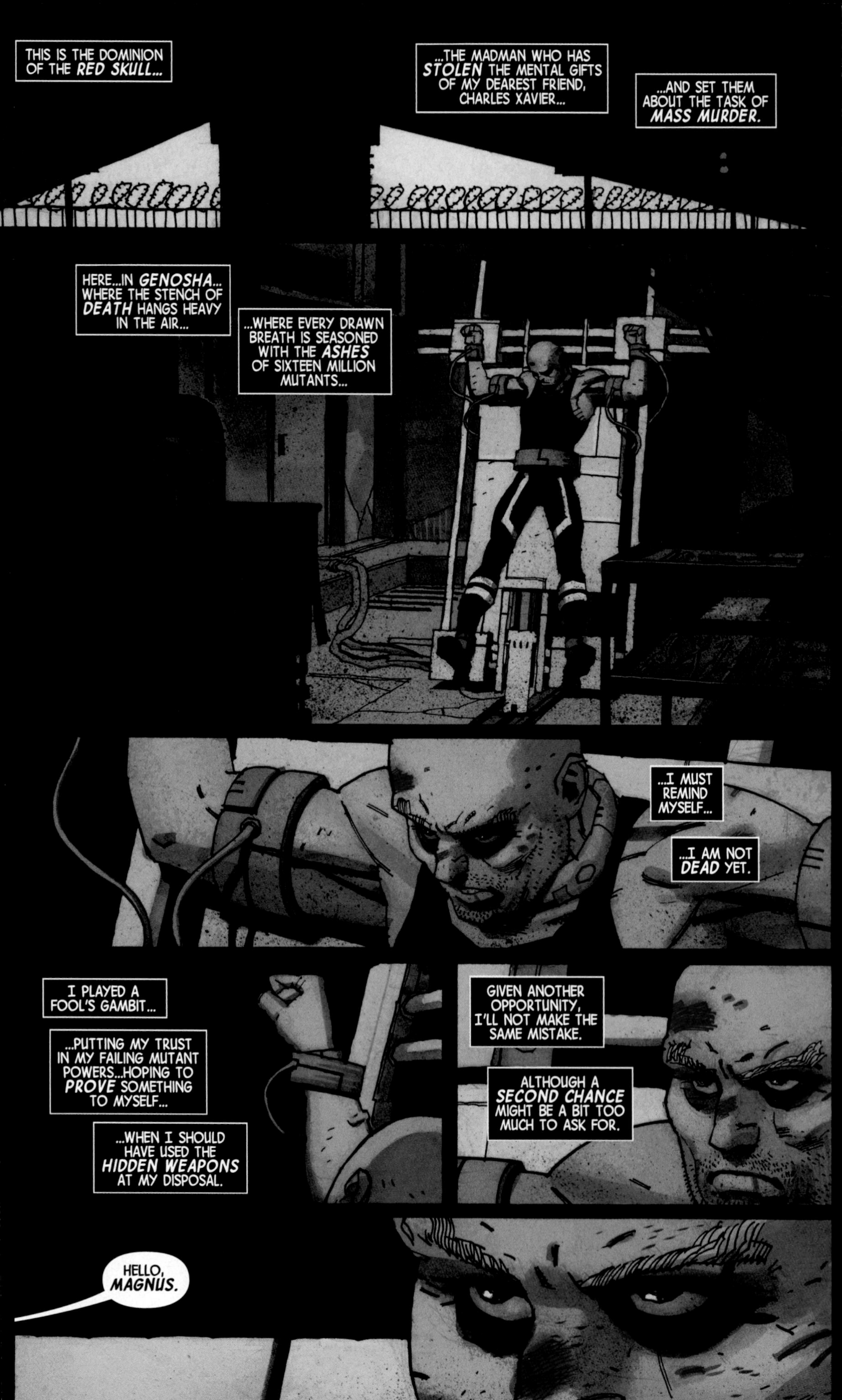
THIS IS THE DOMINION OF THE RED SKULL...
...THE MADMAN WHO HAS STOLEN THE MENTAL GIFTS OF MY DEAREST FRIEND, CHARLES XAVIER...
...AND SET THEM ABOUT THE TASK OF MASS MURDER.
HERE...IN GENOSHA... WHERE THE STENCH OF DEATH HANGS HEAVY IN THE AIR...
...WHERE EVERY DRAWN BREATH IS SEASONED WITH THE ASHES OF SIXTEEN MILLION MUTANTS...
...I MUST REMIND MYSELF...
...I AM NOT DEAD YET.
I PLAYED A FOOL'S GAMBIT...
...PUTTING MY TRUST IN MY FAILING MUTANT POWERS...HOPING TO PROVE SOMETHING TO MYSELF...
...WHEN I SHOULD HAVE USED THE HIDDEN WEAPONS AT MY DISPOSAL.
GIVEN ANOTHER OPPORTUNITY, I'LL NOT MAKE THE SAME MISTAKE.
ALTHOUGH A SECOND CHANCE MIGHT BE A BIT TOO MUCH TO ASK FOR.
HELLO, MAGNUS.

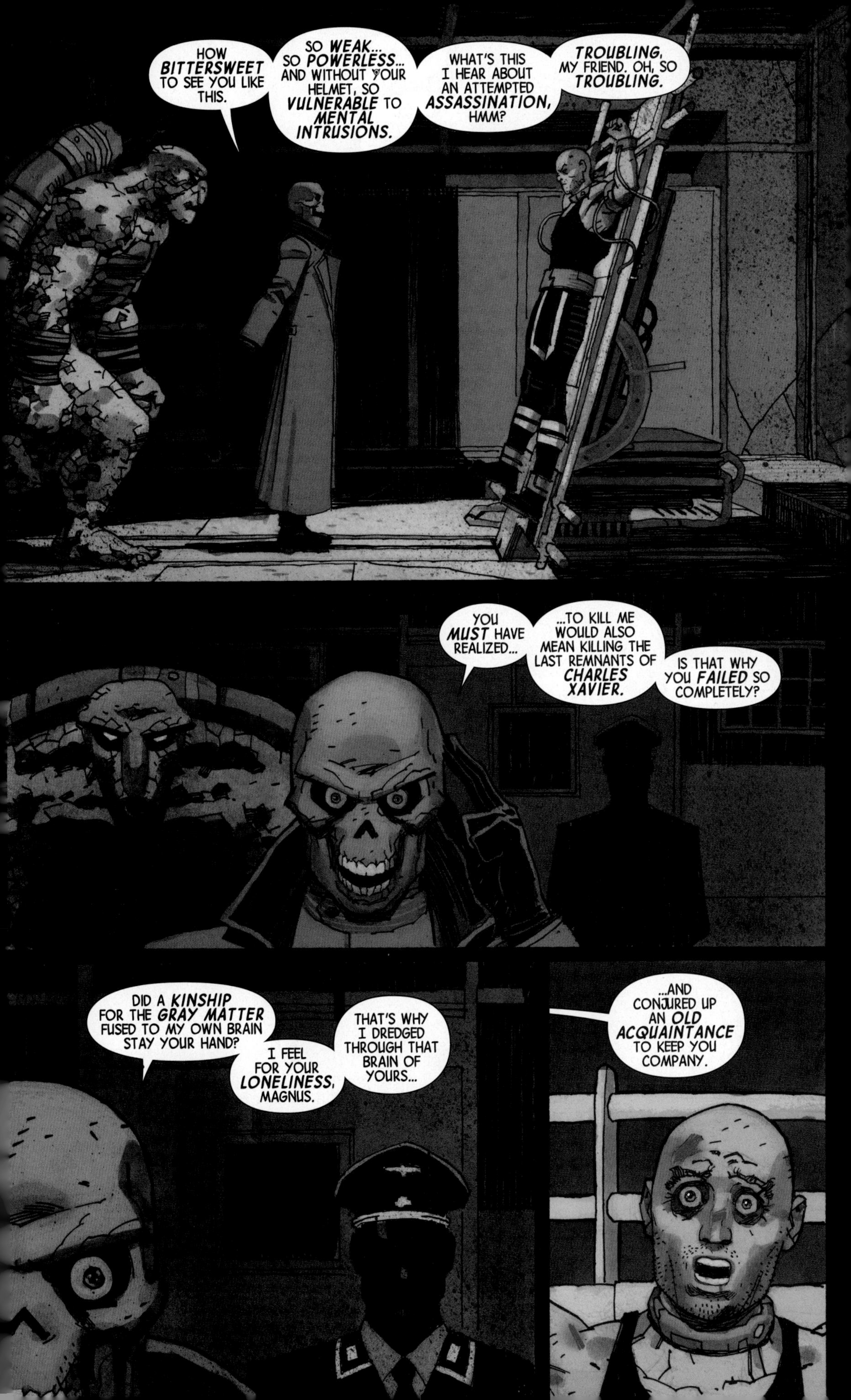
HOW BITTERSWEET TO SEE YOU LIKE THIS.
SO WEAK... SO POWERLESS... AND WITHOUT YOUR HELMET, SO VULNERABLE TO MENTAL INTRUSIONS.
WHAT'S THIS I HEAR ABOUT AN ATTEMPTED ASSASSINATION, HMM?
TROUBLING, MY FRIEND. OH, SO TROUBLING.
YOU MUST HAVE REALIZED...
...TO KILL ME WOULD ALSO MEAN KILLING THE LAST REMNANTS OF CHARLES XAVIER.
IS THAT WHY YOU FAILED SO COMPLETELY?
DID A KINSHIP FOR THE GRAY MATTER FUSED TO MY OWN BRAIN STAY YOUR HAND?
I FEEL FOR YOUR LONELINESS, MAGNUS.
THAT'S WHY I DREDGED THROUGH THAT BRAIN OF YOURS...
...AND CONJURED UP AN OLD ACQUAINTANCE TO KEEP YOU COMPANY.

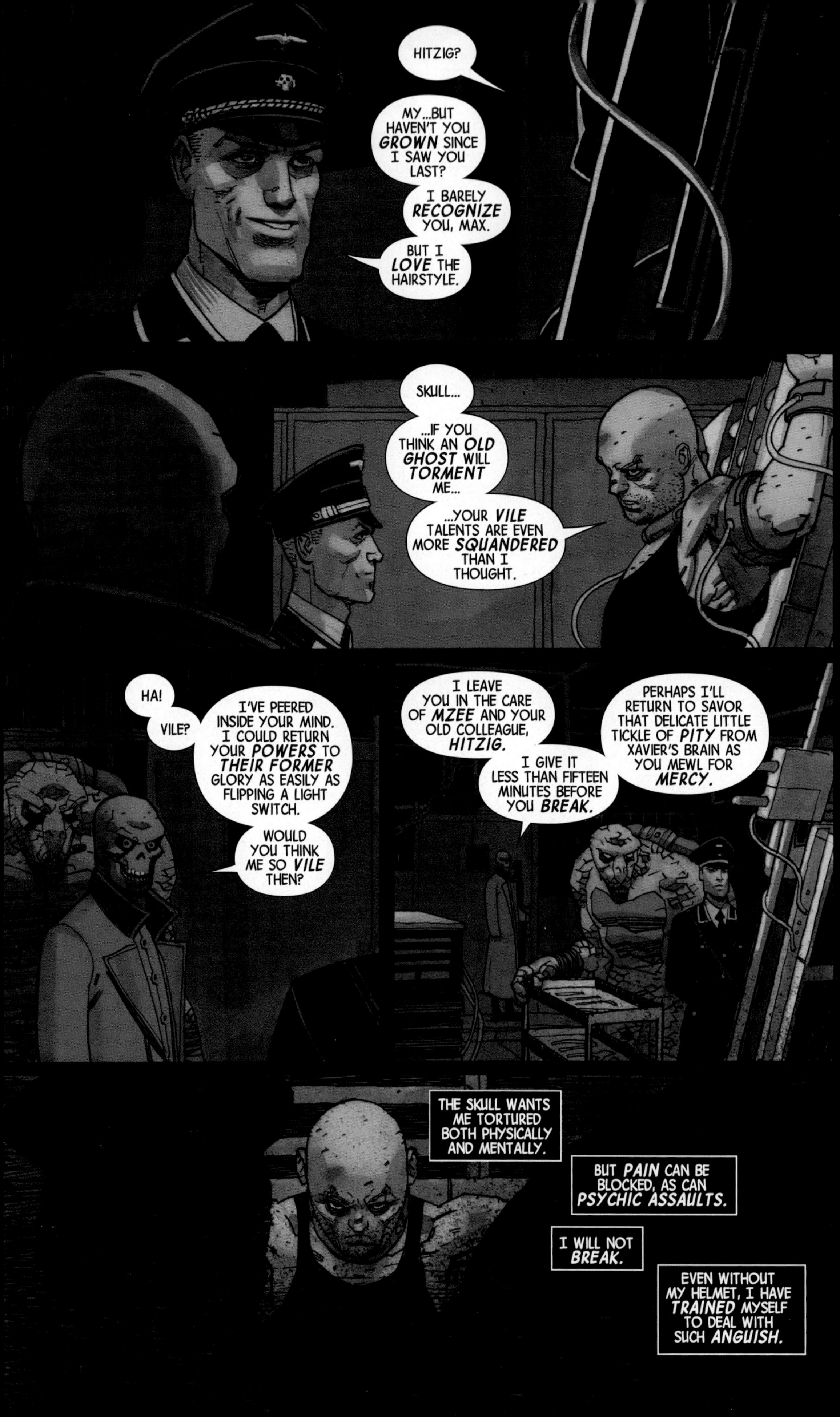
HITZIG?
MY...BUT HAVEN'T YOU GROWN SINCE I SAW YOU LAST?
I BARELY RECOGNIZE YOU, MAX.
BUT I LOVE THE HAIRSTYLE.
SKULL...
...IF YOU THINK AN OLD GHOST WILL TORMENT ME...
...YOUR VILE TALENTS ARE EVEN MORE SQUANDERED THAN I THOUGHT.
HA!
VILE?
I'VE PEERED INSIDE YOUR MIND. I COULD RETURN YOUR POWERS TO THEIR FORMER GLORY AS EASILY AS FLIPPING A LIGHT SWITCH.
WOULD YOU THINK ME SO VILE THEN?
I LEAVE YOU IN THE CARE OF MZEE AND YOUR OLD COLLEAGUE, HITZIG.
I GIVE IT LESS THAN FIFTEEN MINUTES BEFORE YOU BREAK.
PERHAPS I'LL RETURN TO SAVOR THAT DELICATE LITTLE TICKLE OF PITY FROM XAVIER'S BRAIN AS YOU MEWL FOR MERCY.
THE SKULL WANTS ME TORTURED BOTH PHYSICALLY AND MENTALLY.
BUT PAIN CAN BE BLOCKED, AS CAN PSYCHIC ASSAULTS.
I WILL NOT BREAK.
EVEN WITHOUT MY HELMET, I HAVE TRAINED MYSELF TO DEAL WITH SUCH ANGUISH.

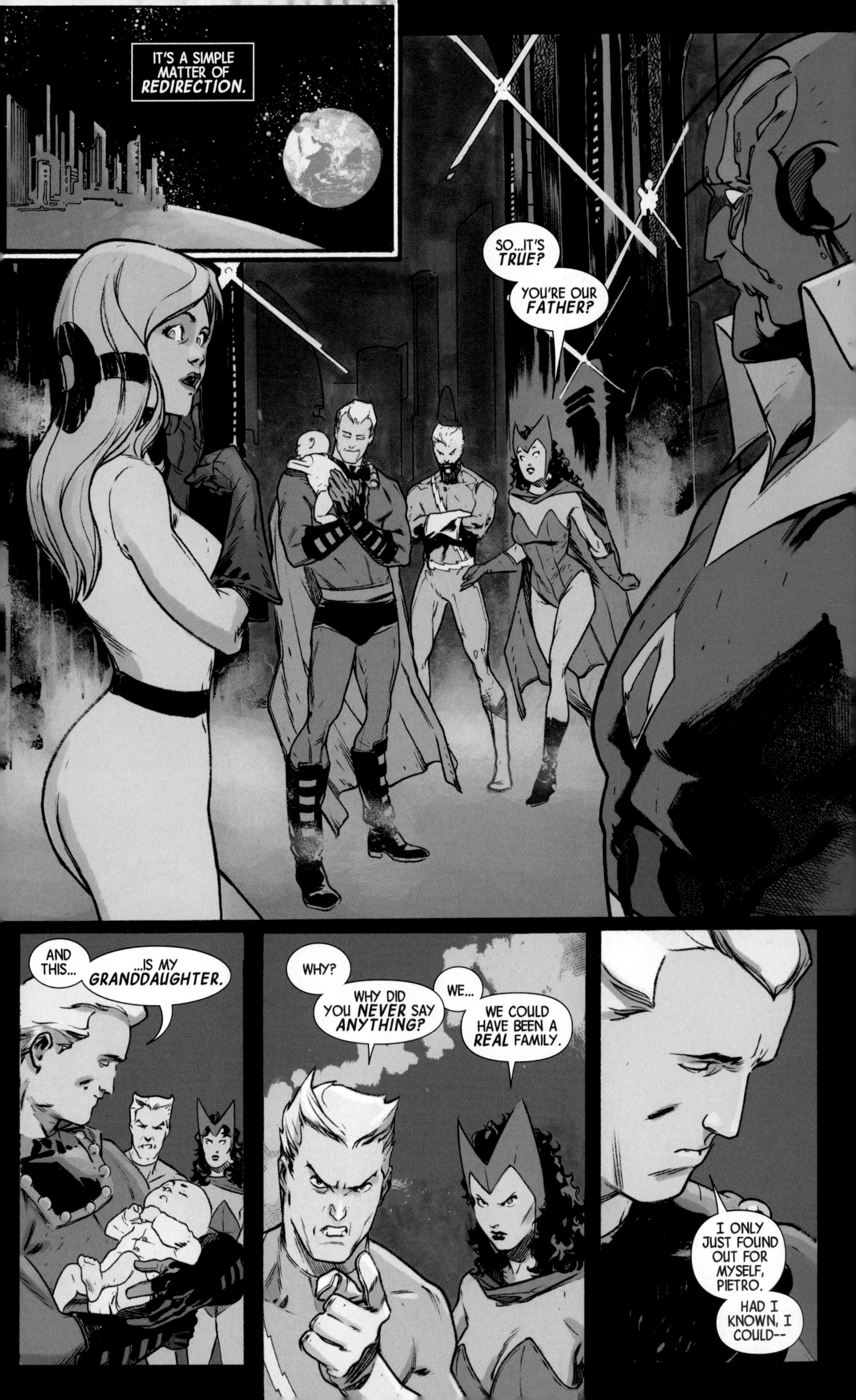
IT'S A SIMPLE MATTER OF REDIRECTION.
SO...IT'S TRUE?
YOU'RE OUR FATHER?
AND THIS...
...IS MY GRANDDAUGHTER.
WHY?
WHY DID YOU NEVER SAY ANYTHING?
WE...
WE COULD HAVE BEEN A REAL FAMILY.
I ONLY JUST FOUND OUT FOR MYSELF, PIETRO.
HAD I KNOWN, I COULD--

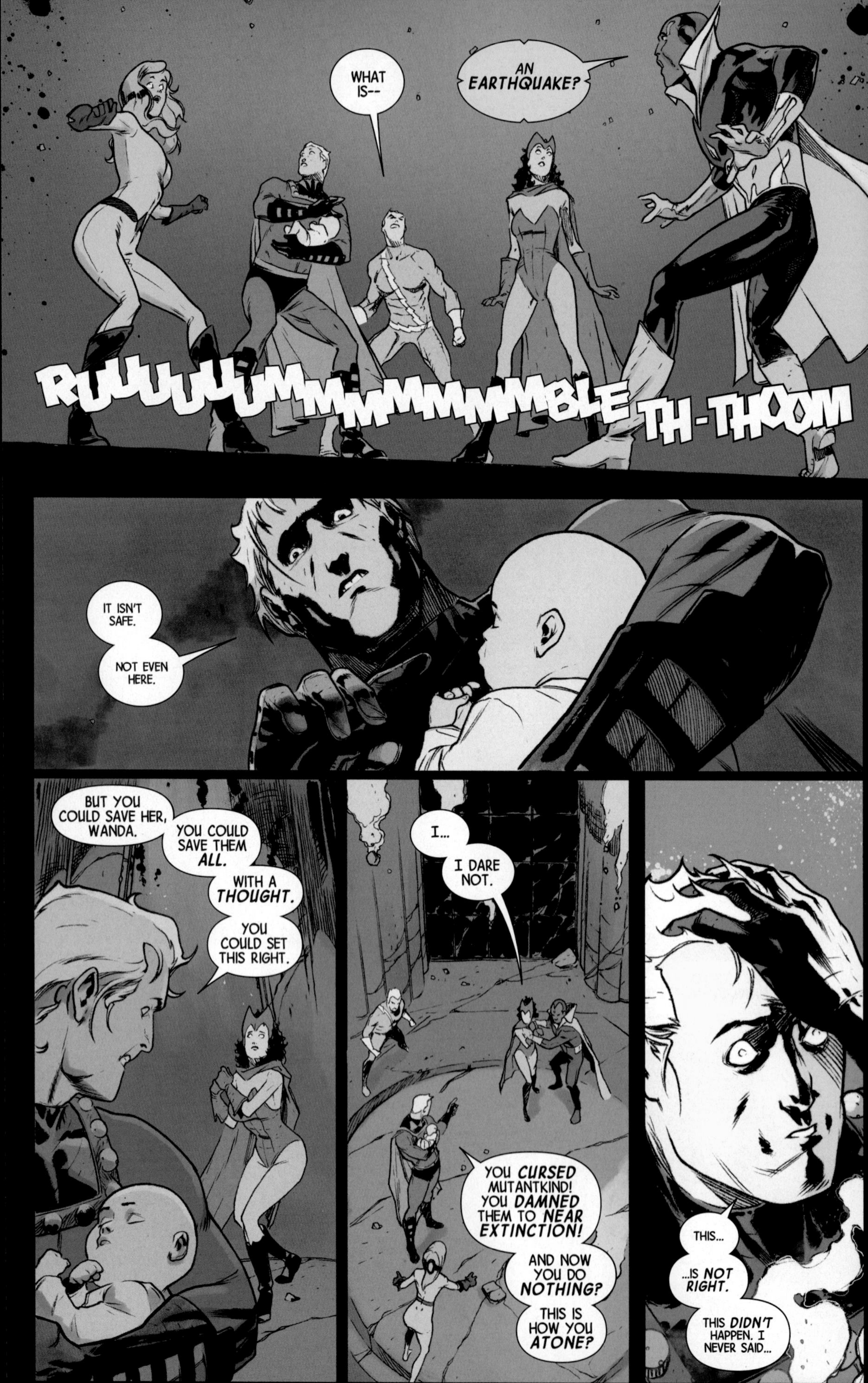
WHAT IS--
AN EARTHQUAKE?
RUUUUUMMMMMMMMMBLE
TH-THOOM
IT ISN'T SAFE.
NOT EVEN HERE.
BUT YOU COULD SAVE HER, WANDA.
YOU COULD SAVE THEM ALL.
WITH A THOUGHT.
YOU COULD SET THIS RIGHT.
I...
I DARE NOT.
YOU CURSED MUTANTKIND! YOU DAMNED THEM TO NEAR EXTINCTION!
AND NOW YOU DO NOTHING?
THIS IS HOW YOU ATONE?
THIS...
...IS NOT RIGHT.
THIS DIDN'T HAPPEN. I NEVER SAID...

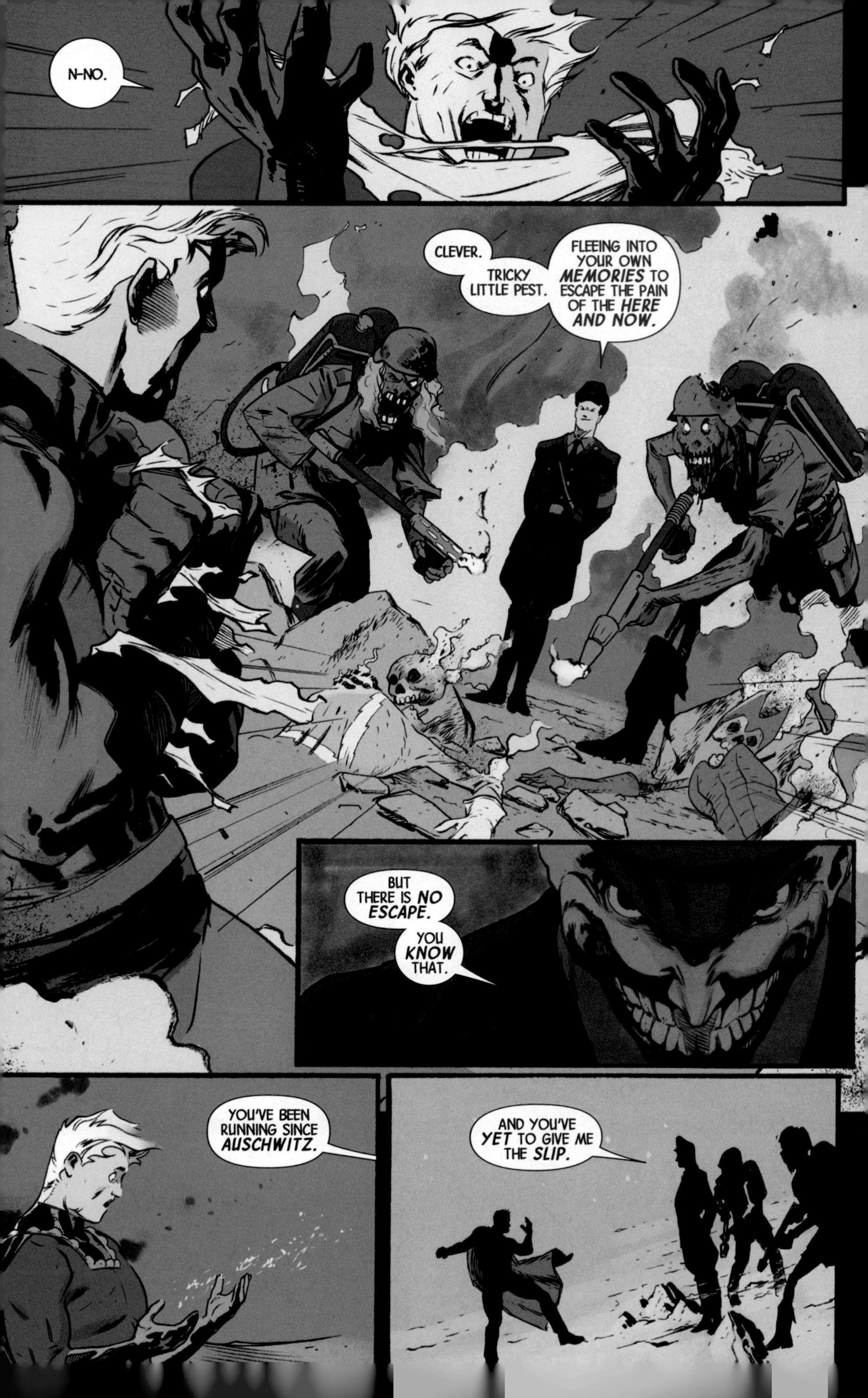
N-NO.
CLEVER.
TRICKY LITTLE PEST.
FLEEING INTO YOUR OWN *MEMORIES* TO ESCAPE THE PAIN OF THE *HERE AND NOW.*
BUT THERE IS *NO ESCAPE.*
YOU *KNOW* THAT.
YOU'VE BEEN RUNNING SINCE *AUSCHWITZ.*
AND YOU'VE *YET* TO GIVE ME THE *SLIP.*

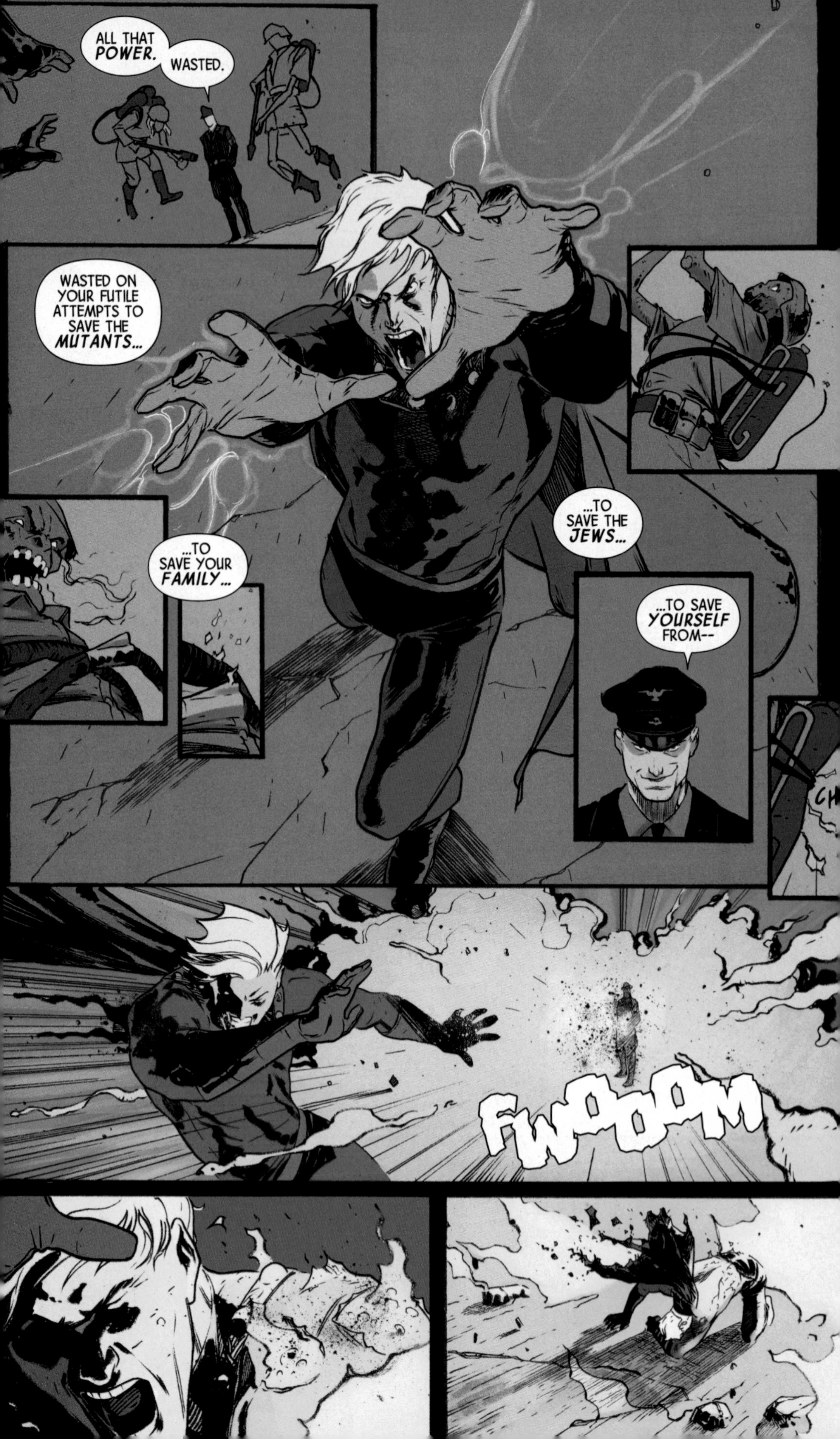
ALL THAT POWER.
WASTED.
WASTED ON YOUR FUTILE ATTEMPTS TO SAVE THE MUTANTS...
...TO SAVE THE JEWS...
...TO SAVE YOUR FAMILY...
...TO SAVE YOURSELF FROM--
FWOOOM

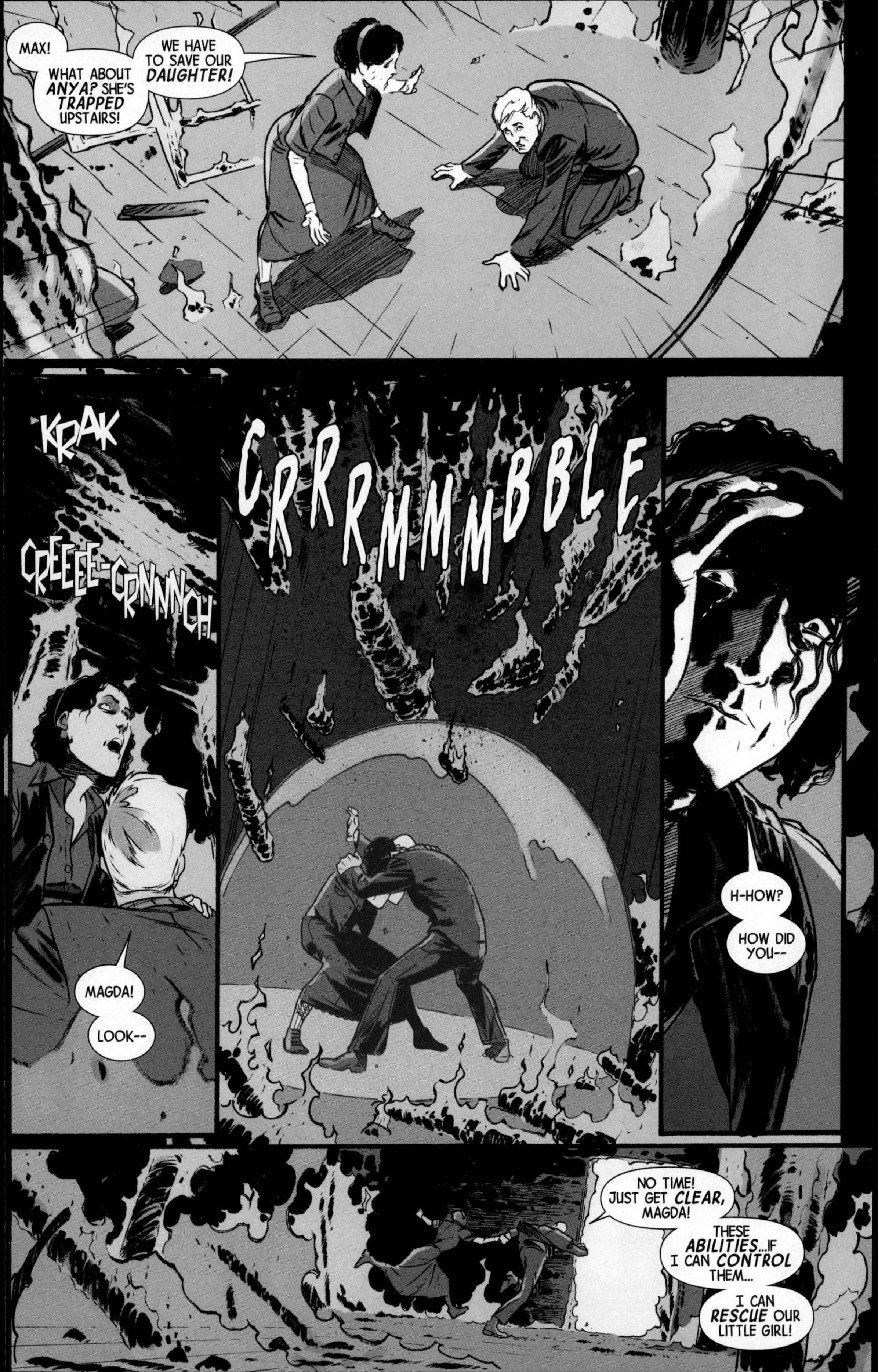
MAX!
WHAT ABOUT ANYA? SHE'S TRAPPED UPSTAIRS!
WE HAVE TO SAVE OUR DAUGHTER!
KRAK
CREEEE-CRNNNCH
MAGDA!
LOOK--
CRRRMMMBBLE
H-HOW?
HOW DID YOU--
NO TIME! JUST GET CLEAR, MAGDA!
THESE ABILITIES...IF I CAN CONTROL THEM...
I CAN RESCUE OUR LITTLE GIRL!

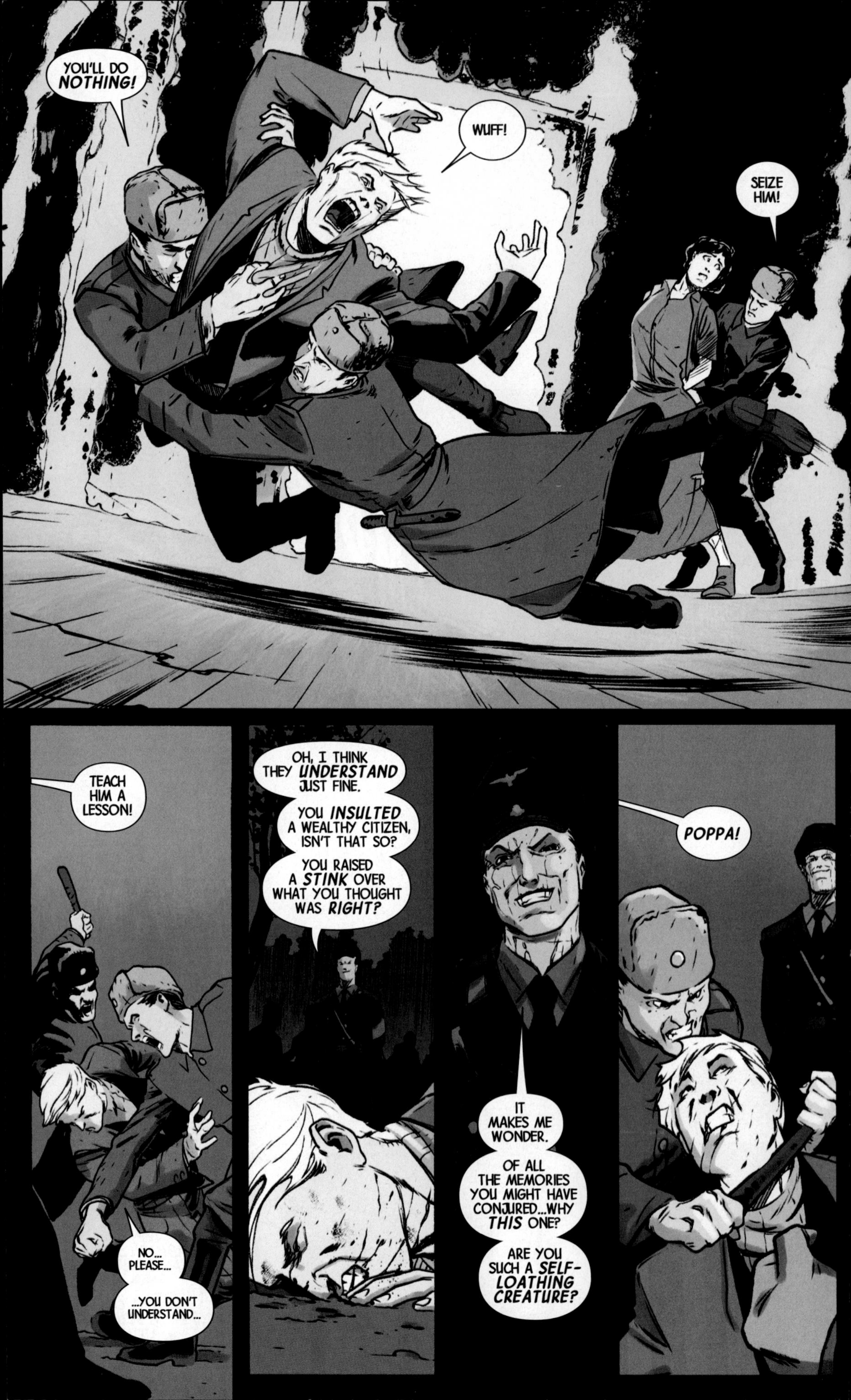
YOU'LL DO NOTHING!
WUFF!
SEIZE HIM!
TEACH HIM A LESSON!
NO... PLEASE...
...YOU DON'T UNDERSTAND...
OH, I THINK THEY UNDERSTAND JUST FINE.
YOU INSULTED A WEALTHY CITIZEN, ISN'T THAT SO?
YOU RAISED A STINK OVER WHAT YOU THOUGHT WAS RIGHT?
IT MAKES ME WONDER.
OF ALL THE MEMORIES YOU MIGHT HAVE CONJURED...WHY THIS ONE?
ARE YOU SUCH A SELF-LOATHING CREATURE?
POPPA!

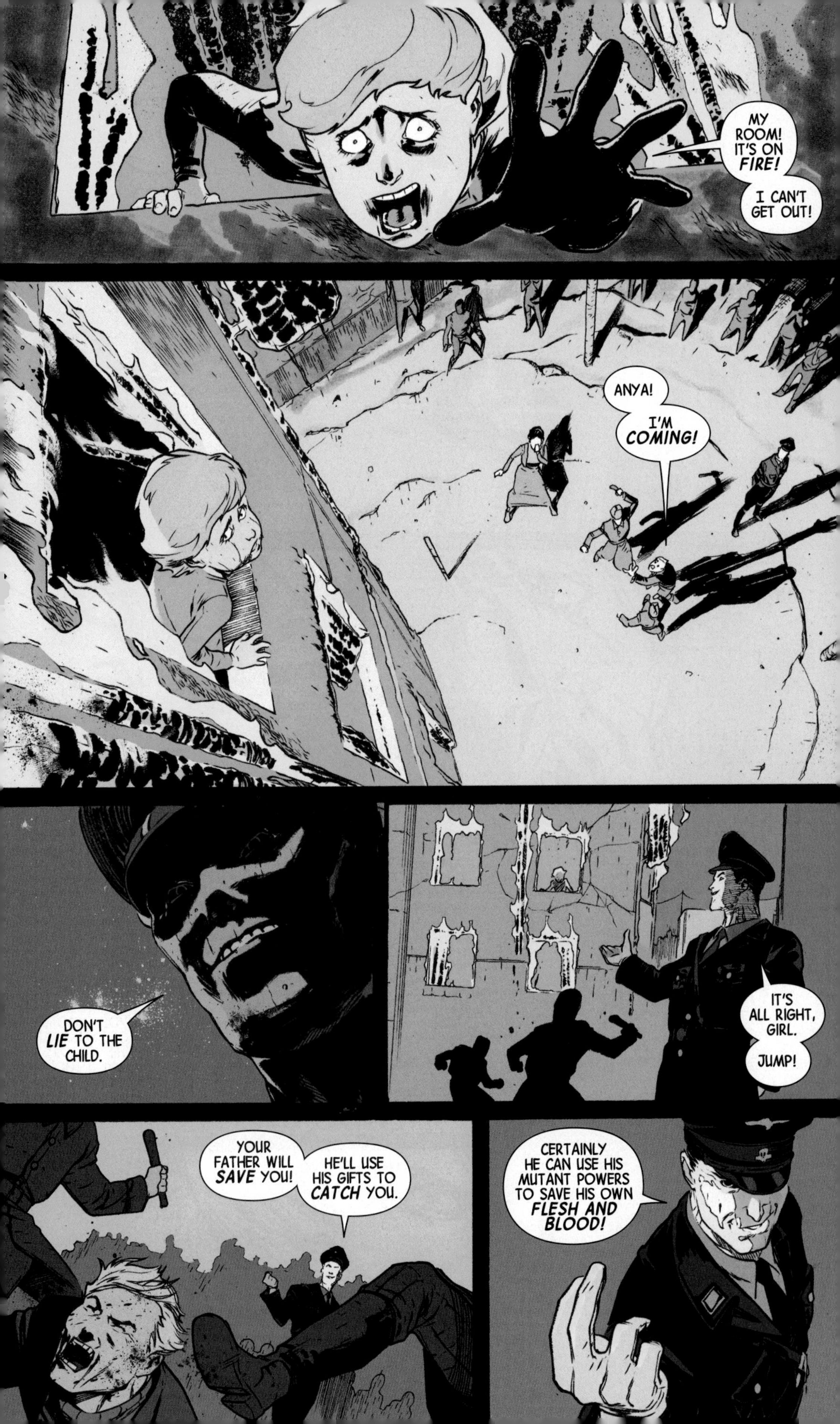
MY ROOM! IT'S ON FIRE!
I CAN'T GET OUT!
ANYA!
I'M COMING!
DON'T LIE TO THE CHILD.
IT'S ALL RIGHT, GIRL.
JUMP!
YOUR FATHER WILL SAVE YOU!
HE'LL USE HIS GIFTS TO CATCH YOU.
CERTAINLY HE CAN USE HIS MUTANT POWERS TO SAVE HIS OWN FLESH AND BLOOD!

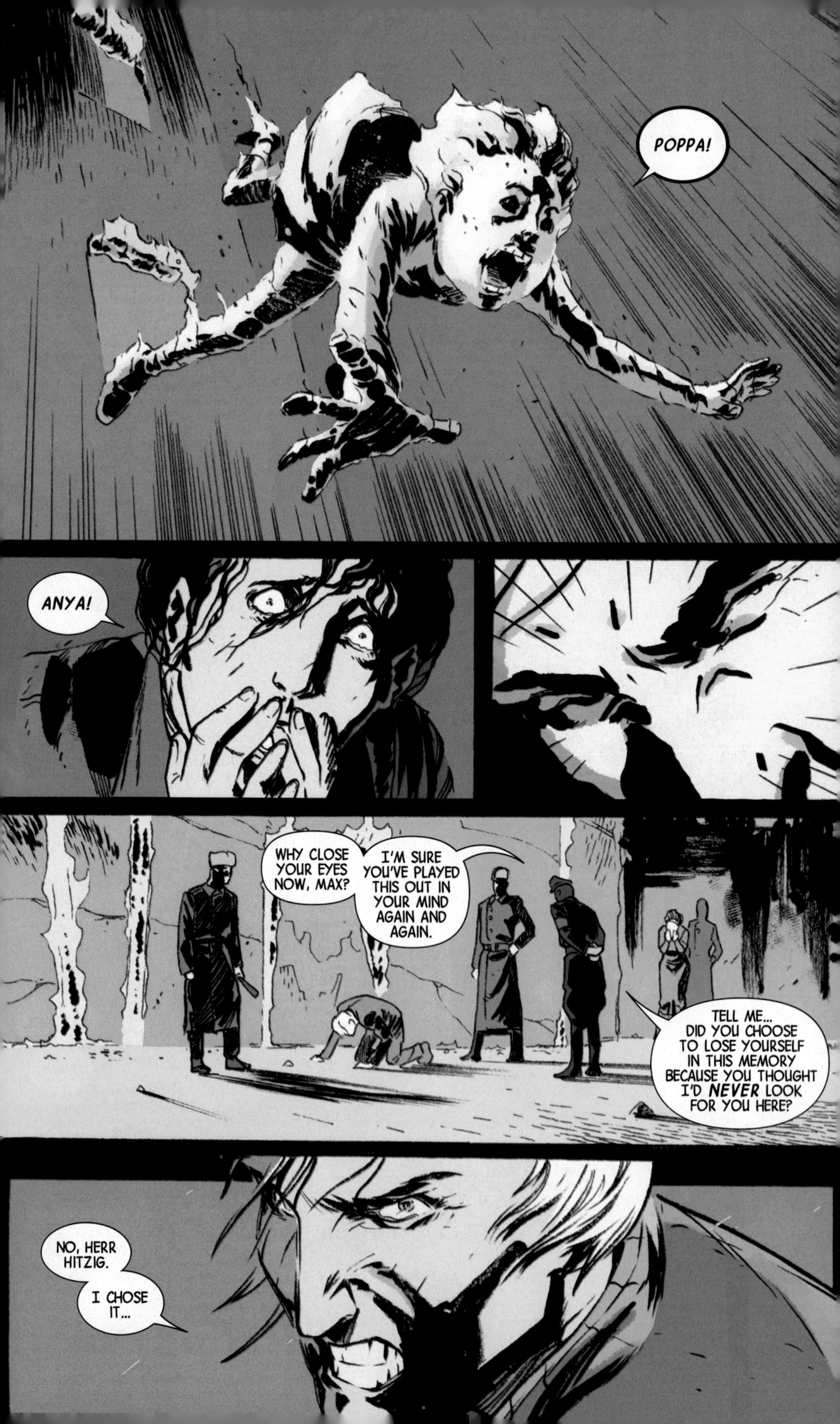
POPPA!
ANYA!
WHY CLOSE YOUR EYES NOW, MAX?
I'M SURE YOU'VE PLAYED THIS OUT IN YOUR MIND AGAIN AND AGAIN.
TELL ME... DID YOU CHOOSE TO LOSE YOURSELF IN THIS MEMORY BECAUSE YOU THOUGHT I'D NEVER LOOK FOR YOU HERE?
NO, HERR HITZIG.
I CHOSE IT...

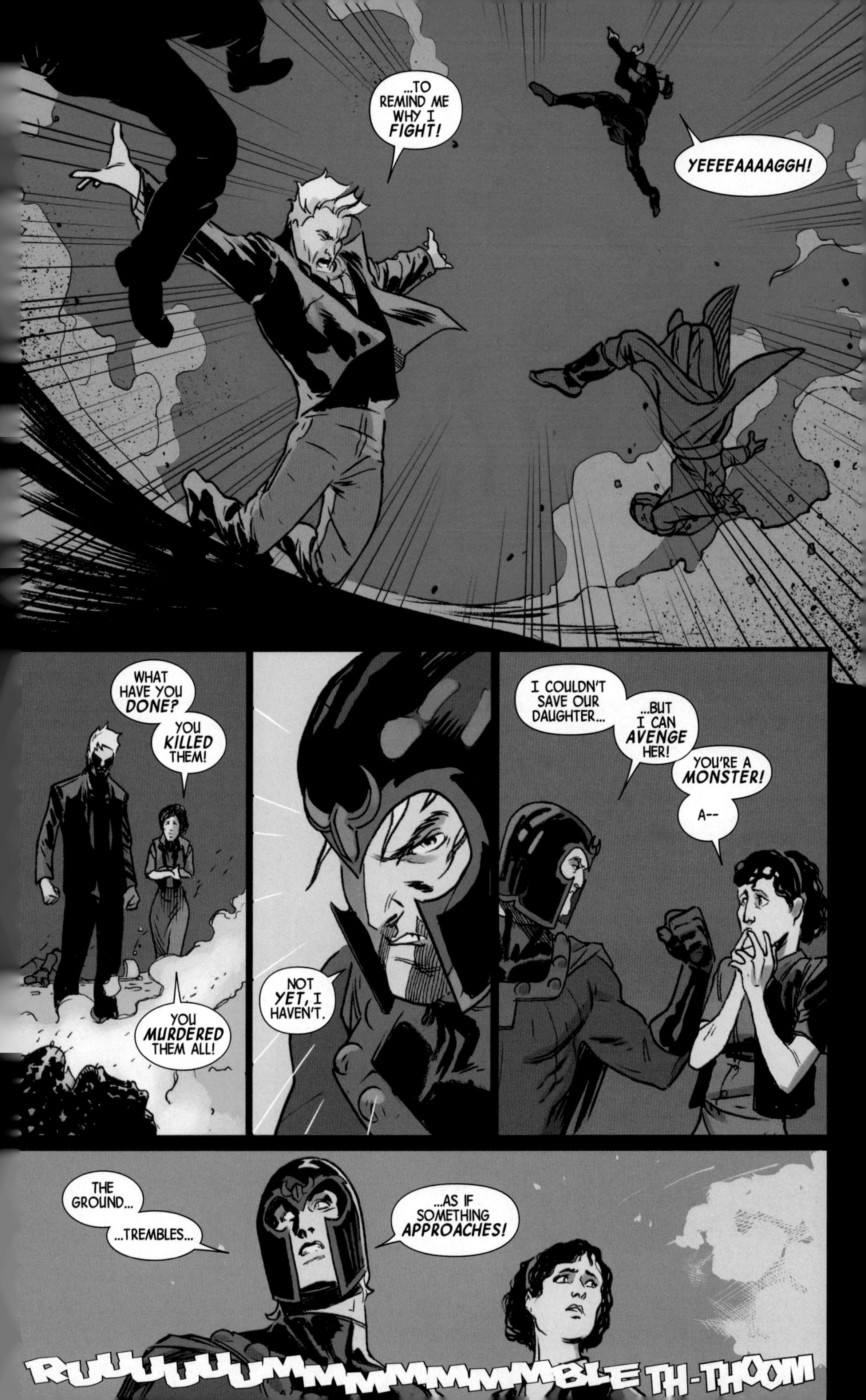
...TO REMIND ME WHY I FIGHT!
YEEEEAAAAGGH!
WHAT HAVE YOU DONE?
YOU KILLED THEM!
YOU MURDERED THEM ALL!
NOT YET, I HAVEN'T.
I COULDN'T SAVE OUR DAUGHTER...
...BUT I CAN AVENGE HER!
YOU'RE A MONSTER!
A--
THE GROUND...
...TREMBLES...
...AS IF SOMETHING APPROACHES!
RUUUUUUMMMMMMMMBLE TH-THOOM

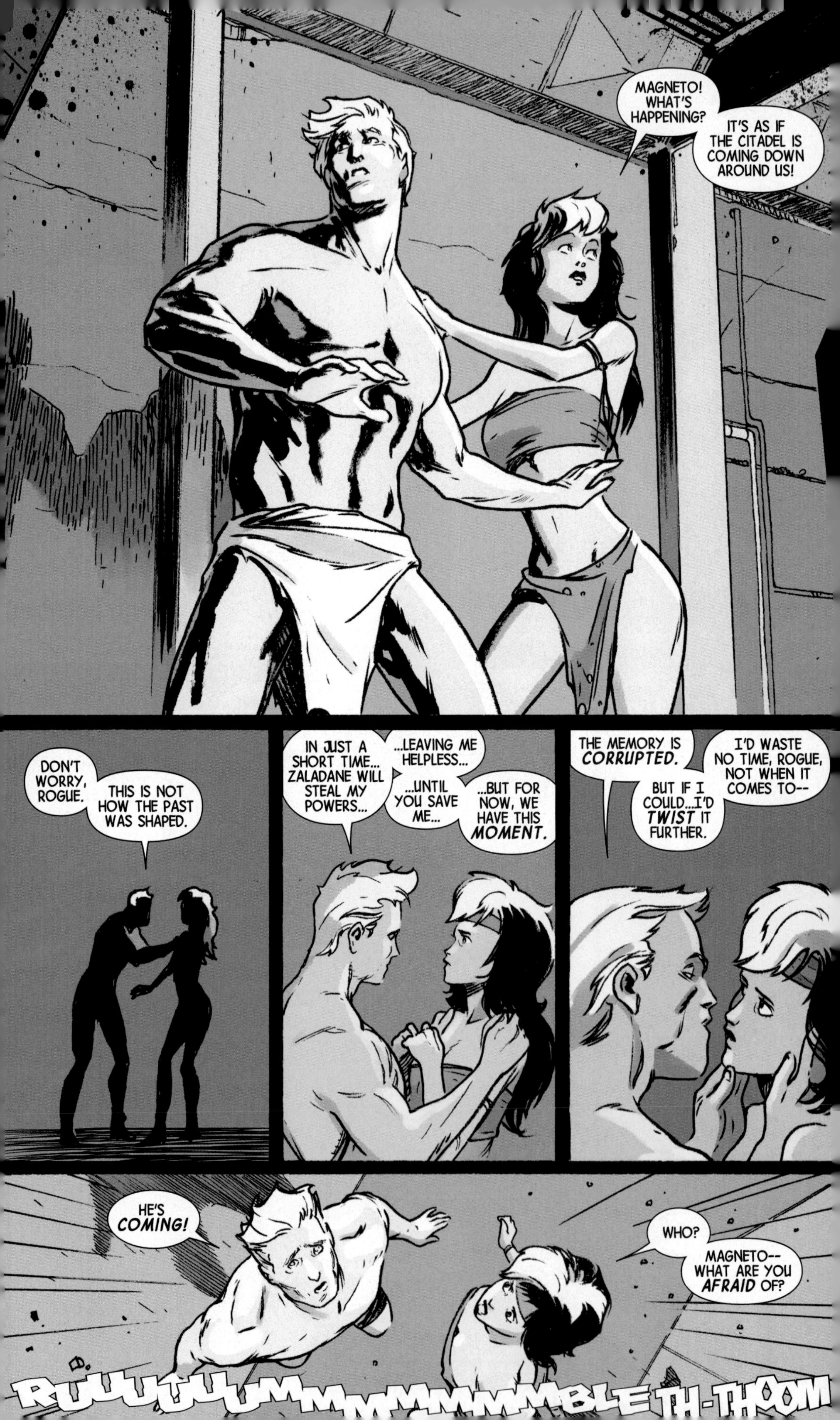
MAGNETO! WHAT'S HAPPENING?
IT'S AS IF THE CITADEL IS COMING DOWN AROUND US!
DON'T WORRY, ROGUE.
THIS IS NOT HOW THE PAST WAS SHAPED.
IN JUST A SHORT TIME... ZALADANE WILL STEAL MY POWERS...
...LEAVING ME HELPLESS...
...UNTIL YOU SAVE ME...
...BUT FOR NOW, WE HAVE THIS MOMENT.
THE MEMORY IS CORRUPTED.
BUT IF I COULD...I'D TWIST IT FURTHER.
I'D WASTE NO TIME, ROGUE, NOT WHEN IT COMES TO--
HE'S COMING!
WHO?
MAGNETO-- WHAT ARE YOU AFRAID OF?
RUUUUUMMMMMMMMMBLETH-THOOM

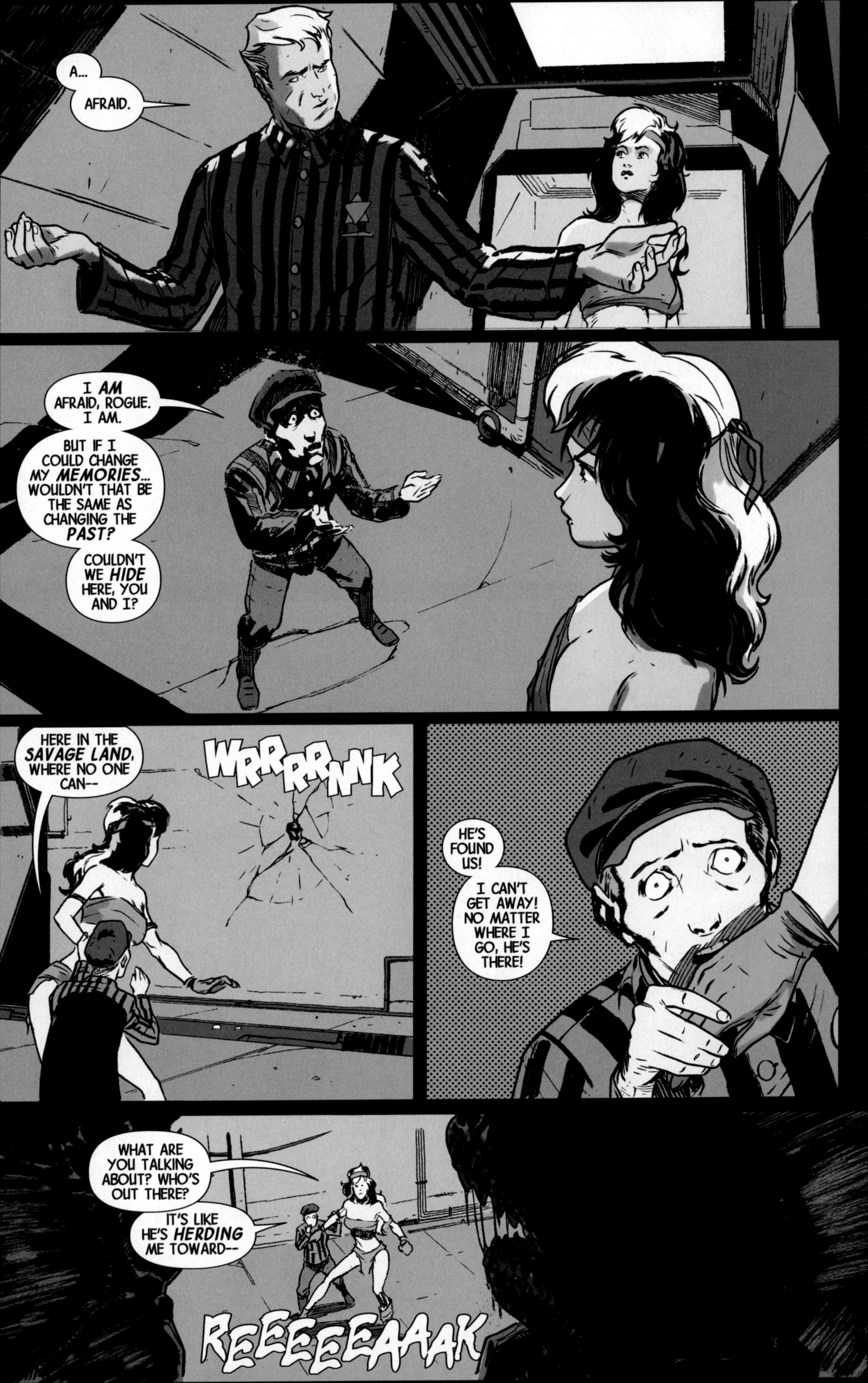
A...
AFRAID.
I AM AFRAID, ROGUE. I AM.
BUT IF I COULD CHANGE MY MEMORIES... WOULDN'T THAT BE THE SAME AS CHANGING THE PAST?
COULDN'T WE HIDE HERE, YOU AND I?
HERE IN THE SAVAGE LAND, WHERE NO ONE CAN--
WRRRRNNK
HE'S FOUND US!
I CAN'T GET AWAY! NO MATTER WHERE I GO, HE'S THERE!
WHAT ARE YOU TALKING ABOUT? WHO'S OUT THERE?
IT'S LIKE HE'S HERDING ME TOWARD--
REEEEEEAAAK

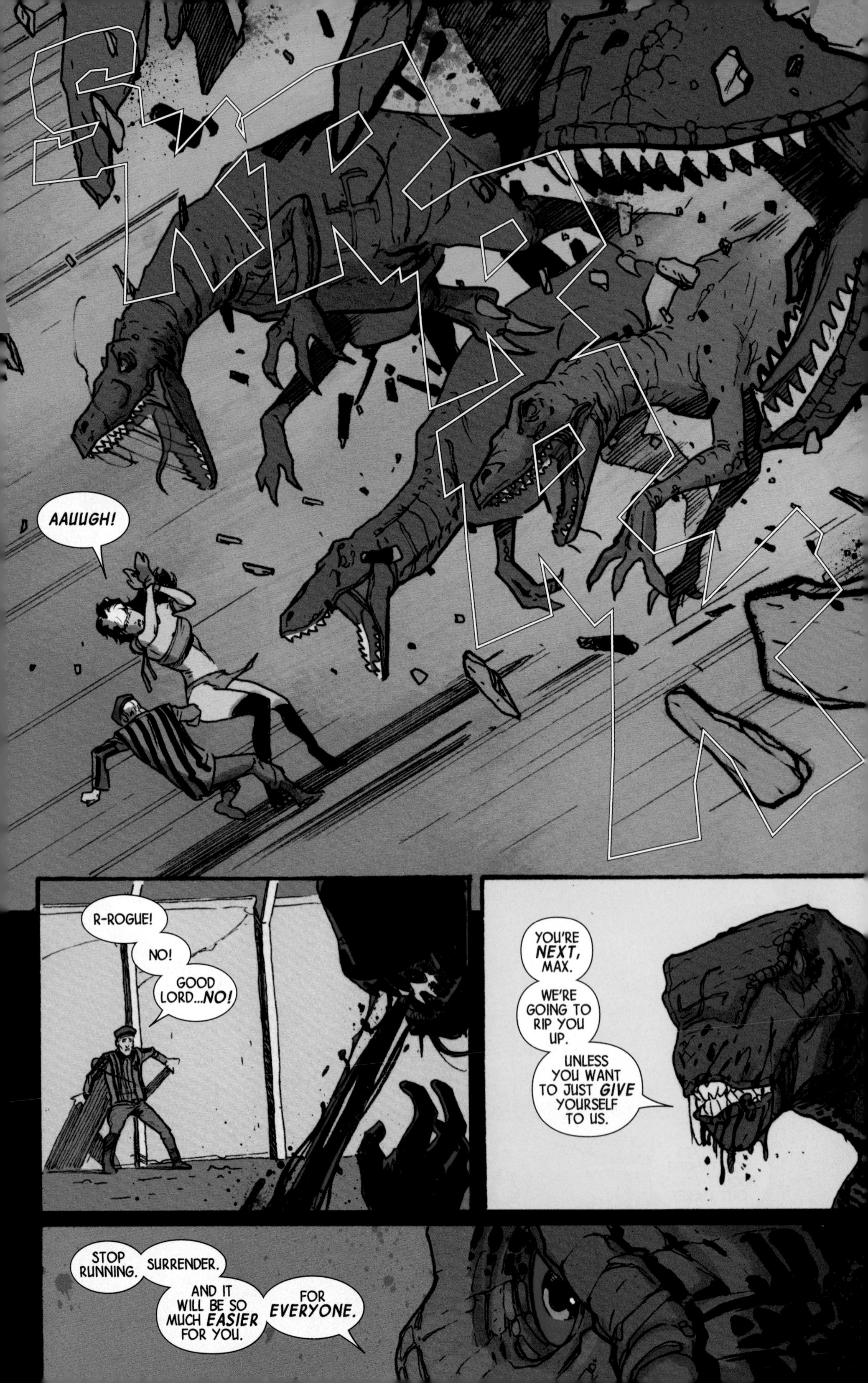
AAUUGH!
R-ROGUE!
NO!
GOOD LORD...NO!
YOU'RE NEXT, MAX.
WE'RE GOING TO RIP YOU UP.
UNLESS YOU WANT TO JUST GIVE YOURSELF TO US.
STOP RUNNING.
SURRENDER.
AND IT WILL BE SO MUCH EASIER FOR YOU.
FOR EVERYONE.

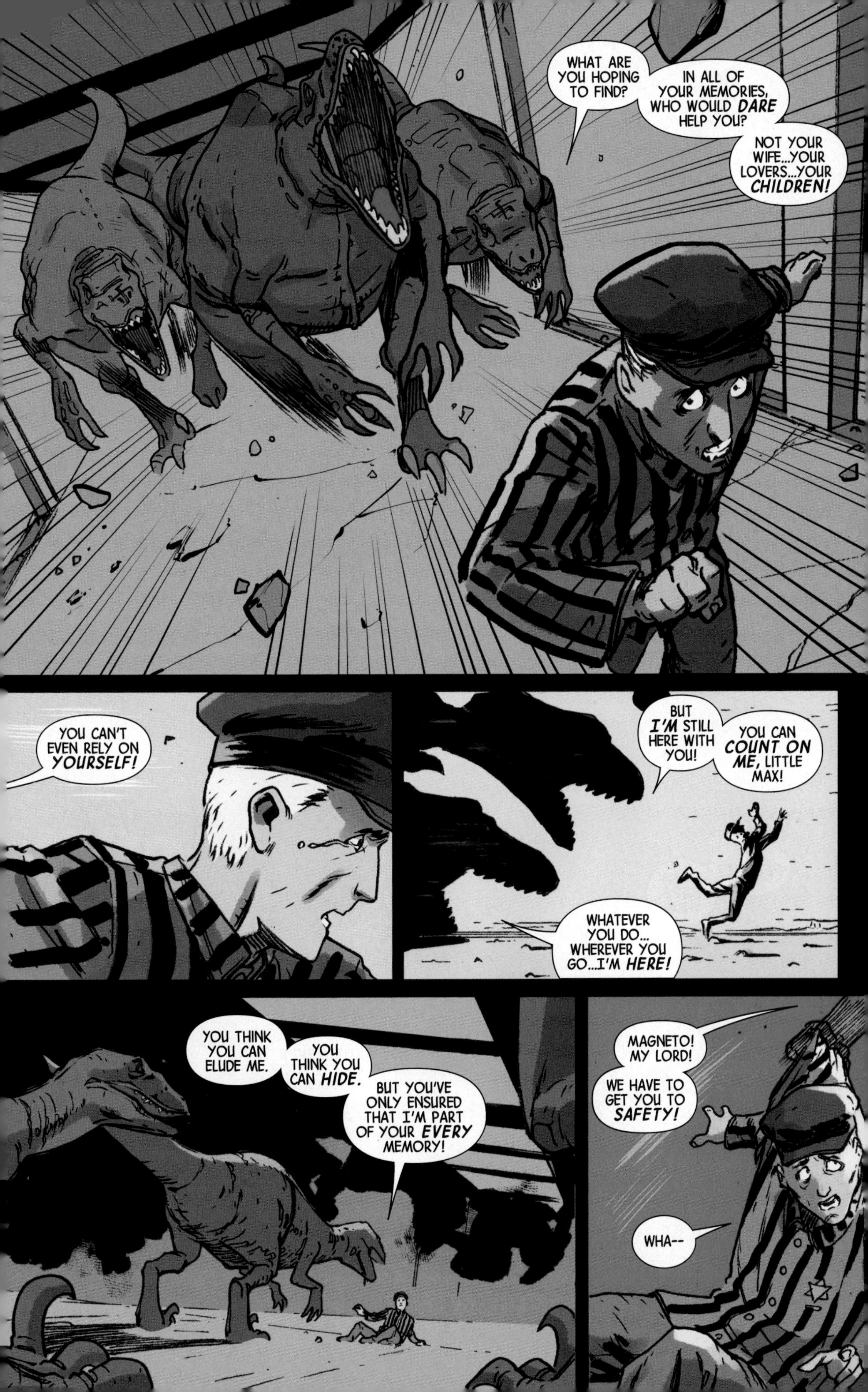
WHAT ARE YOU HOPING TO FIND?
IN ALL OF YOUR MEMORIES, WHO WOULD DARE HELP YOU?
NOT YOUR WIFE...YOUR LOVERS...YOUR CHILDREN!
YOU CAN'T EVEN RELY ON YOURSELF!
BUT I'M STILL HERE WITH YOU!
YOU CAN COUNT ON ME, LITTLE MAX!
WHATEVER YOU DO... WHEREVER YOU GO...I'M HERE!
YOU THINK YOU CAN ELUDE ME.
YOU THINK YOU CAN HIDE.
BUT YOU'VE ONLY ENSURED THAT I'M PART OF YOUR EVERY MEMORY!
MAGNETO! MY LORD!
WE HAVE TO GET YOU TO SAFETY!
WHA--

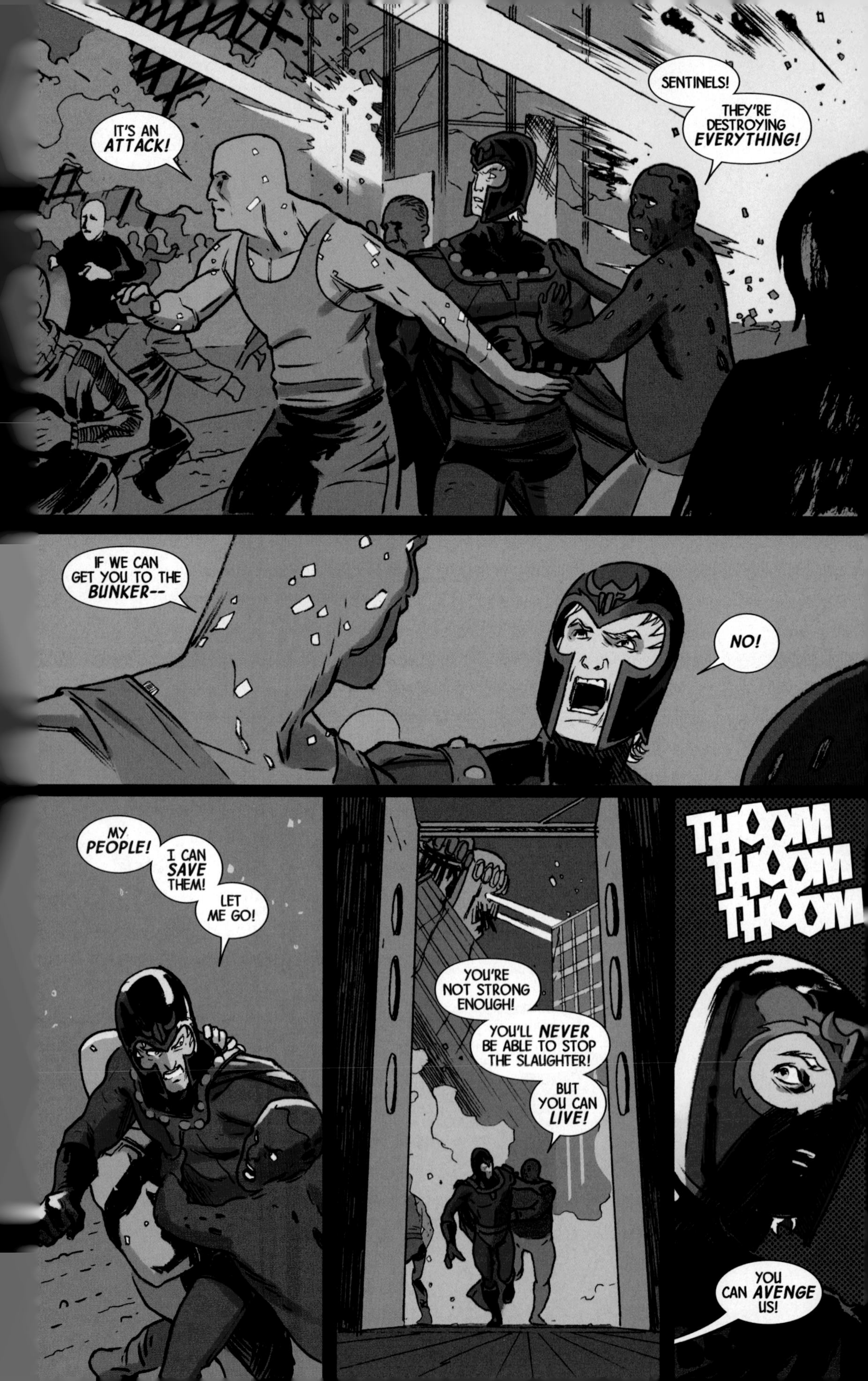
IT'S AN ATTACK!
SENTINELS!
THEY'RE DESTROYING EVERYTHING!
IF WE CAN GET YOU TO THE BUNKER--
NO!
MY PEOPLE!
I CAN SAVE THEM!
LET ME GO!
YOU'RE NOT STRONG ENOUGH!
YOU'LL NEVER BE ABLE TO STOP THE SLAUGHTER!
BUT YOU CAN LIVE!
THOOM THOOM THOOM
YOU CAN AVENGE US!

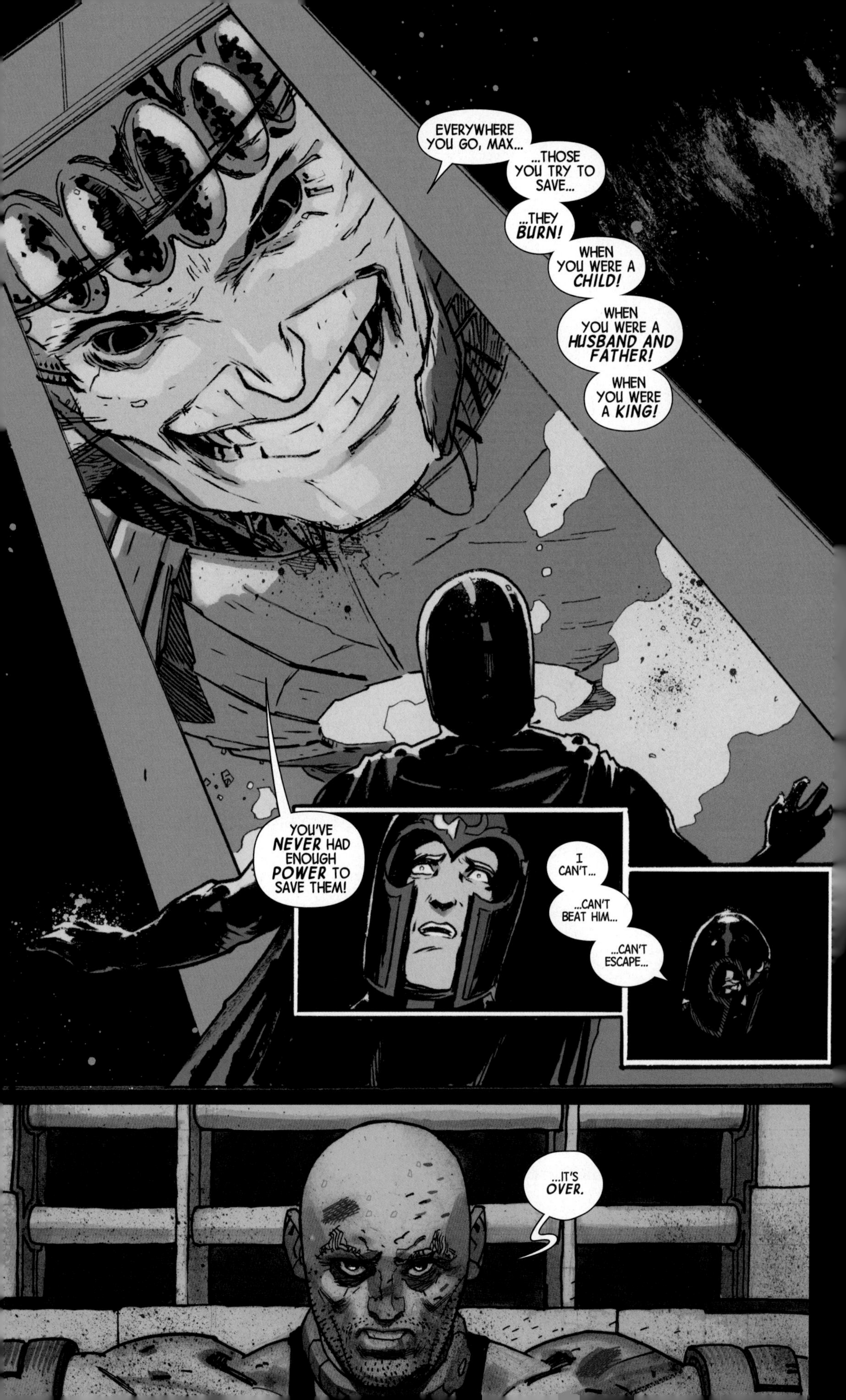
EVERYWHERE YOU GO, MAX...
...THOSE YOU TRY TO SAVE...
...THEY *BURN!*
WHEN YOU WERE A *CHILD!*
WHEN YOU WERE A *HUSBAND AND FATHER!*
WHEN YOU WERE A *KING!*
YOU'VE *NEVER* HAD ENOUGH *POWER* TO SAVE THEM!
I CAN'T...
...CAN'T BEAT HIM...
...CAN'T ESCAPE...
...IT'S *OVER.*

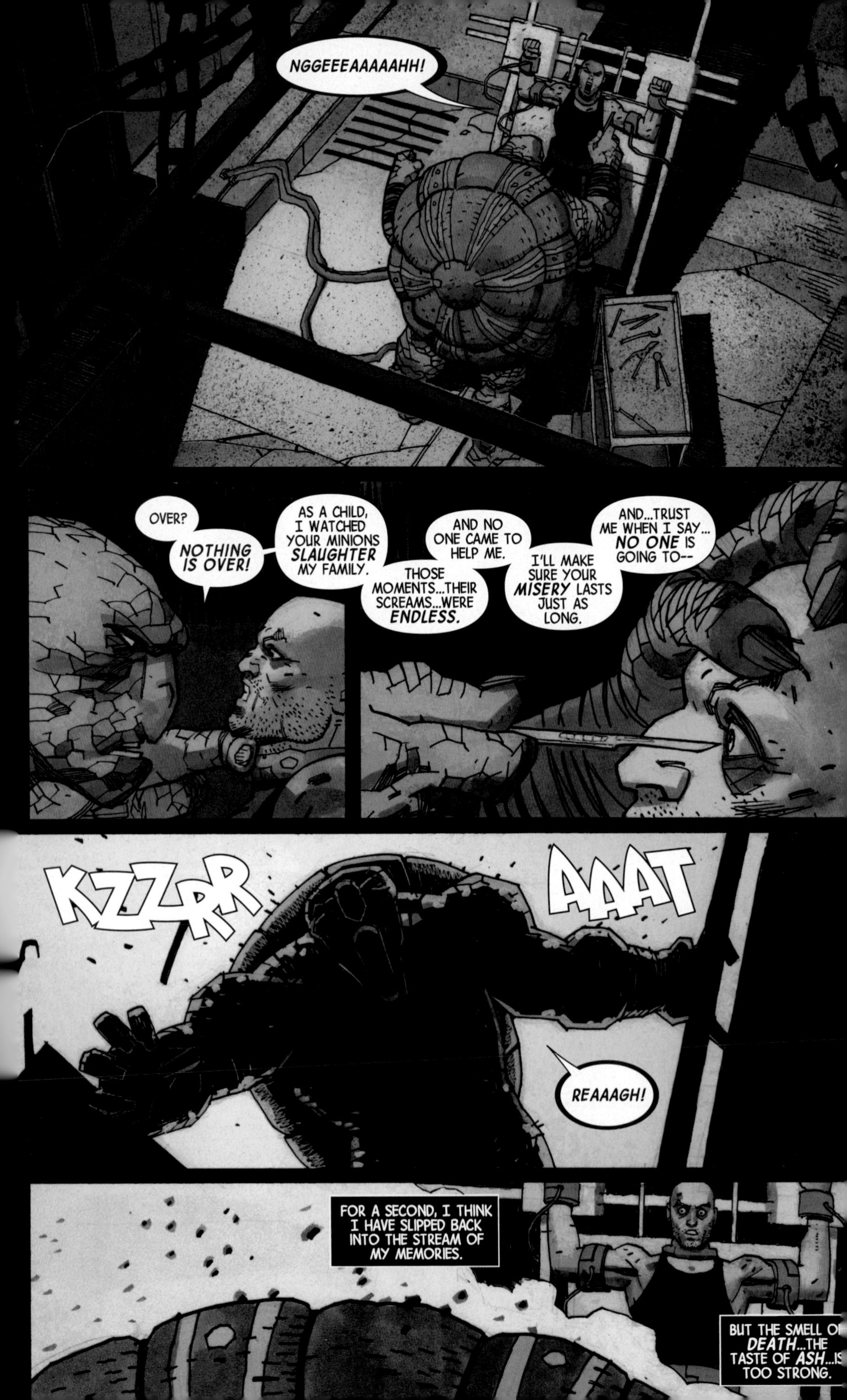
NGGEEEAAAAAHH!
OVER? NOTHING IS OVER!
AS A CHILD, I WATCHED YOUR MINIONS SLAUGHTER MY FAMILY.
THOSE MOMENTS...THEIR SCREAMS...WERE ENDLESS.
AND NO ONE CAME TO HELP ME.
I'LL MAKE SURE YOUR MISERY LASTS JUST AS LONG.
AND...TRUST ME WHEN I SAY... NO ONE IS GOING TO--
KZZRR
AAAT
REAAAGH!
FOR A SECOND, I THINK I HAVE SLIPPED BACK INTO THE STREAM OF MY MEMORIES.
BUT THE SMELL OF DEATH...THE TASTE OF ASH...IS TOO STRONG.

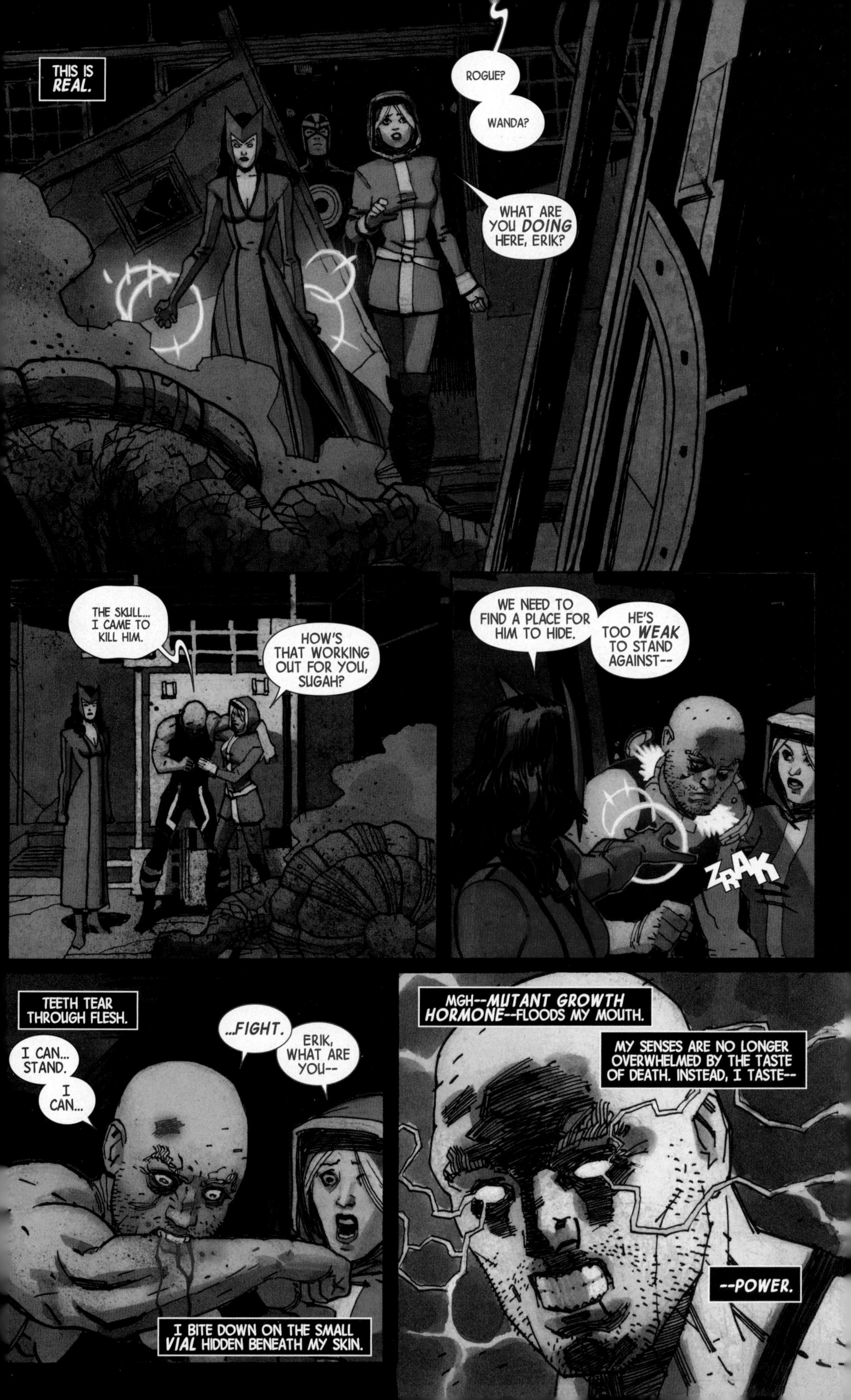

THIS IS REAL.
ROGUE?
WANDA?
WHAT ARE YOU DOING HERE, ERIK?
THE SKULL... I CAME TO KILL HIM.
HOW'S THAT WORKING OUT FOR YOU, SUGAH?
WE NEED TO FIND A PLACE FOR HIM TO HIDE.
HE'S TOO WEAK TO STAND AGAINST--
ZRAK
TEETH TEAR THROUGH FLESH.
I CAN... STAND.
I CAN...
...FIGHT.
ERIK, WHAT ARE YOU--
I BITE DOWN ON THE SMALL VIAL HIDDEN BENEATH MY SKIN.
MGH--MUTANT GROWTH HORMONE--FLOODS MY MOUTH.
MY SENSES ARE NO LONGER OVERWHELMED BY THE TASTE OF DEATH. INSTEAD, I TASTE--
--POWER.

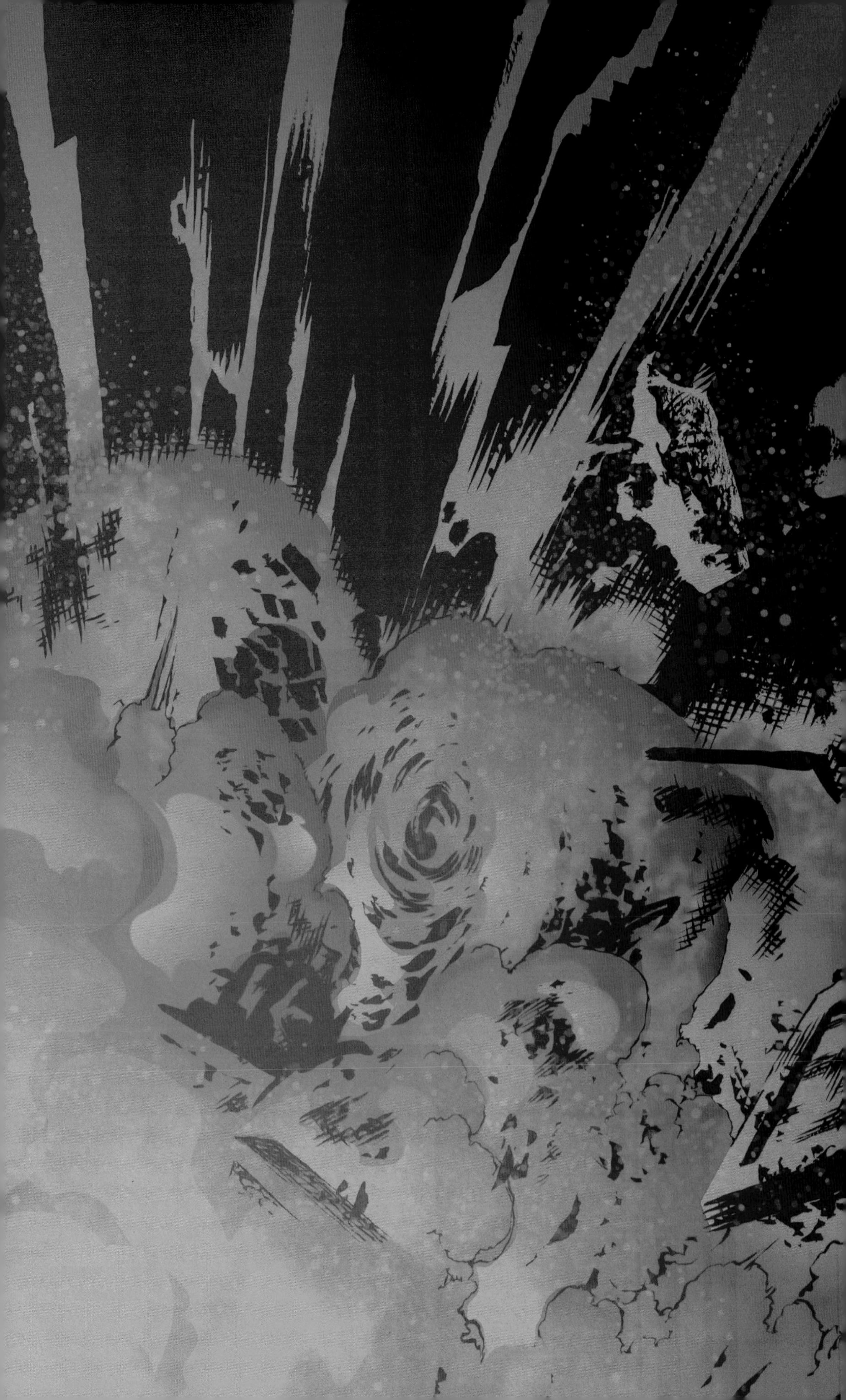

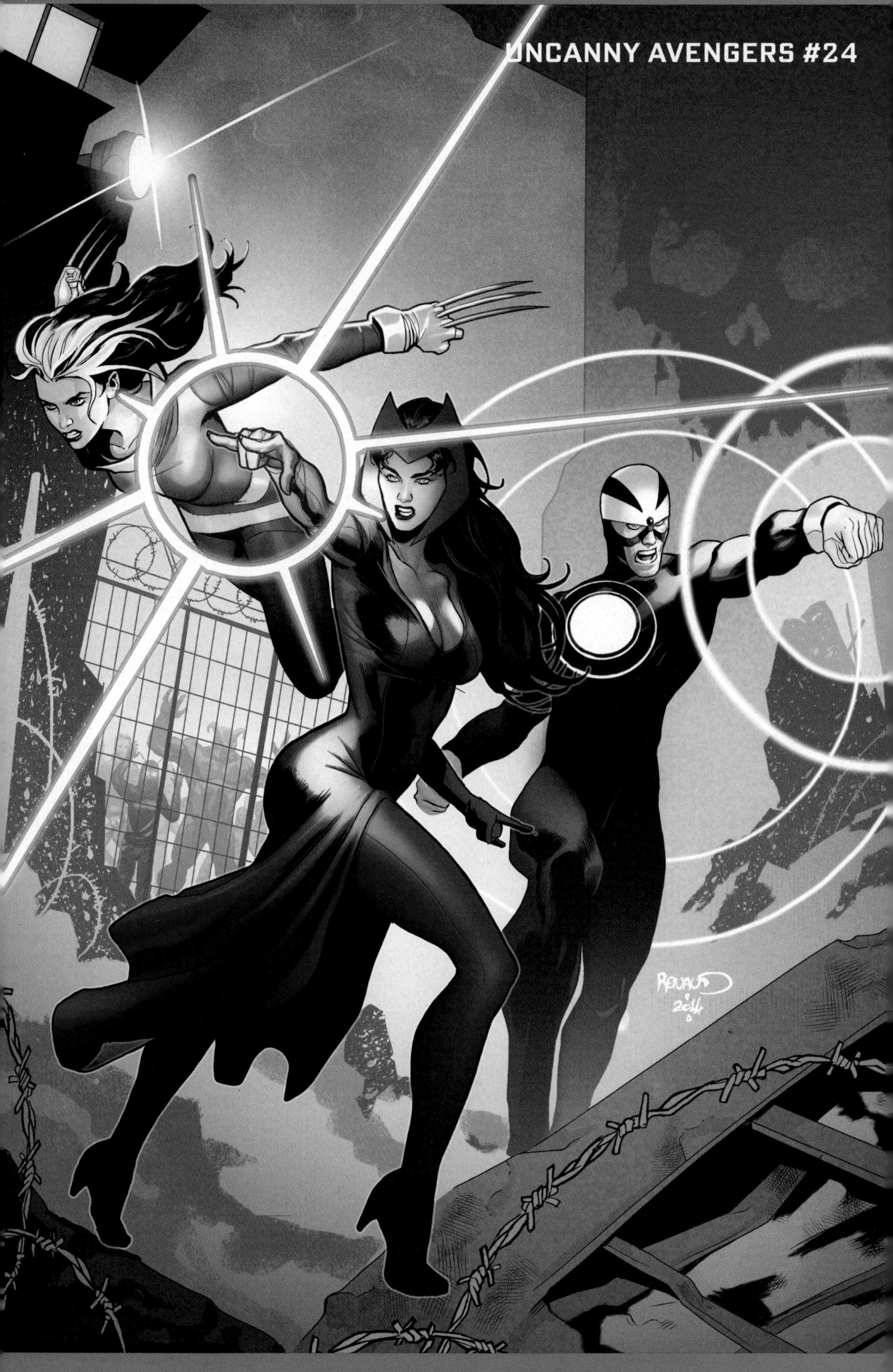
UNCANNY AVENGERS #24

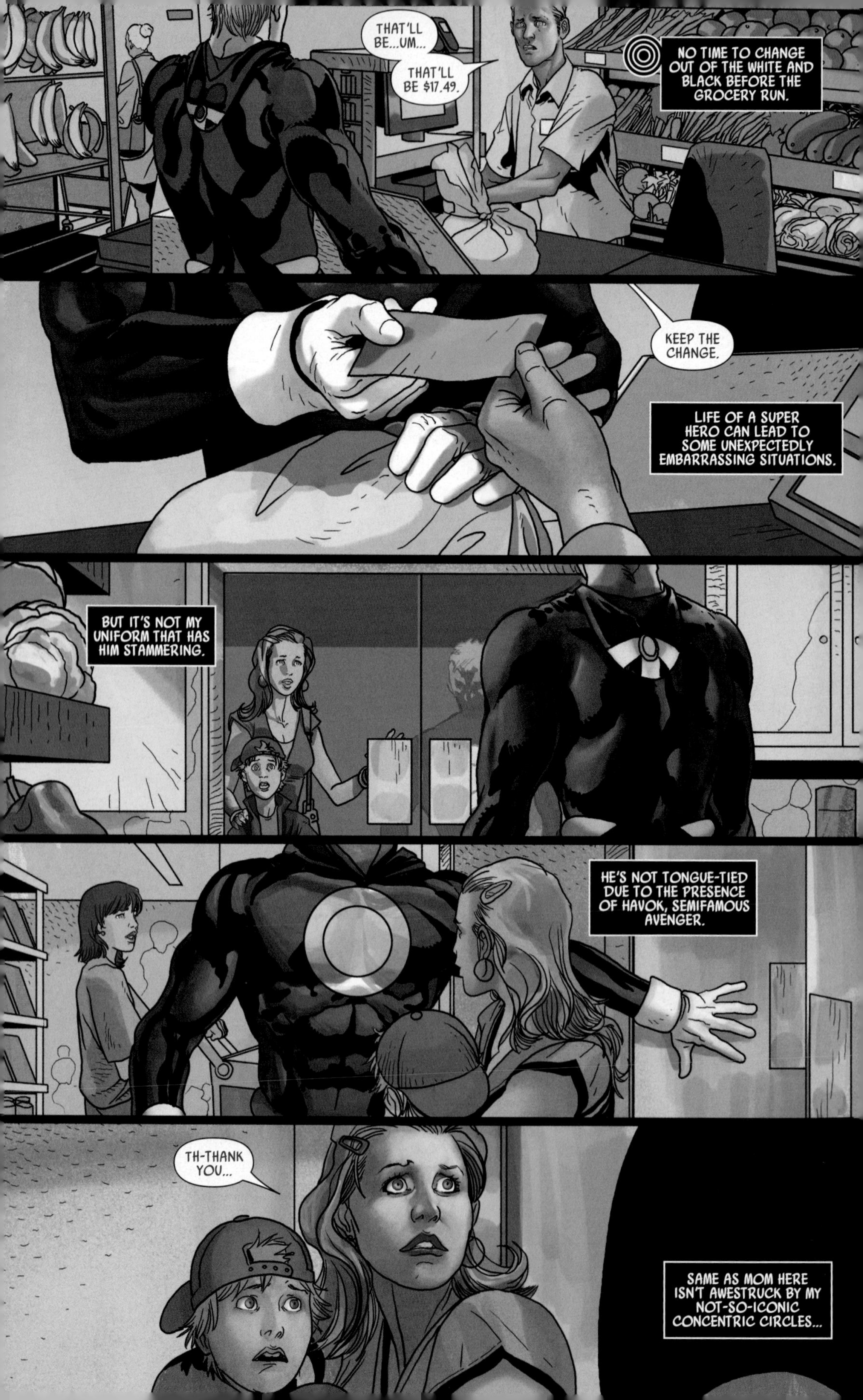
THAT'LL BE...UM...
THAT'LL BE $17.49.
NO TIME TO CHANGE OUT OF THE WHITE AND BLACK BEFORE THE GROCERY RUN.
KEEP THE CHANGE.
LIFE OF A SUPER HERO CAN LEAD TO SOME UNEXPECTEDLY EMBARRASSING SITUATIONS.
BUT IT'S NOT MY UNIFORM THAT HAS HIM STAMMERING.
HE'S NOT TONGUE-TIED DUE TO THE PRESENCE OF HAVOK, SEMIFAMOUS AVENGER.
TH-THANK YOU...
SAME AS MOM HERE ISN'T AWESTRUCK BY MY NOT-SO-ICONIC CONCENTRIC CIRCLES...

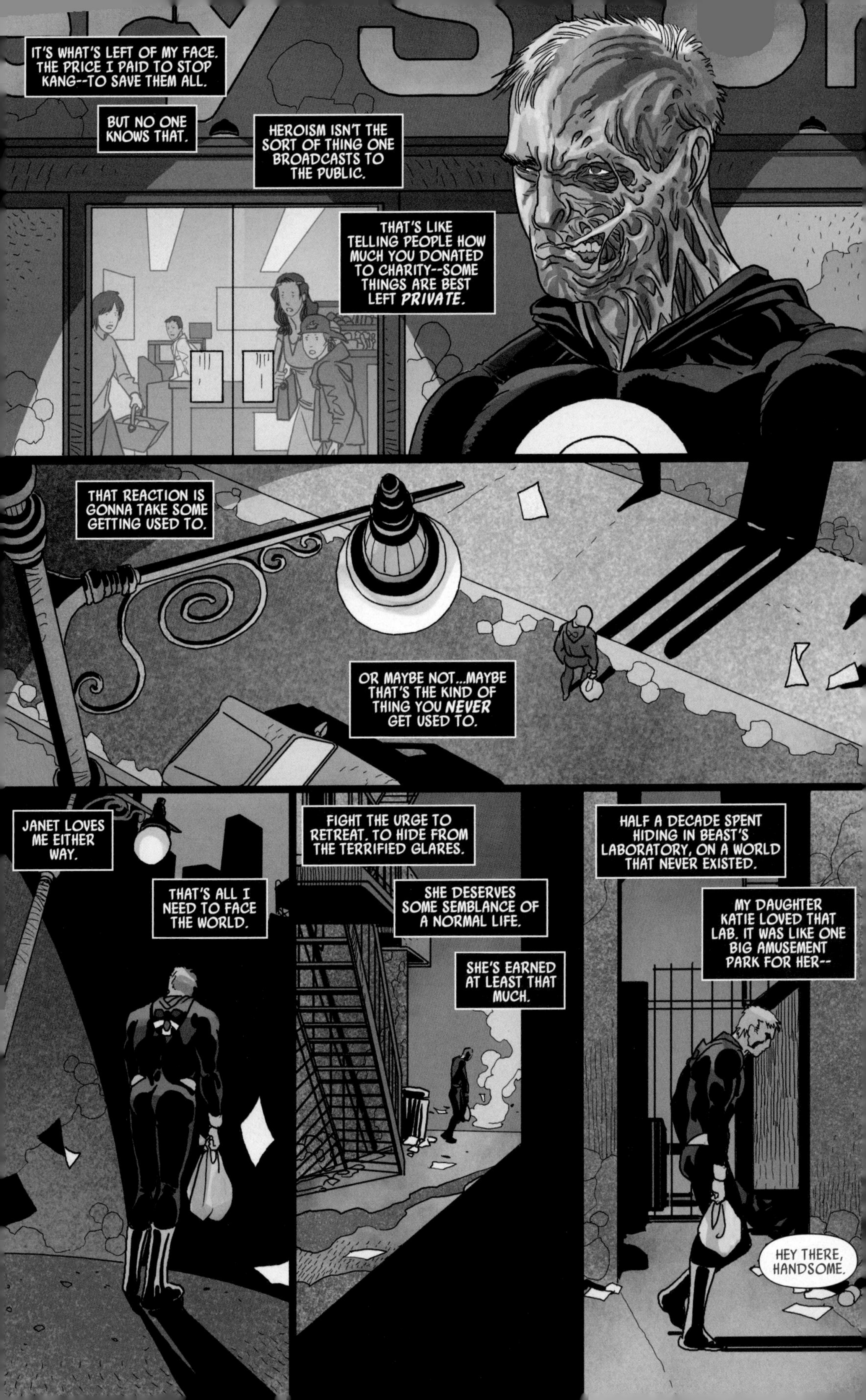
IT'S WHAT'S LEFT OF MY FACE. THE PRICE I PAID TO STOP KANG--TO SAVE THEM ALL.
BUT NO ONE KNOWS THAT.
HEROISM ISN'T THE SORT OF THING ONE BROADCASTS TO THE PUBLIC.
THAT'S LIKE TELLING PEOPLE HOW MUCH YOU DONATED TO CHARITY--SOME THINGS ARE BEST LEFT *PRIVATE.*
THAT REACTION IS GONNA TAKE SOME GETTING USED TO.
OR MAYBE NOT...MAYBE THAT'S THE KIND OF THING YOU *NEVER* GET USED TO.
JANET LOVES ME EITHER WAY.
THAT'S ALL I NEED TO FACE THE WORLD.
FIGHT THE URGE TO RETREAT. TO HIDE FROM THE TERRIFIED GLARES.
SHE DESERVES SOME SEMBLANCE OF A NORMAL LIFE.
SHE'S EARNED AT LEAST THAT MUCH.
HALF A DECADE SPENT HIDING IN BEAST'S LABORATORY, ON A WORLD THAT NEVER EXISTED.
MY DAUGHTER KATIE LOVED THAT LAB. IT WAS LIKE ONE BIG AMUSEMENT PARK FOR HER--
HEY THERE, HANDSOME.

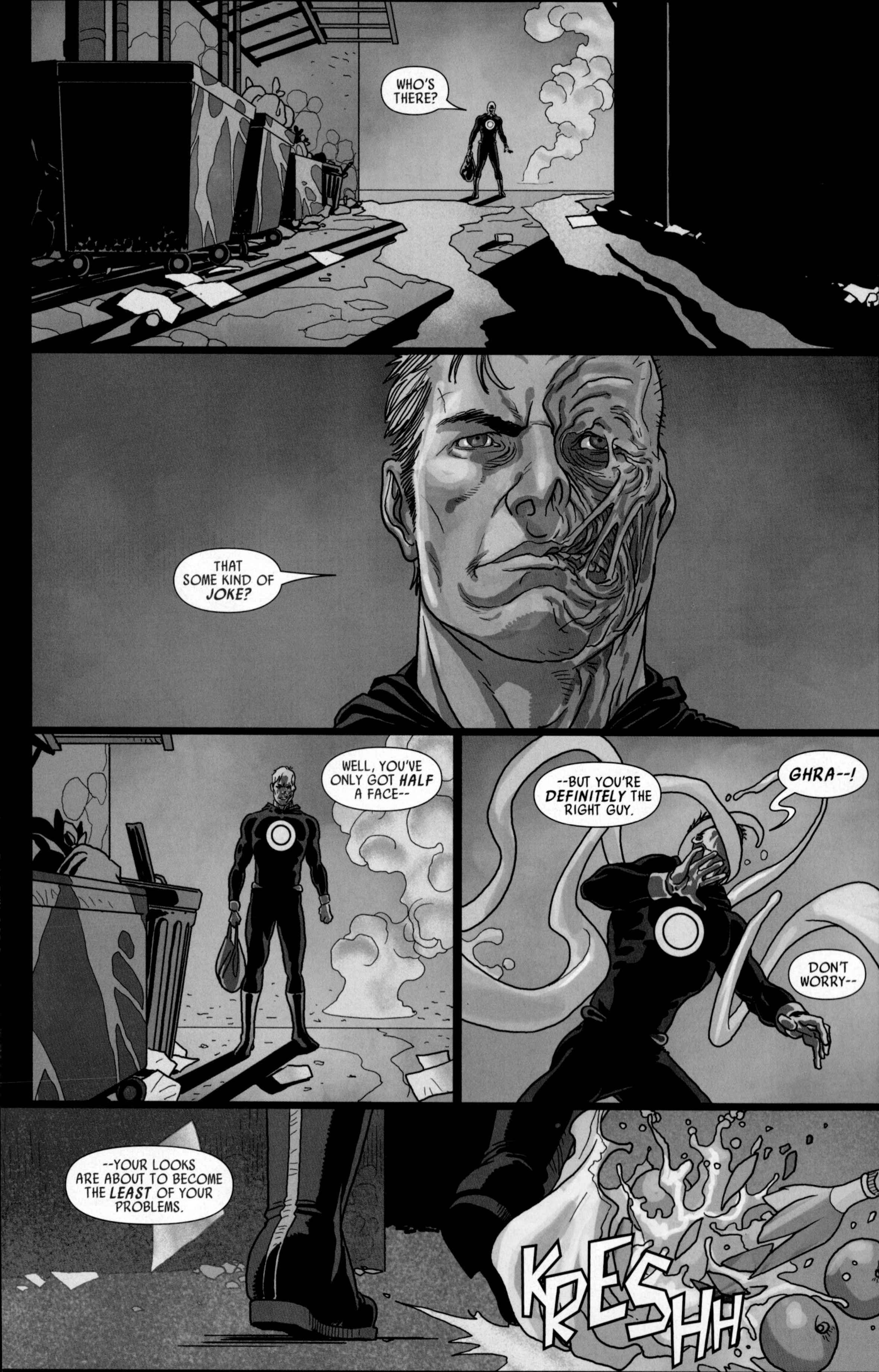
WHO'S THERE?
THAT SOME KIND OF JOKE?
WELL, YOU'VE ONLY GOT HALF A FACE--
--BUT YOU'RE DEFINITELY THE RIGHT GUY.
GHRA--!
DON'T WORRY--
--YOUR LOOKS ARE ABOUT TO BECOME THE LEAST OF YOUR PROBLEMS.
KRESHH

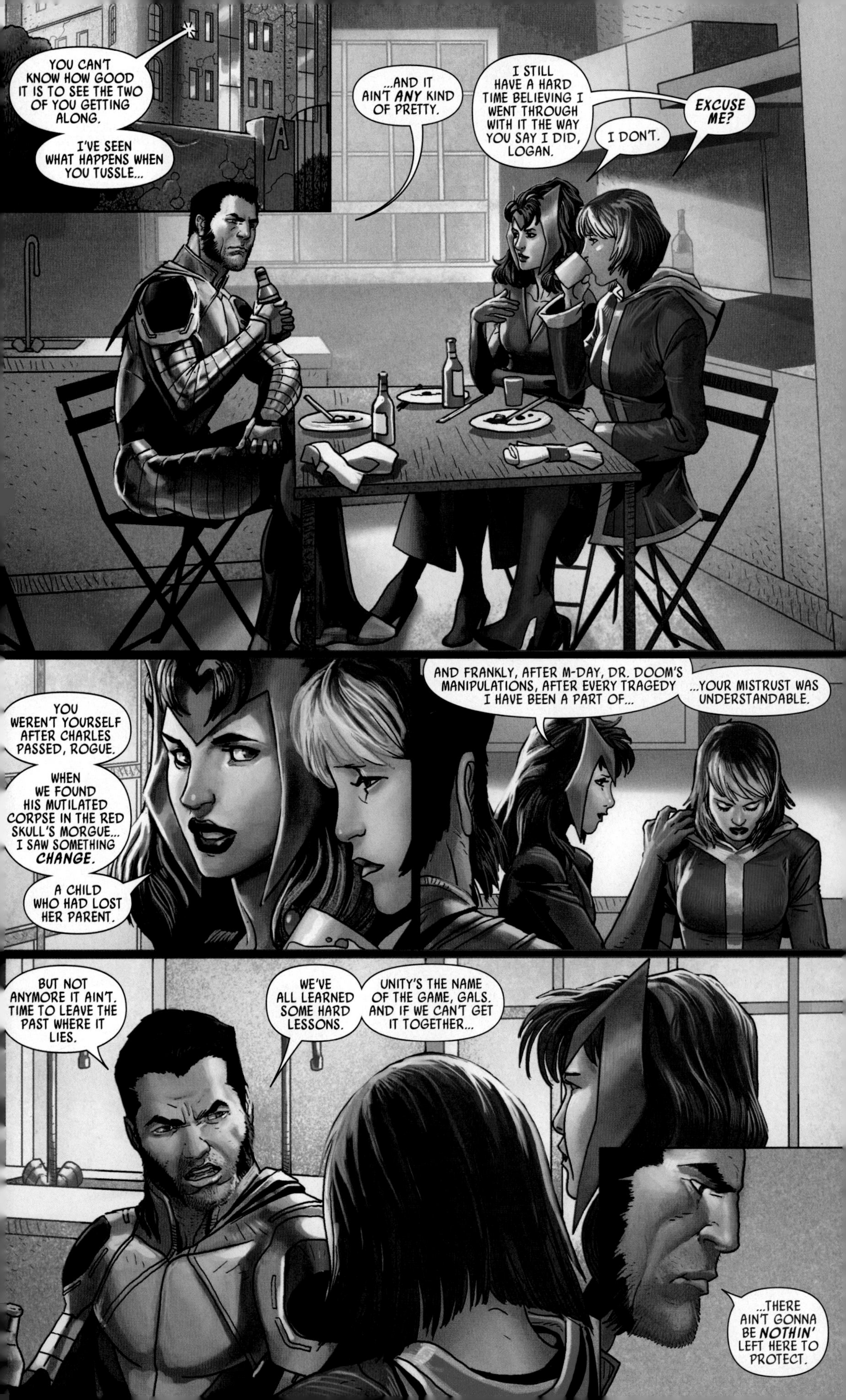
YOU CAN'T KNOW HOW GOOD IT IS TO SEE THE TWO OF YOU GETTING ALONG.
I'VE SEEN WHAT HAPPENS WHEN YOU TUSSLE...
...AND IT AIN'T ANY KIND OF PRETTY.
I STILL HAVE A HARD TIME BELIEVING I WENT THROUGH WITH IT THE WAY YOU SAY I DID, LOGAN.
I DON'T.
EXCUSE ME?
YOU WEREN'T YOURSELF AFTER CHARLES PASSED, ROGUE.
WHEN WE FOUND HIS MUTILATED CORPSE IN THE RED SKULL'S MORGUE... I SAW SOMETHING CHANGE.
A CHILD WHO HAD LOST HER PARENT.
AND FRANKLY, AFTER M-DAY, DR. DOOM'S MANIPULATIONS, AFTER EVERY TRAGEDY I HAVE BEEN A PART OF...
...YOUR MISTRUST WAS UNDERSTANDABLE.
BUT NOT ANYMORE IT AIN'T. TIME TO LEAVE THE PAST WHERE IT LIES.
WE'VE ALL LEARNED SOME HARD LESSONS.
UNITY'S THE NAME OF THE GAME, GALS. AND IF WE CAN'T GET IT TOGETHER...
...THERE AIN'T GONNA BE NOTHIN' LEFT HERE TO PROTECT.

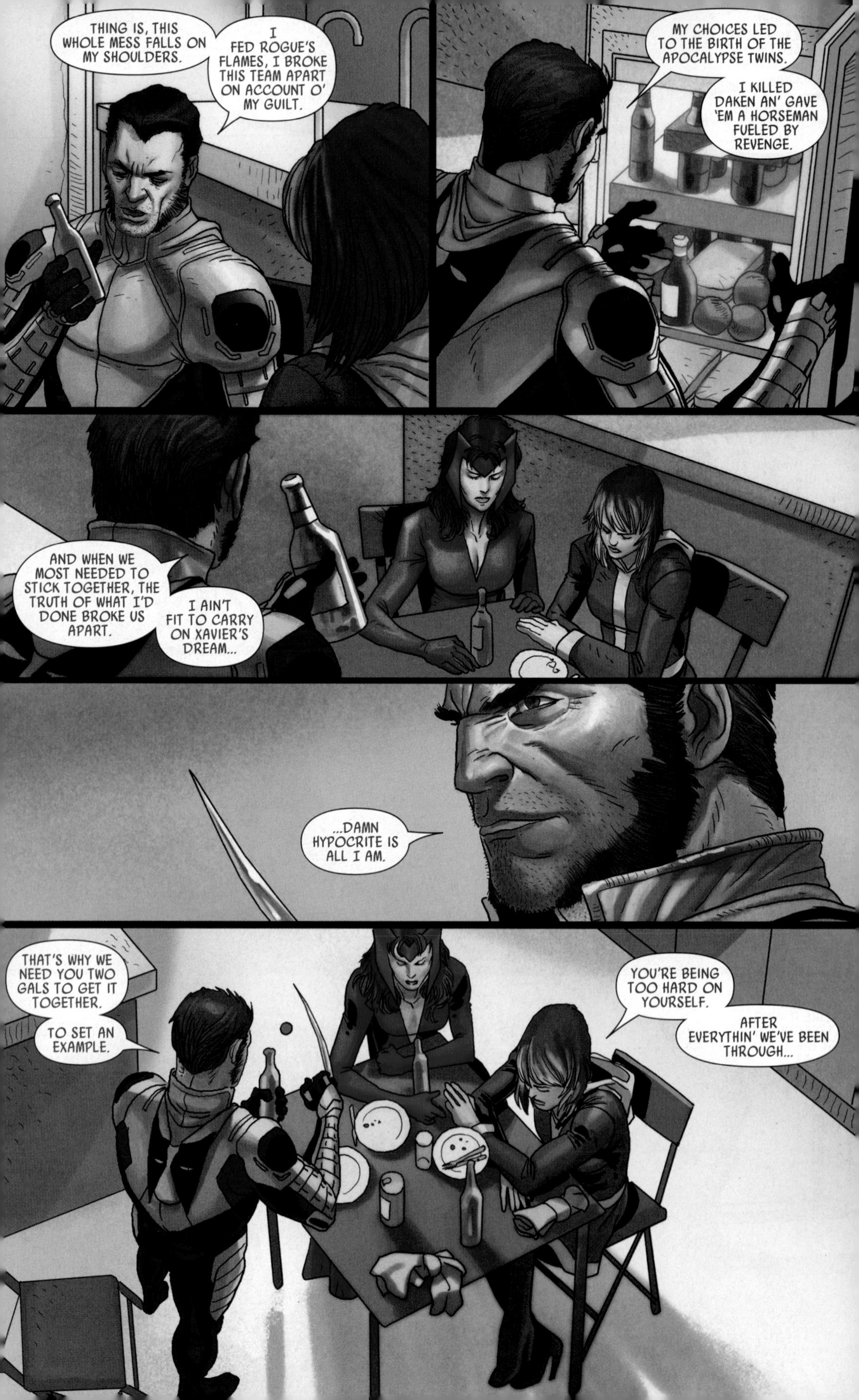
THING IS, THIS WHOLE MESS FALLS ON MY SHOULDERS.
I FED ROGUE'S FLAMES, I BROKE THIS TEAM APART ON ACCOUNT O' MY GUILT.
MY CHOICES LED TO THE BIRTH OF THE APOCALYPSE TWINS.
I KILLED DAKEN AN' GAVE 'EM A HORSEMAN FUELED BY REVENGE.
AND WHEN WE MOST NEEDED TO STICK TOGETHER, THE TRUTH OF WHAT I'D DONE BROKE US APART.
I AIN'T FIT TO CARRY ON XAVIER'S DREAM...
...DAMN HYPOCRITE IS ALL I AM.
THAT'S WHY WE NEED YOU TWO GALS TO GET IT TOGETHER.
TO SET AN EXAMPLE.
YOU'RE BEING TOO HARD ON YOURSELF.
AFTER EVERYTHIN' WE'VE BEEN THROUGH...

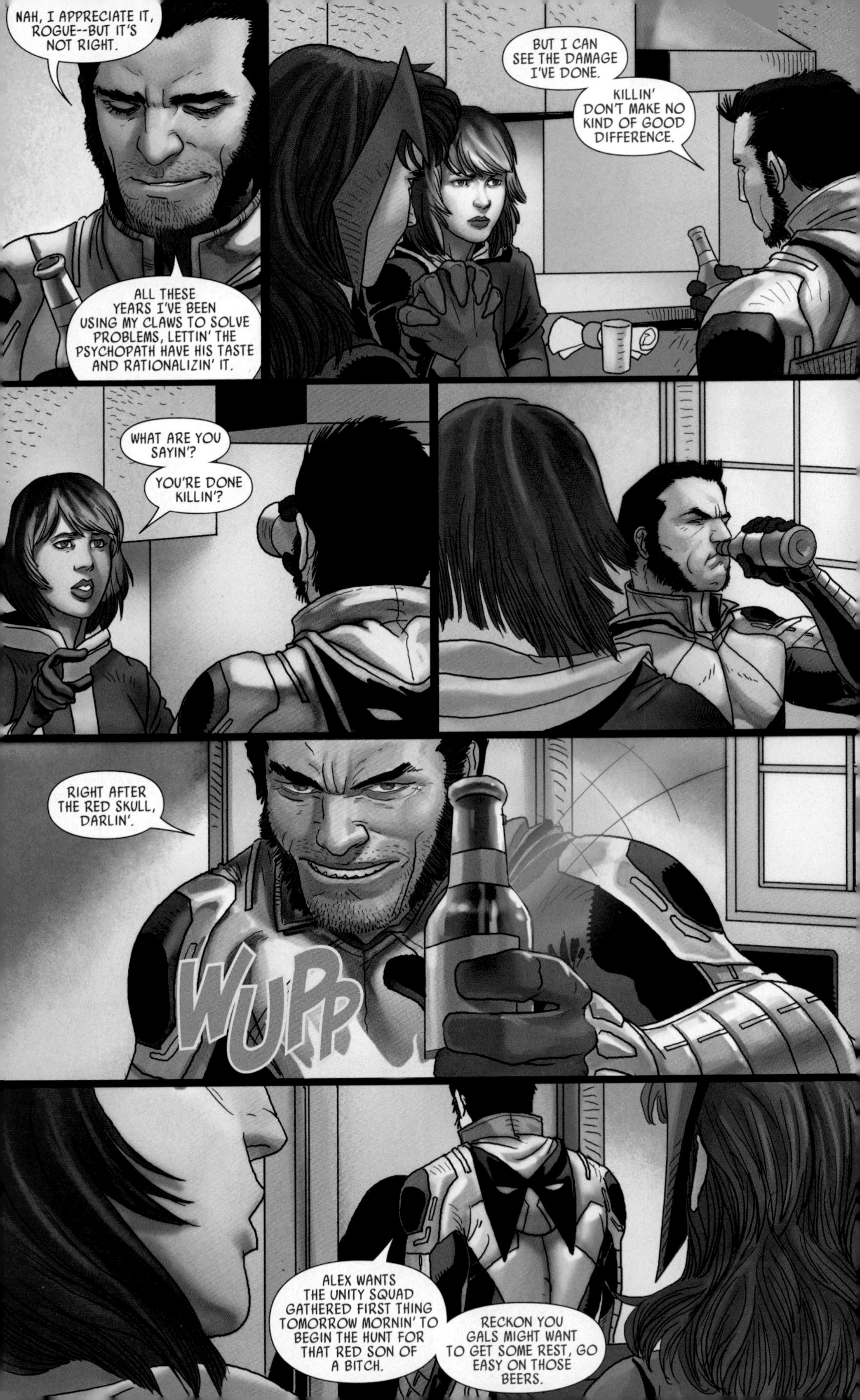
NAH, I APPRECIATE IT, ROGUE--BUT IT'S NOT RIGHT.
ALL THESE YEARS I'VE BEEN USING MY CLAWS TO SOLVE PROBLEMS, LETTIN' THE PSYCHOPATH HAVE HIS TASTE AND RATIONALIZIN' IT.
BUT I CAN SEE THE DAMAGE I'VE DONE.
KILLIN' DON'T MAKE NO KIND OF GOOD DIFFERENCE.
WHAT ARE YOU SAYIN'?
YOU'RE DONE KILLIN'?
RIGHT AFTER THE RED SKULL, DARLIN'.
WUPP.
ALEX WANTS THE UNITY SQUAD GATHERED FIRST THING TOMORROW MORNIN' TO BEGIN THE HUNT FOR THAT RED SON OF A BITCH.
RECKON YOU GALS MIGHT WANT TO GET SOME REST, GO EASY ON THOSE BEERS.

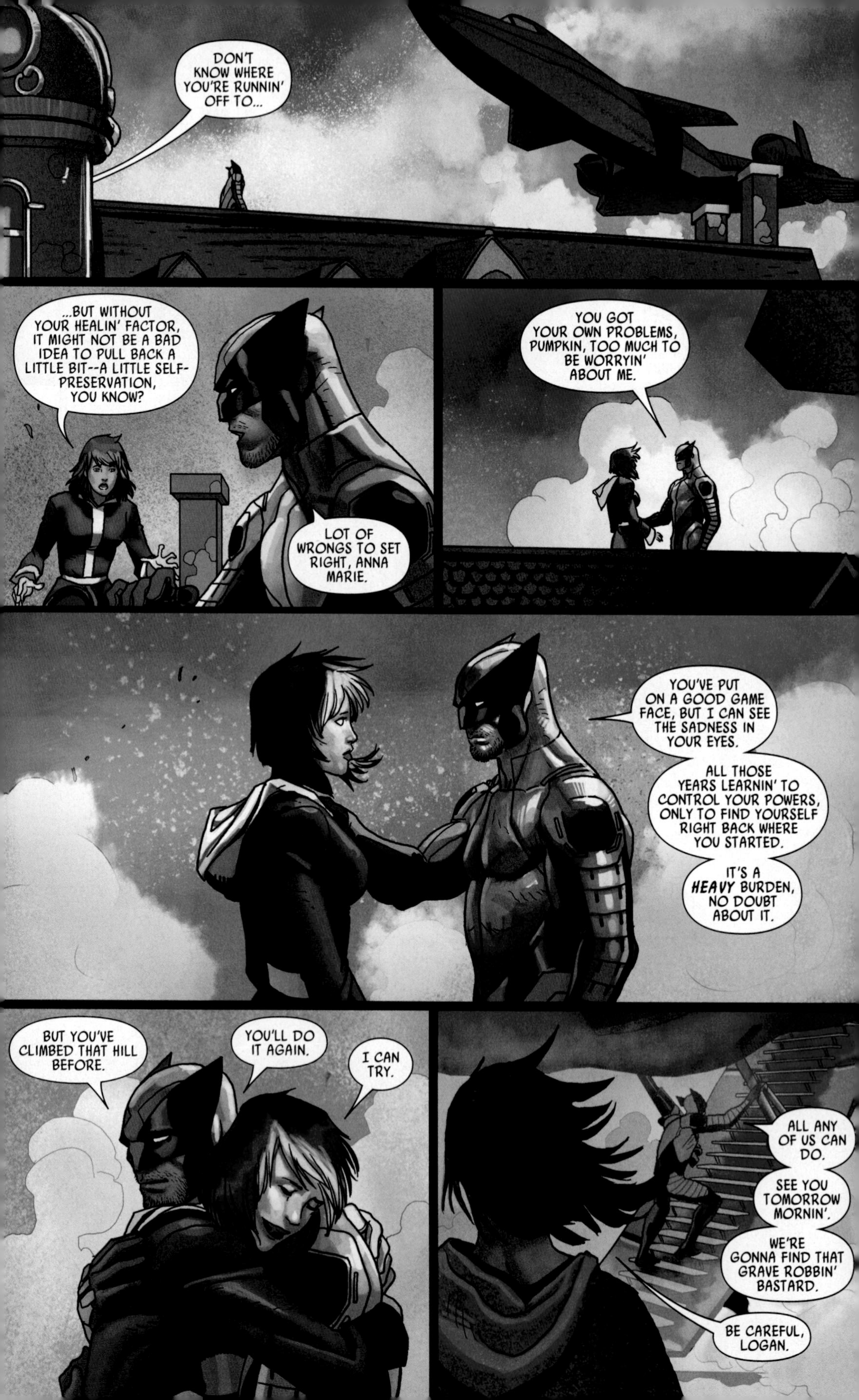
DON'T KNOW WHERE YOU'RE RUNNIN' OFF TO...
...BUT WITHOUT YOUR HEALIN' FACTOR, IT MIGHT NOT BE A BAD IDEA TO PULL BACK A LITTLE BIT--A LITTLE SELF-PRESERVATION, YOU KNOW?
LOT OF WRONGS TO SET RIGHT, ANNA MARIE.
YOU GOT YOUR OWN PROBLEMS, PUMPKIN, TOO MUCH TO BE WORRYIN' ABOUT ME.
YOU'VE PUT ON A GOOD GAME FACE, BUT I CAN SEE THE SADNESS IN YOUR EYES.
ALL THOSE YEARS LEARNIN' TO CONTROL YOUR POWERS, ONLY TO FIND YOURSELF RIGHT BACK WHERE YOU STARTED.
IT'S A HEAVY BURDEN, NO DOUBT ABOUT IT.
BUT YOU'VE CLIMBED THAT HILL BEFORE.
YOU'LL DO IT AGAIN.
I CAN TRY.
ALL ANY OF US CAN DO.
SEE YOU TOMORROW MORNIN'.
WE'RE GONNA FIND THAT GRAVE ROBBIN' BASTARD.
BE CAREFUL, LOGAN.

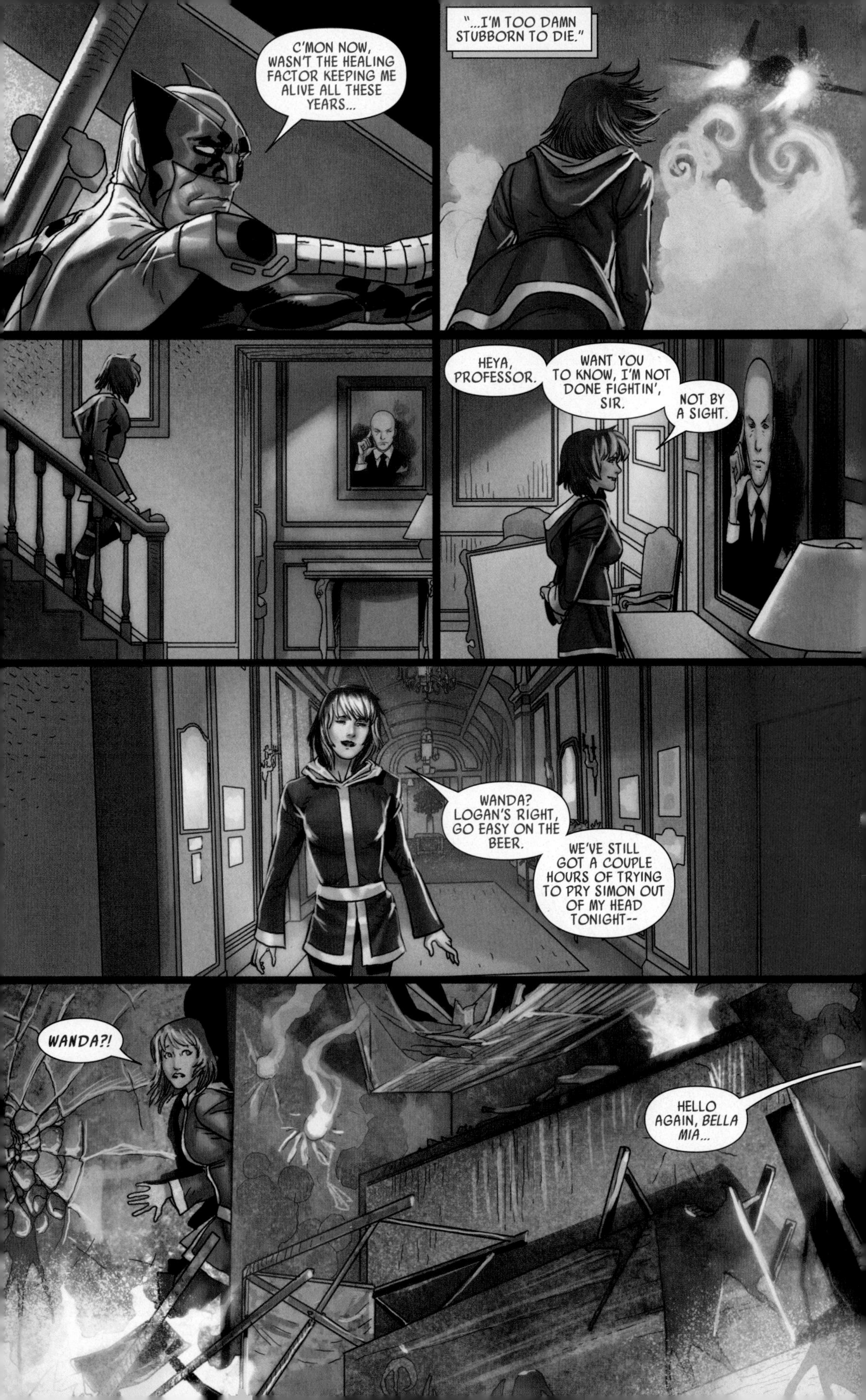
C'MON NOW, WASN'T THE HEALING FACTOR KEEPING ME ALIVE ALL THESE YEARS...
"...I'M TOO DAMN STUBBORN TO DIE."
HEYA, PROFESSOR.
WANT YOU TO KNOW, I'M NOT DONE FIGHTIN', SIR.
NOT BY A SIGHT.
WANDA? LOGAN'S RIGHT, GO EASY ON THE BEER.
WE'VE STILL GOT A COUPLE HOURS OF TRYING TO PRY SIMON OUT OF MY HEAD TONIGHT--
WANDA?!
HELLO AGAIN, BELLA MIA...

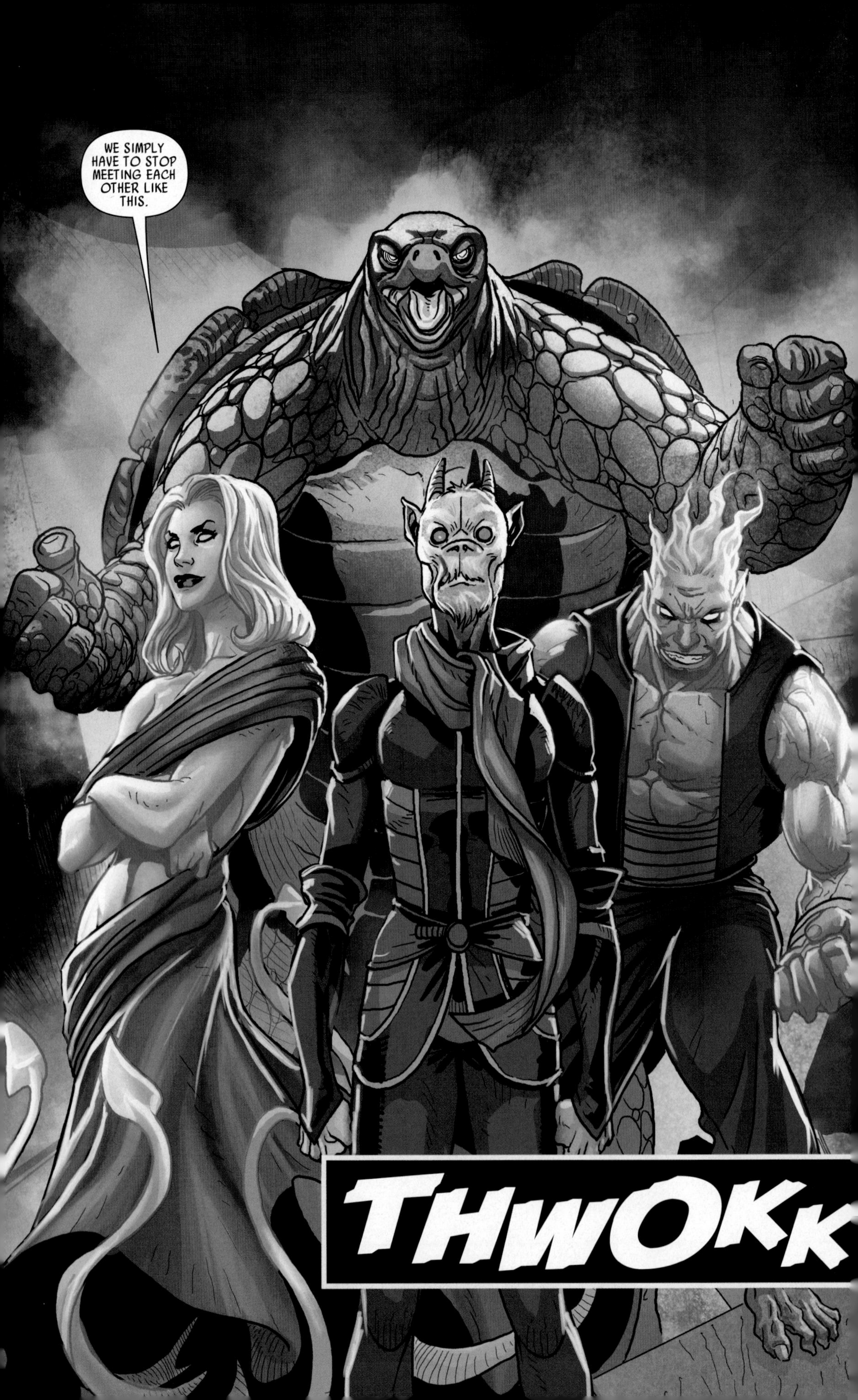
WE SIMPLY HAVE TO STOP MEETING EACH OTHER LIKE THIS.
THWOKK

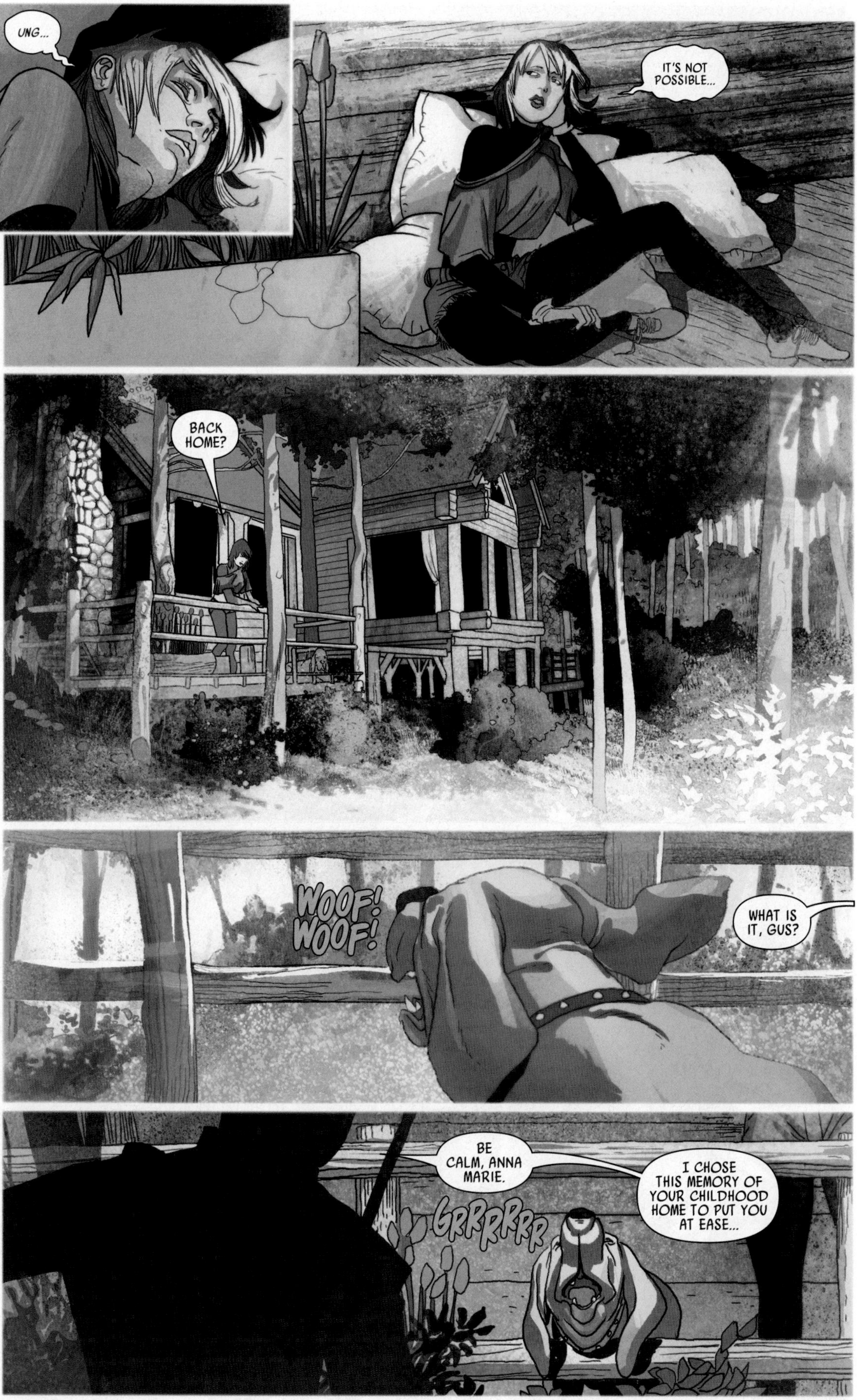
UNG...
IT'S NOT POSSIBLE...
BACK HOME?
WOOF! WOOF!
WHAT IS IT, GUS?
BE CALM, ANNA MARIE.
I CHOSE THIS MEMORY OF YOUR CHILDHOOD HOME TO PUT YOU AT EASE...
GRRRRRR

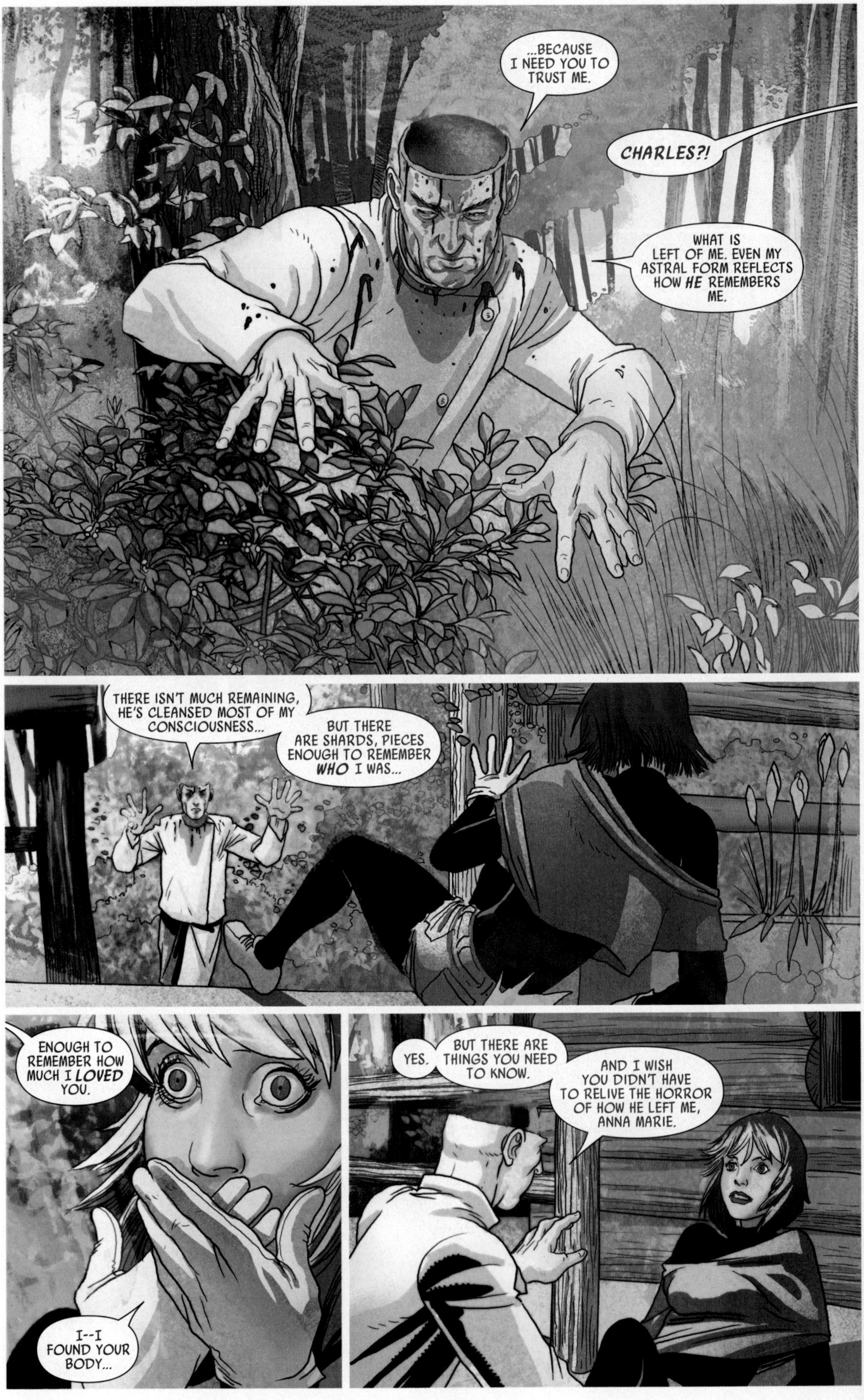
...BECAUSE I NEED YOU TO TRUST ME.
CHARLES?!
WHAT IS LEFT OF ME. EVEN MY ASTRAL FORM REFLECTS HOW HE REMEMBERS ME.
THERE ISN'T MUCH REMAINING, HE'S CLEANSED MOST OF MY CONSCIOUSNESS...
BUT THERE ARE SHARDS, PIECES ENOUGH TO REMEMBER WHO I WAS...
ENOUGH TO REMEMBER HOW MUCH I LOVED YOU.
I--I FOUND YOUR BODY...
YES.
BUT THERE ARE THINGS YOU NEED TO KNOW.
AND I WISH YOU DIDN'T HAVE TO RELIVE THE HORROR OF HOW HE LEFT ME, ANNA MARIE.

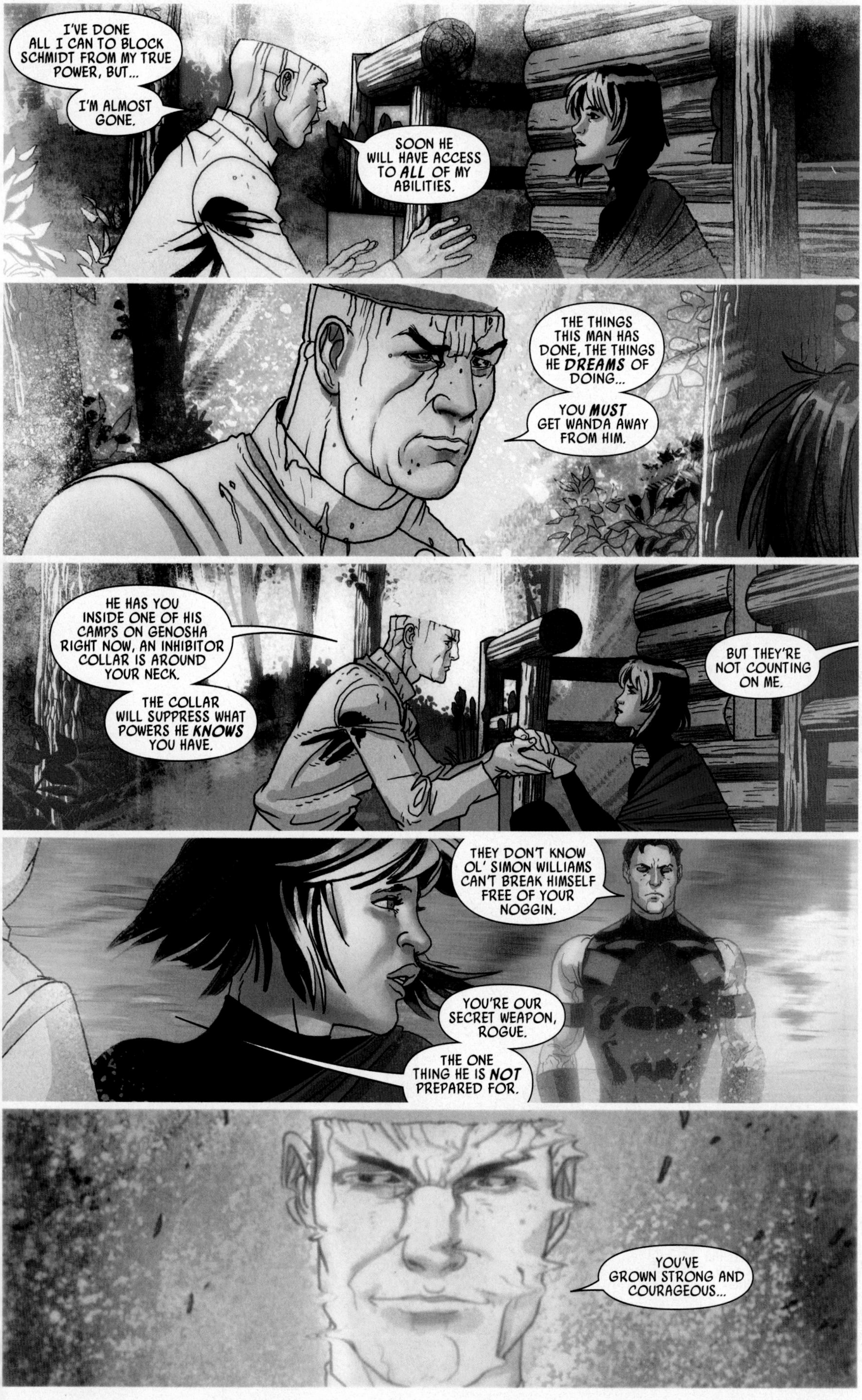
I'VE DONE ALL I CAN TO BLOCK SCHMIDT FROM MY TRUE POWER, BUT...
I'M ALMOST GONE.
SOON HE WILL HAVE ACCESS TO ALL OF MY ABILITIES.
THE THINGS THIS MAN HAS DONE, THE THINGS HE DREAMS OF DOING...
YOU MUST GET WANDA AWAY FROM HIM.
HE HAS YOU INSIDE ONE OF HIS CAMPS ON GENOSHA RIGHT NOW, AN INHIBITOR COLLAR IS AROUND YOUR NECK.
THE COLLAR WILL SUPPRESS WHAT POWERS HE KNOWS YOU HAVE.
BUT THEY'RE NOT COUNTING ON ME.
THEY DON'T KNOW OL' SIMON WILLIAMS CAN'T BREAK HIMSELF FREE OF YOUR NOGGIN.
YOU'RE OUR SECRET WEAPON, ROGUE.
THE ONE THING HE IS NOT PREPARED FOR.
YOU'VE GROWN STRONG AND COURAGEOUS...

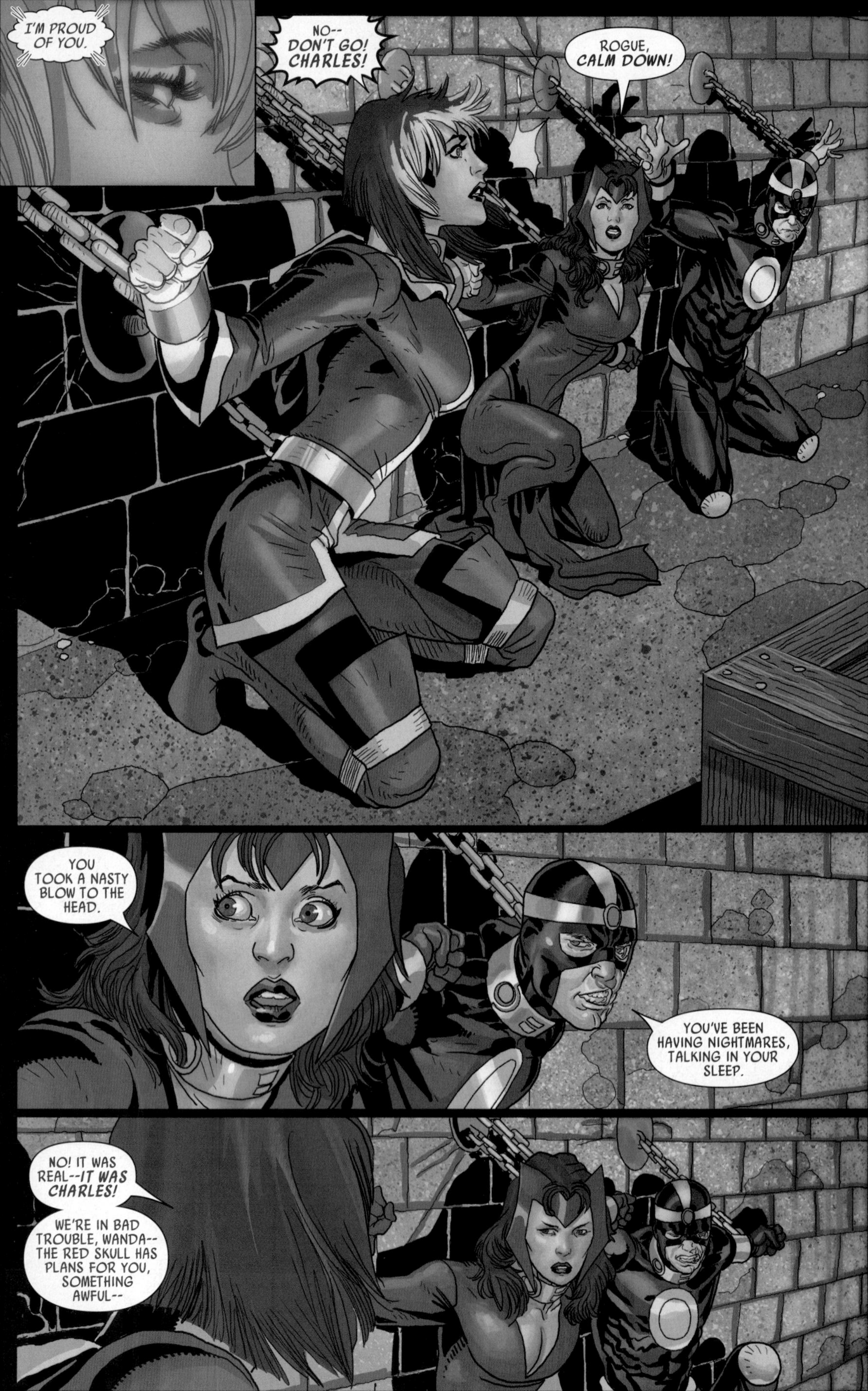
I'M PROUD OF YOU.
NO-- DON'T GO! CHARLES!
ROGUE, CALM DOWN!
YOU TOOK A NASTY BLOW TO THE HEAD.
YOU'VE BEEN HAVING NIGHTMARES, TALKING IN YOUR SLEEP.
NO! IT WAS REAL--IT WAS CHARLES!
WE'RE IN BAD TROUBLE, WANDA-- THE RED SKULL HAS PLANS FOR YOU, SOMETHING AWFUL--

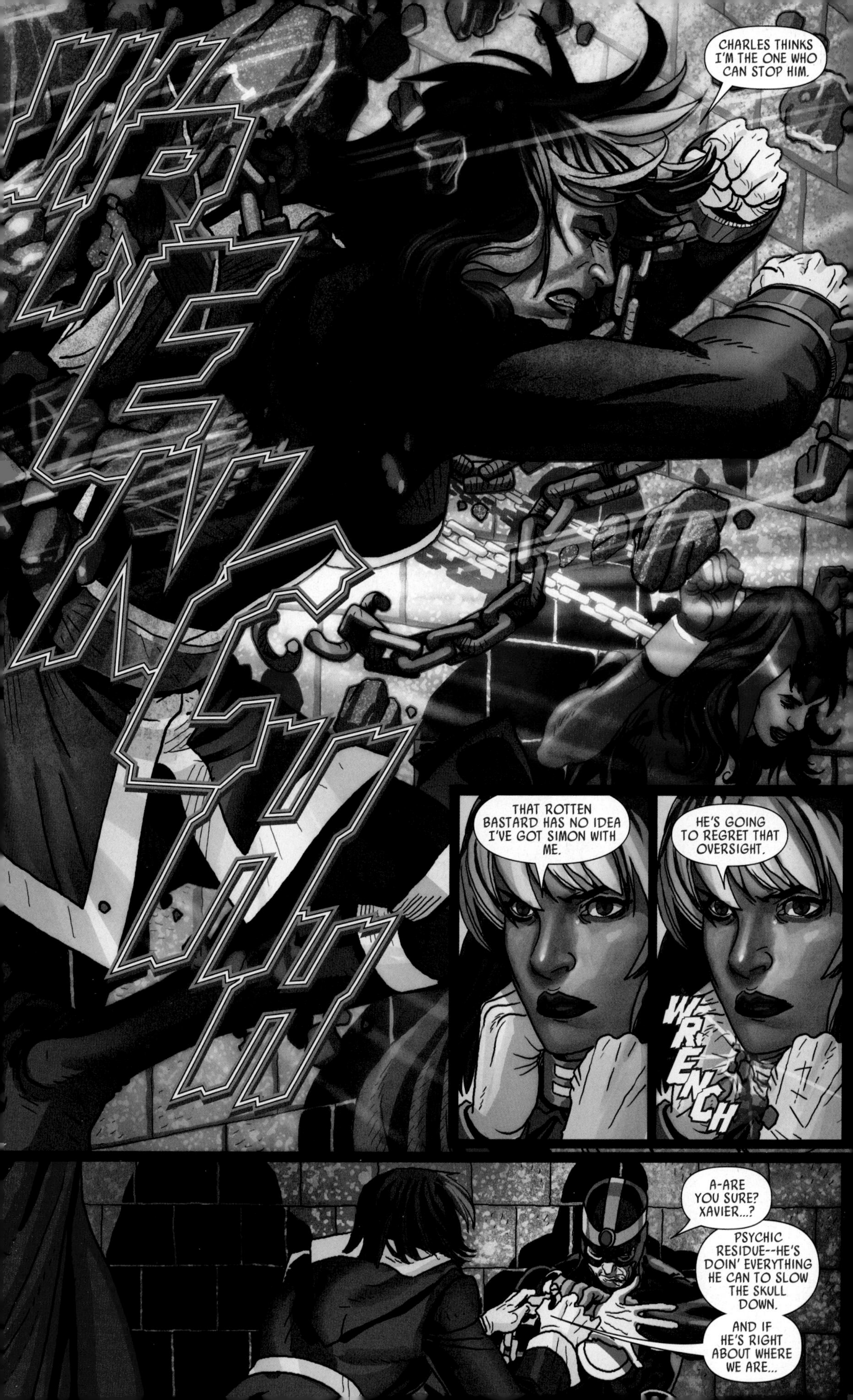
CHARLES THINKS I'M THE ONE WHO CAN STOP HIM.
THAT ROTTEN BASTARD HAS NO IDEA I'VE GOT SIMON WITH ME.
HE'S GOING TO REGRET THAT OVERSIGHT.
WRENCH
A-ARE YOU SURE? XAVIER...?
PSYCHIC RESIDUE--HE'S DOIN' EVERYTHING HE CAN TO SLOW THE SKULL DOWN.
AND IF HE'S RIGHT ABOUT WHERE WE ARE...

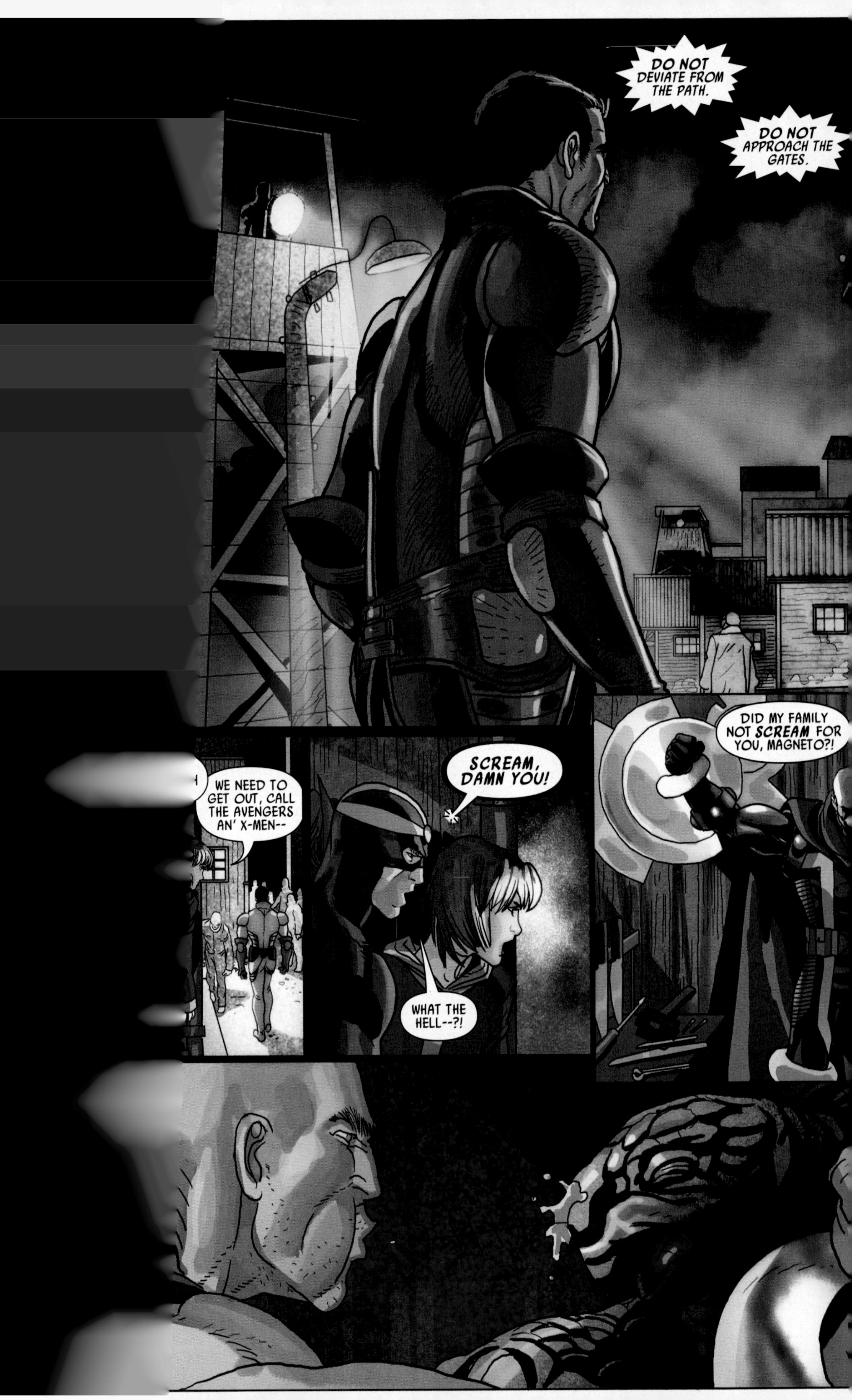
DO NOT DEVIATE FROM THE PATH.
DO NOT APPROACH THE GATES.
WE NEED TO GET OUT, CALL THE AVENGERS AN' X-MEN--
SCREAM, DAMN YOU!
WHAT THE HELL--?!
DID MY FAMILY NOT SCREAM FOR YOU, MAGNETO?!

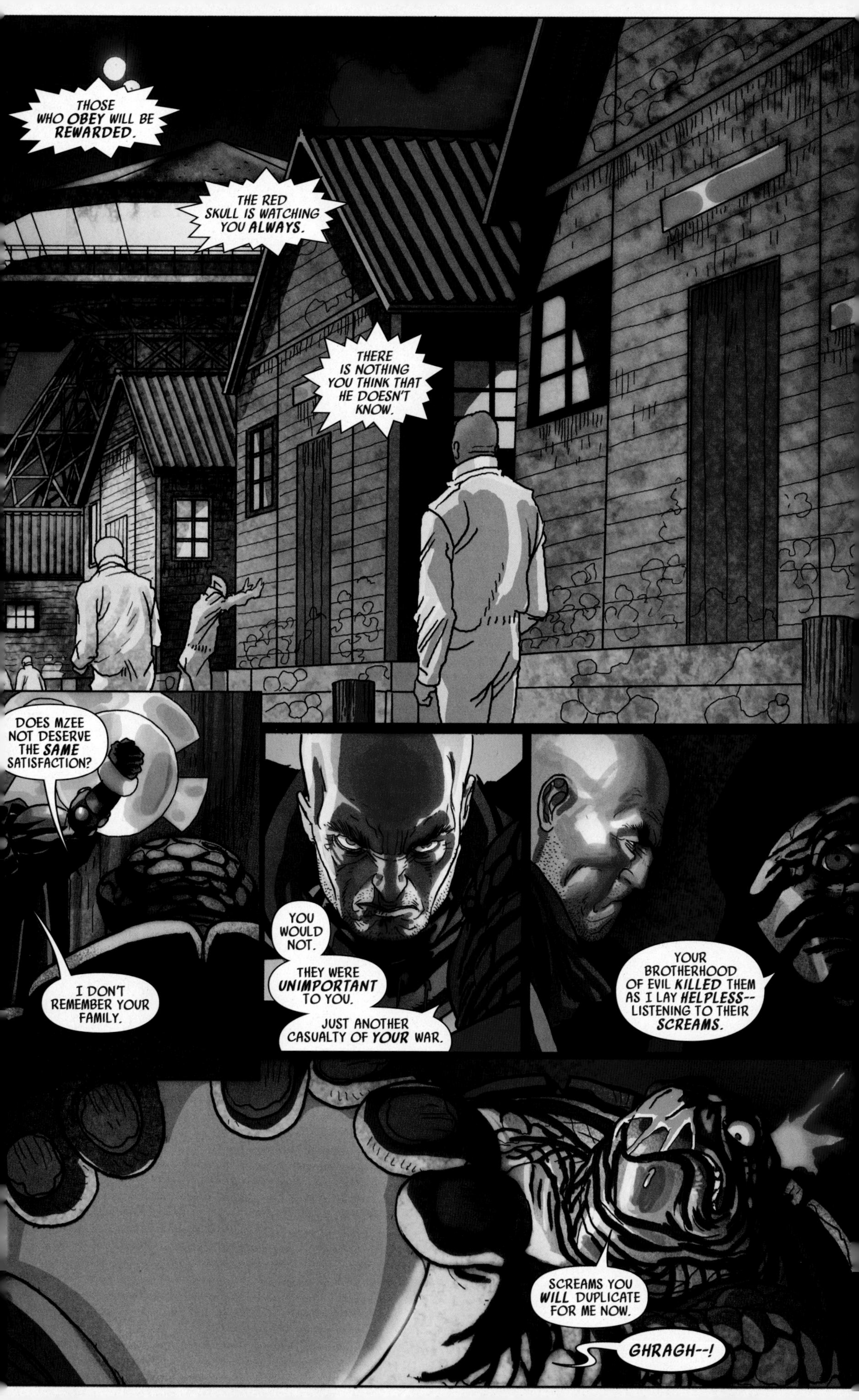
THOSE WHO OBEY WILL BE REWARDED.
THE RED SKULL IS WATCHING YOU ALWAYS.
THERE IS NOTHING YOU THINK THAT HE DOESN'T KNOW.
DOES MZEE NOT DESERVE THE SAME SATISFACTION?
I DON'T REMEMBER YOUR FAMILY.
YOU WOULD NOT.
THEY WERE UNIMPORTANT TO YOU.
JUST ANOTHER CASUALTY OF YOUR WAR.
YOUR BROTHERHOOD OF EVIL KILLED THEM AS I LAY HELPLESS--LISTENING TO THEIR SCREAMS.
SCREAMS YOU WILL DUPLICATE FOR ME NOW.
GHRAGH--!

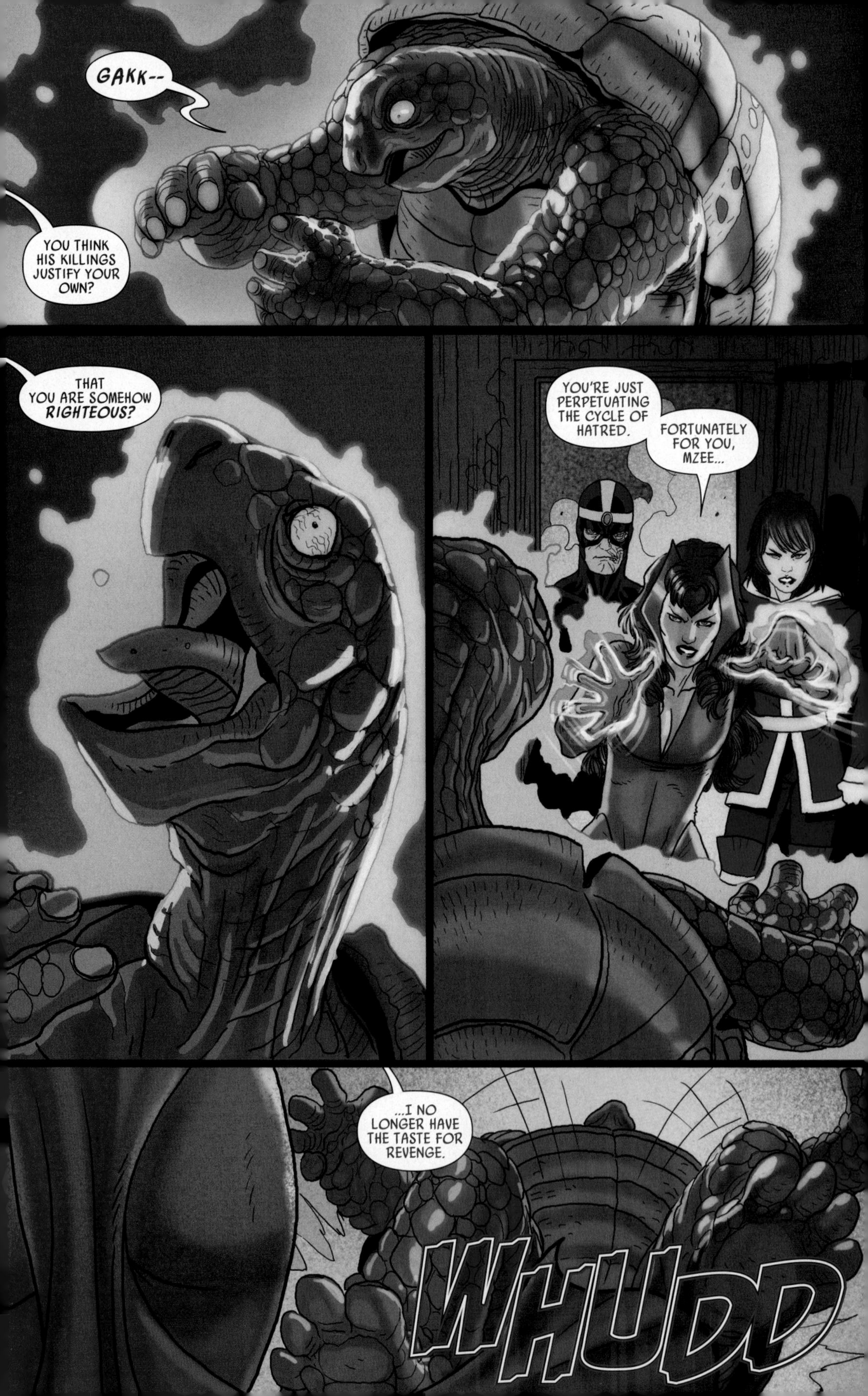
GAKK--
YOU THINK HIS KILLINGS JUSTIFY YOUR OWN?
THAT YOU ARE SOMEHOW *RIGHTEOUS?*
YOU'RE JUST PERPETUATING THE CYCLE OF HATRED.
FORTUNATELY FOR YOU, MZEE...
...I NO LONGER HAVE THE TASTE FOR REVENGE.
WHUDD

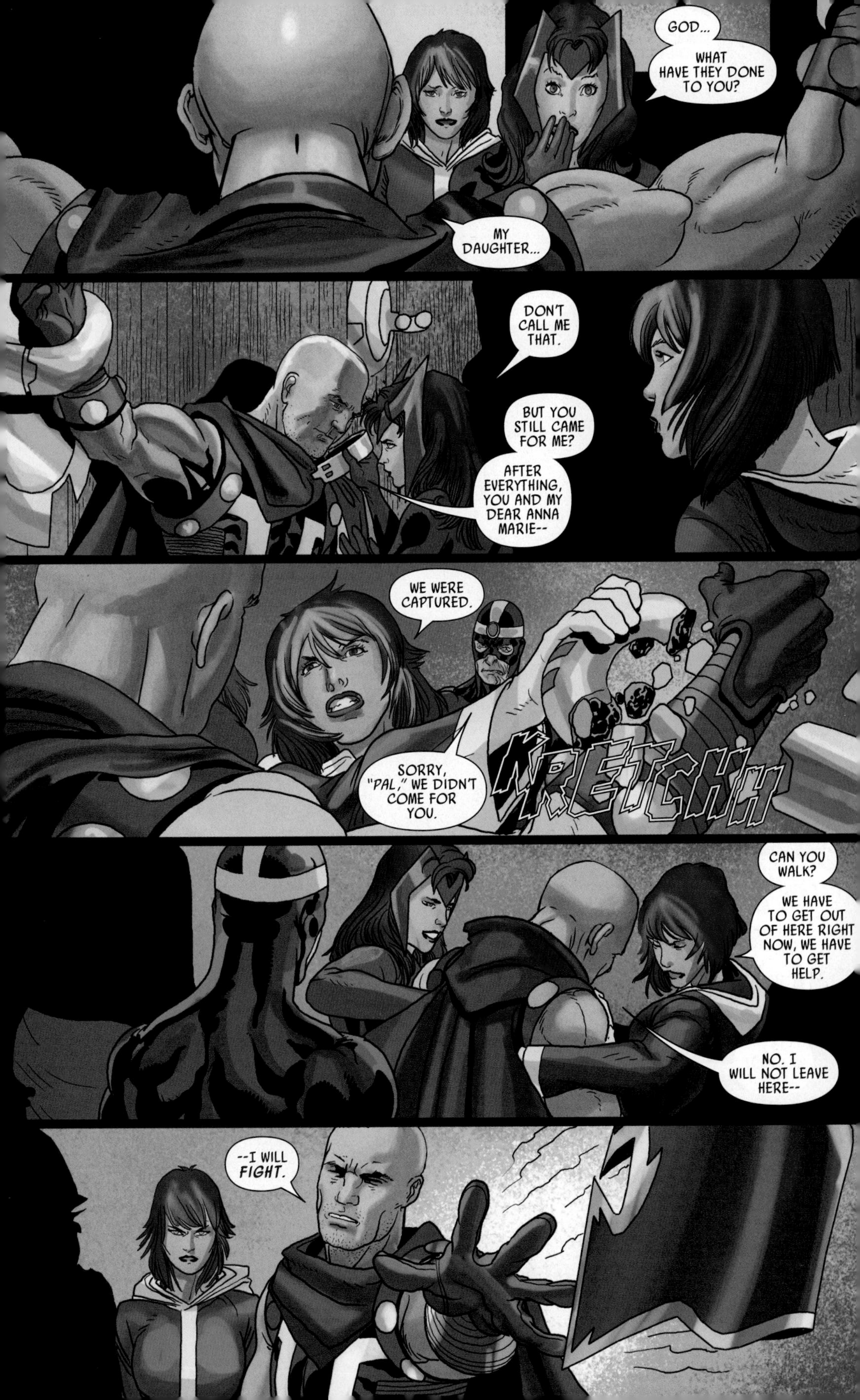
GOD... WHAT HAVE THEY DONE TO YOU?
MY DAUGHTER...
DON'T CALL ME THAT.
BUT YOU STILL CAME FOR ME?
AFTER EVERYTHING, YOU AND MY DEAR ANNA MARIE--
WE WERE CAPTURED.
SORRY, "PAL," WE DIDN'T COME FOR YOU.
KRETCHH
CAN YOU WALK?
WE HAVE TO GET OUT OF HERE RIGHT NOW, WE HAVE TO GET HELP.
NO. I WILL NOT LEAVE HERE--
--I WILL FIGHT.

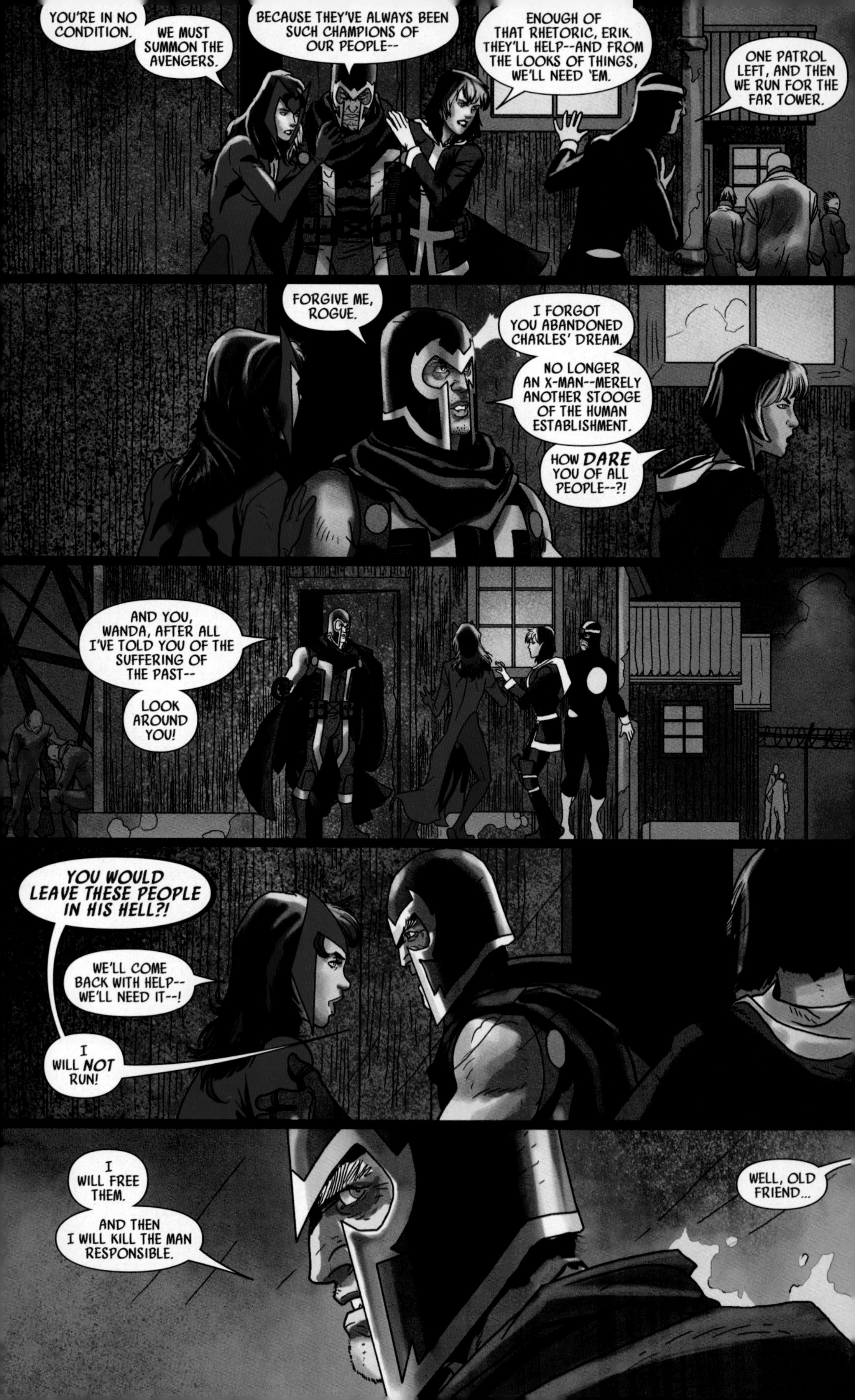
YOU'RE IN NO CONDITION.
WE MUST SUMMON THE AVENGERS.
BECAUSE THEY'VE ALWAYS BEEN SUCH CHAMPIONS OF OUR PEOPLE--
ENOUGH OF THAT RHETORIC, ERIK. THEY'LL HELP--AND FROM THE LOOKS OF THINGS, WE'LL NEED 'EM.
ONE PATROL LEFT, AND THEN WE RUN FOR THE FAR TOWER.
FORGIVE ME, ROGUE.
I FORGOT YOU ABANDONED CHARLES' DREAM.
NO LONGER AN X-MAN--MERELY ANOTHER STOOGE OF THE HUMAN ESTABLISHMENT.
HOW DARE YOU OF ALL PEOPLE--?!
AND YOU, WANDA, AFTER ALL I'VE TOLD YOU OF THE SUFFERING OF THE PAST--
LOOK AROUND YOU!
YOU WOULD LEAVE THESE PEOPLE IN HIS HELL?!
WE'LL COME BACK WITH HELP-- WE'LL NEED IT--!
I WILL NOT RUN!
I WILL FREE THEM.
AND THEN I WILL KILL THE MAN RESPONSIBLE.
WELL, OLD FRIEND...

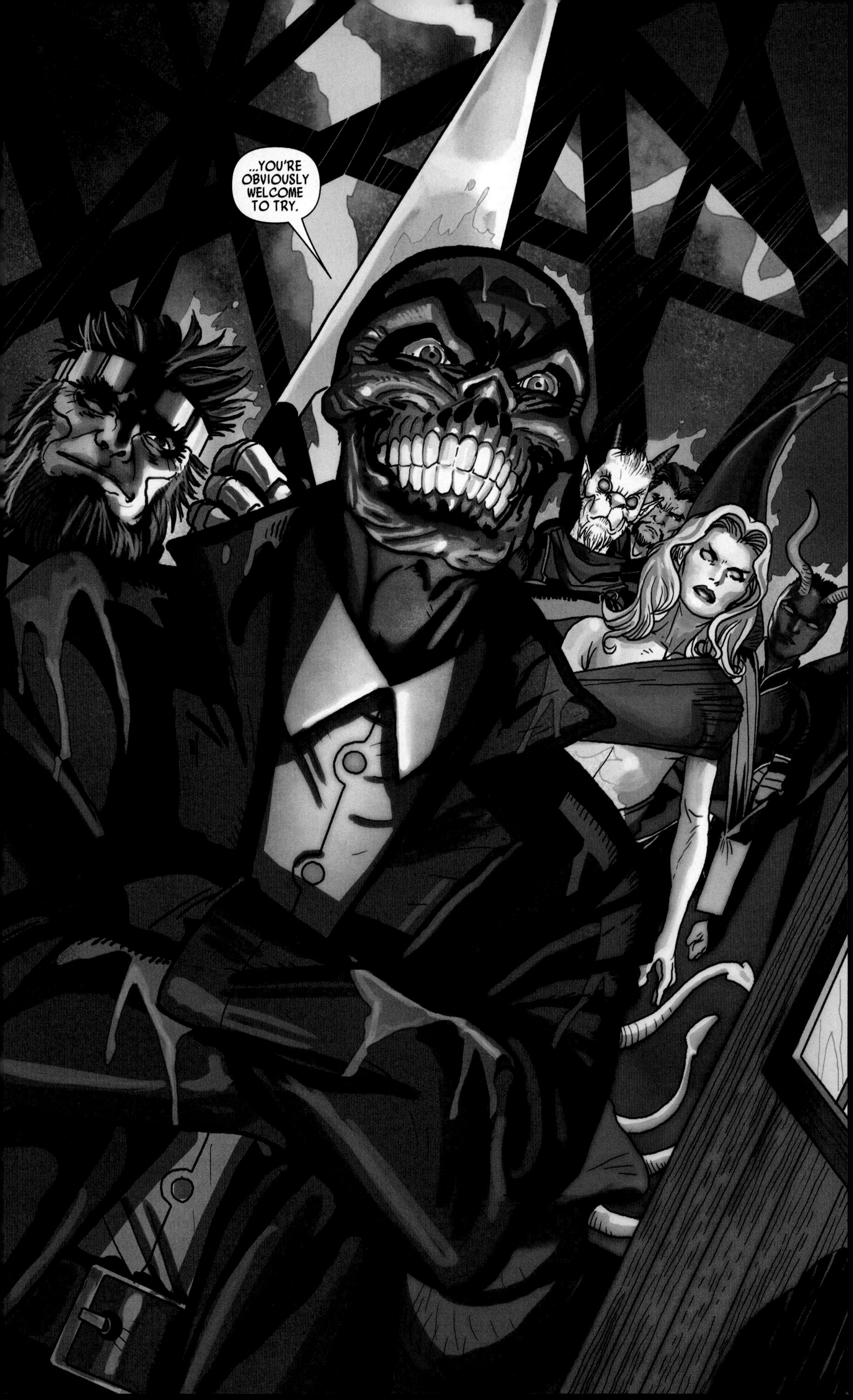
...YOU'RE OBVIOUSLY WELCOME TO TRY.

UNCANNY AVENGERS #25

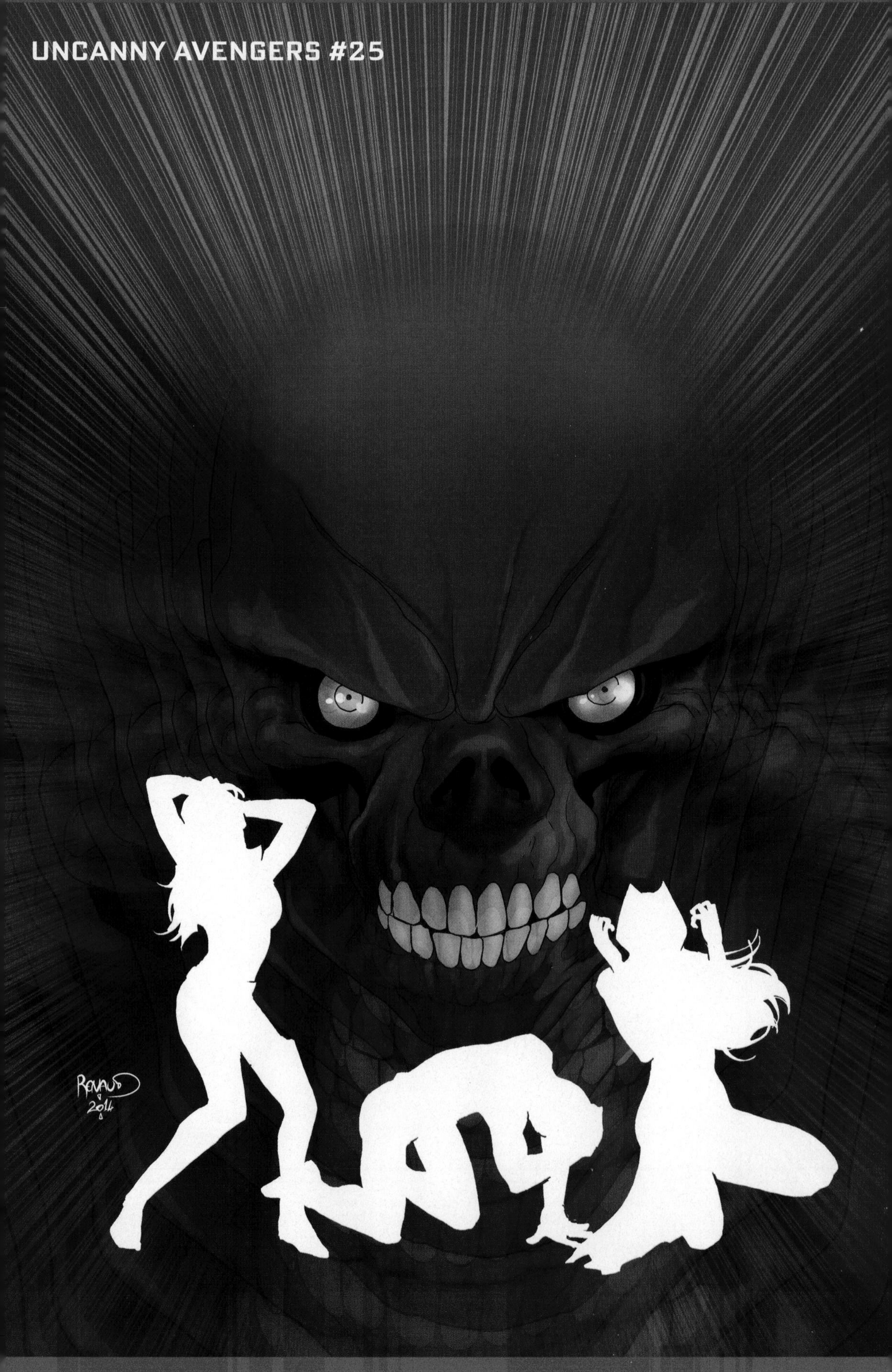

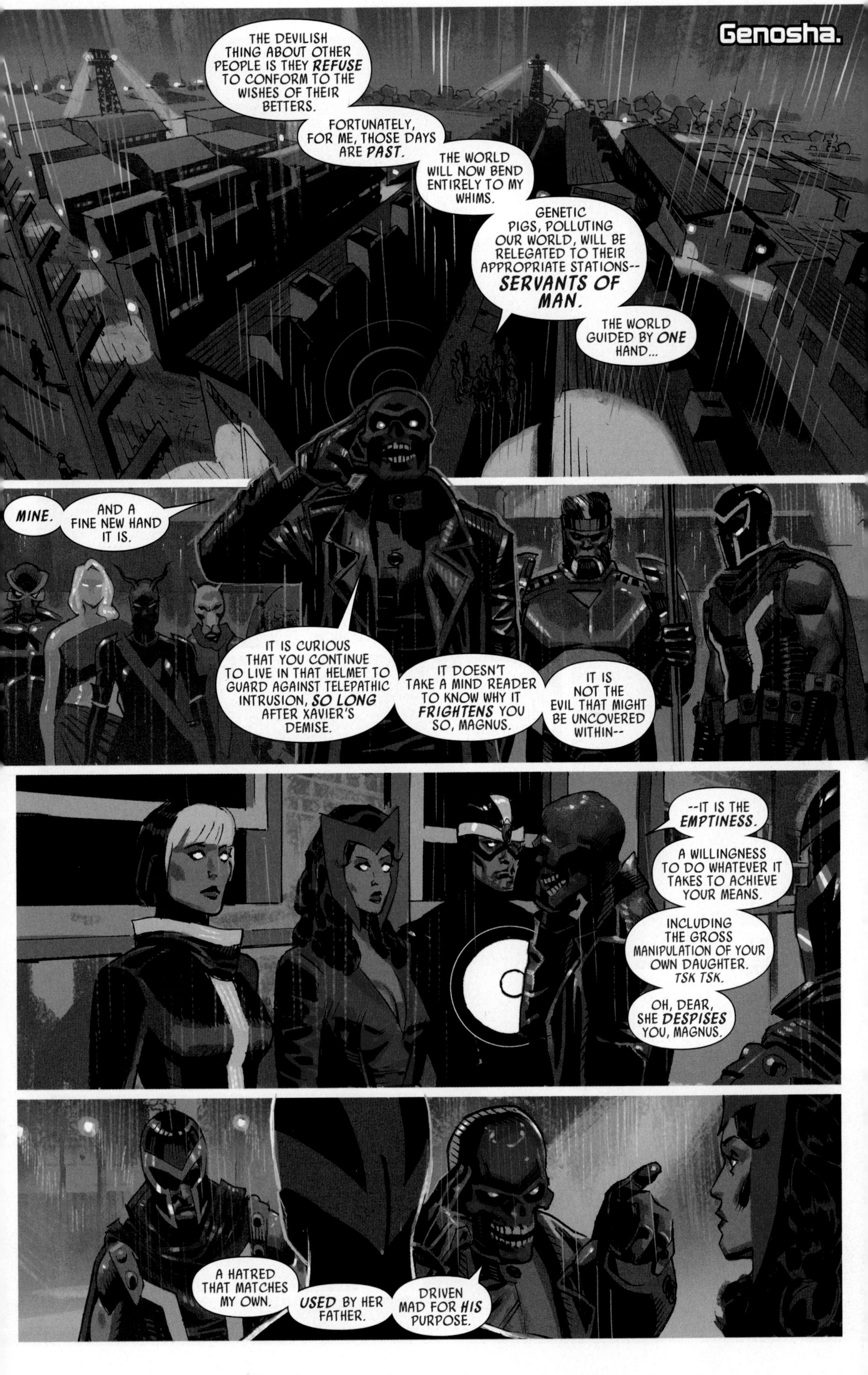
Genosha.
THE DEVILISH THING ABOUT OTHER PEOPLE IS THEY REFUSE TO CONFORM TO THE WISHES OF THEIR BETTERS.
FORTUNATELY, FOR ME, THOSE DAYS ARE PAST.
THE WORLD WILL NOW BEND ENTIRELY TO MY WHIMS.
GENETIC PIGS, POLLUTING OUR WORLD, WILL BE RELEGATED TO THEIR APPROPRIATE STATIONS-- SERVANTS OF MAN.
THE WORLD GUIDED BY ONE HAND...
MINE.
AND A FINE NEW HAND IT IS.
IT IS CURIOUS THAT YOU CONTINUE TO LIVE IN THAT HELMET TO GUARD AGAINST TELEPATHIC INTRUSION, SO LONG AFTER XAVIER'S DEMISE.
IT DOESN'T TAKE A MIND READER TO KNOW WHY IT FRIGHTENS YOU SO, MAGNUS.
IT IS NOT THE EVIL THAT MIGHT BE UNCOVERED WITHIN--
--IT IS THE EMPTINESS.
A WILLINGNESS TO DO WHATEVER IT TAKES TO ACHIEVE YOUR MEANS.
INCLUDING THE GROSS MANIPULATION OF YOUR OWN DAUGHTER. TSK TSK.
OH, DEAR, SHE DESPISES YOU, MAGNUS.
A HATRED THAT MATCHES MY OWN.
USED BY HER FATHER.
DRIVEN MAD FOR HIS PURPOSE.

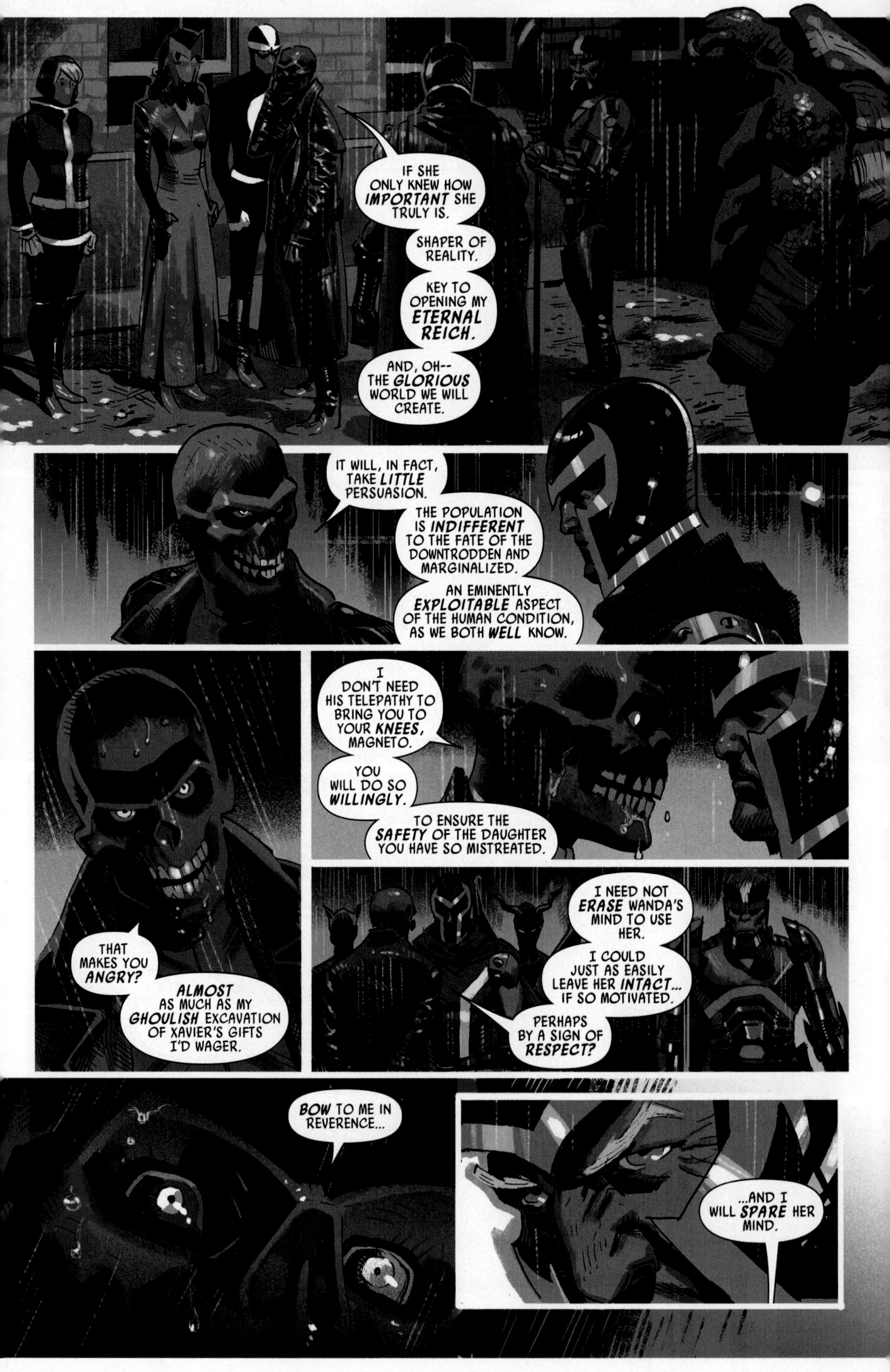
IF SHE ONLY KNEW HOW IMPORTANT SHE TRULY IS.
SHAPER OF REALITY.
KEY TO OPENING MY ETERNAL REICH.
AND, OH-- THE GLORIOUS WORLD WE WILL CREATE.
IT WILL, IN FACT, TAKE LITTLE PERSUASION.
THE POPULATION IS INDIFFERENT TO THE FATE OF THE DOWNTRODDEN AND MARGINALIZED.
AN EMINENTLY EXPLOITABLE ASPECT OF THE HUMAN CONDITION, AS WE BOTH WELL KNOW.
THAT MAKES YOU ANGRY?
ALMOST AS MUCH AS MY GHOULISH EXCAVATION OF XAVIER'S GIFTS I'D WAGER.
I DON'T NEED HIS TELEPATHY TO BRING YOU TO YOUR KNEES, MAGNETO.
YOU WILL DO SO WILLINGLY.
TO ENSURE THE SAFETY OF THE DAUGHTER YOU HAVE SO MISTREATED.
I NEED NOT ERASE WANDA'S MIND TO USE HER.
I COULD JUST AS EASILY LEAVE HER INTACT... IF SO MOTIVATED.
PERHAPS BY A SIGN OF RESPECT?
BOW TO ME IN REVERENCE...
...AND I WILL SPARE HER MIND.

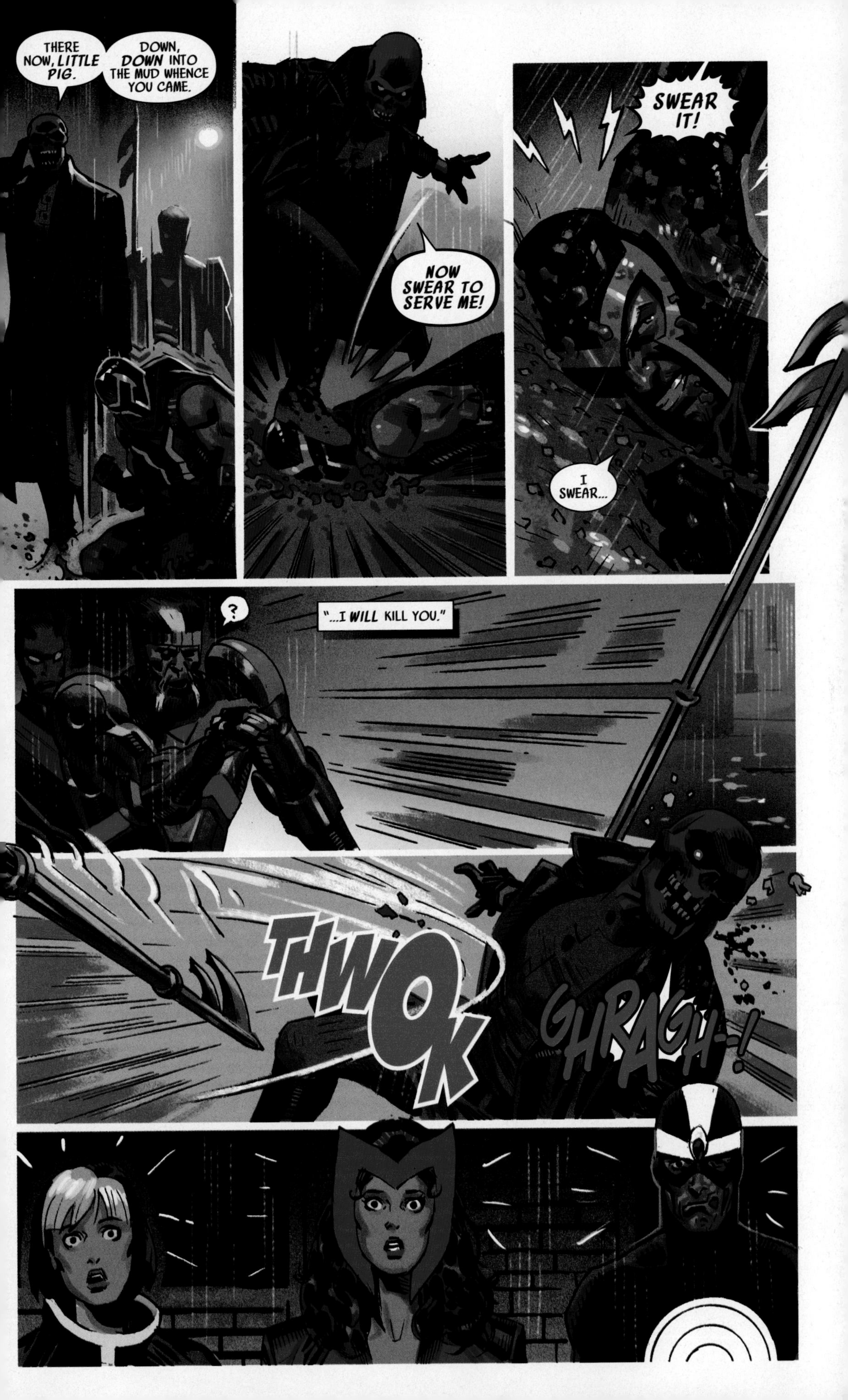
THERE NOW, LITTLE PIG.
DOWN, DOWN INTO THE MUD WHENCE YOU CAME.
NOW SWEAR TO SERVE ME!
SWEAR IT!
I SWEAR...
?
"...I WILL KILL YOU."
THWOK
GHRAGH--!

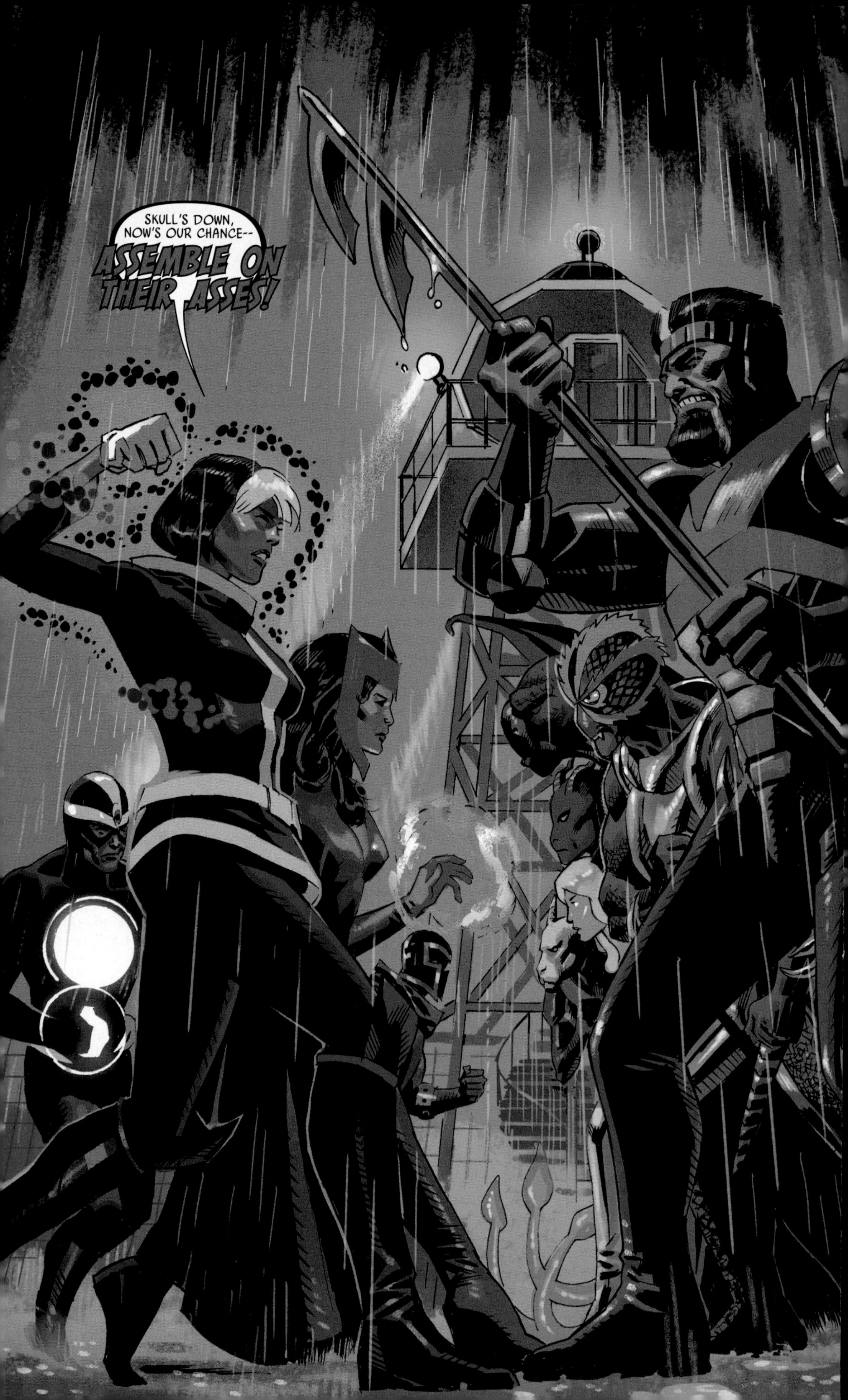
SKULL'S DOWN, NOW'S OUR CHANCE--
ASSEMBLE ON THEIR ASSES!

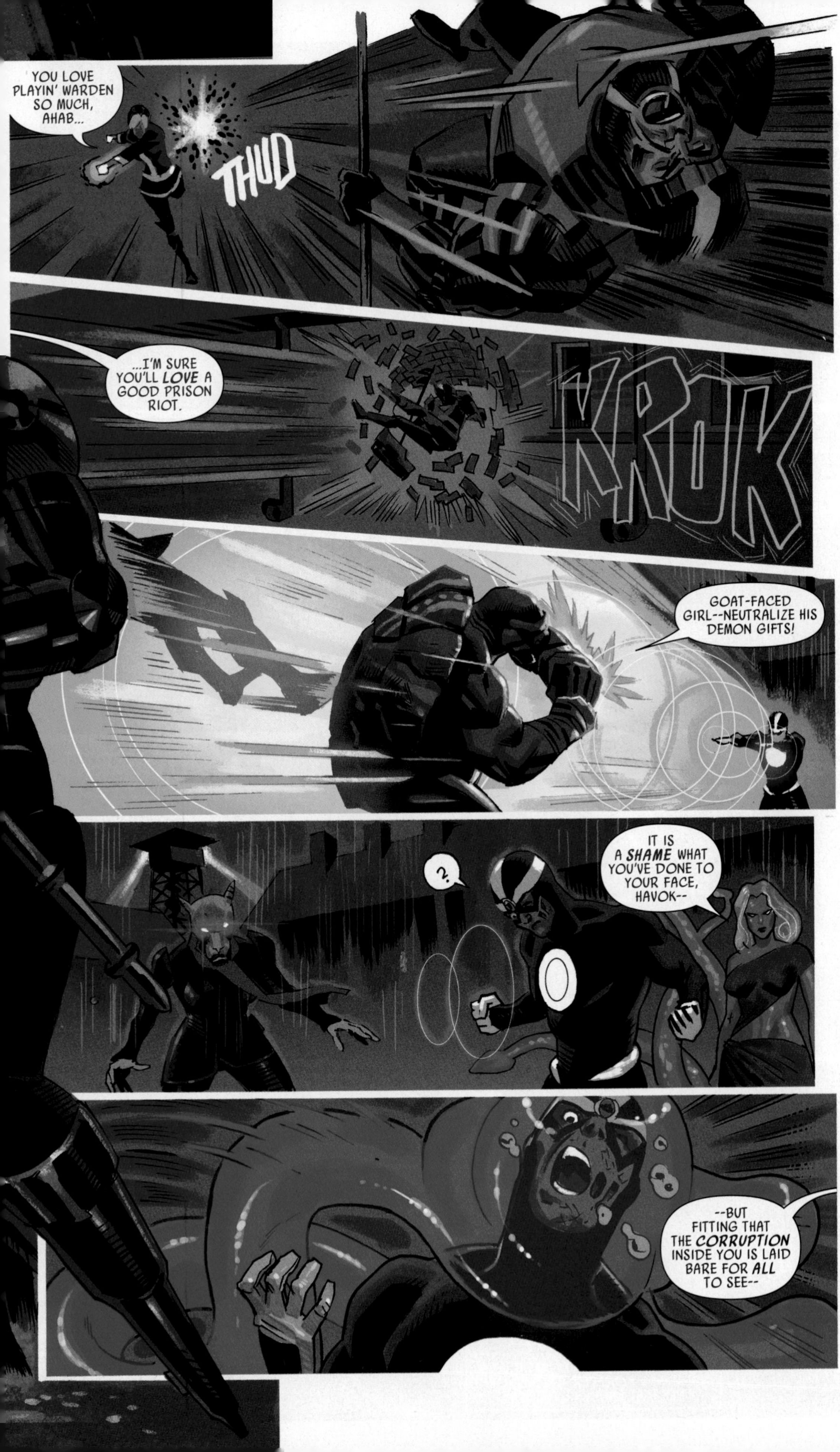
YOU LOVE PLAYIN' WARDEN SO MUCH, AHAB...
THUD
...I'M SURE YOU'LL LOVE A GOOD PRISON RIOT.
KROK
GOAT-FACED GIRL--NEUTRALIZE HIS DEMON GIFTS!
?
IT IS A SHAME WHAT YOU'VE DONE TO YOUR FACE, HAVOK--
--BUT FITTING THAT THE CORRUPTION INSIDE YOU IS LAID BARE FOR ALL TO SEE--

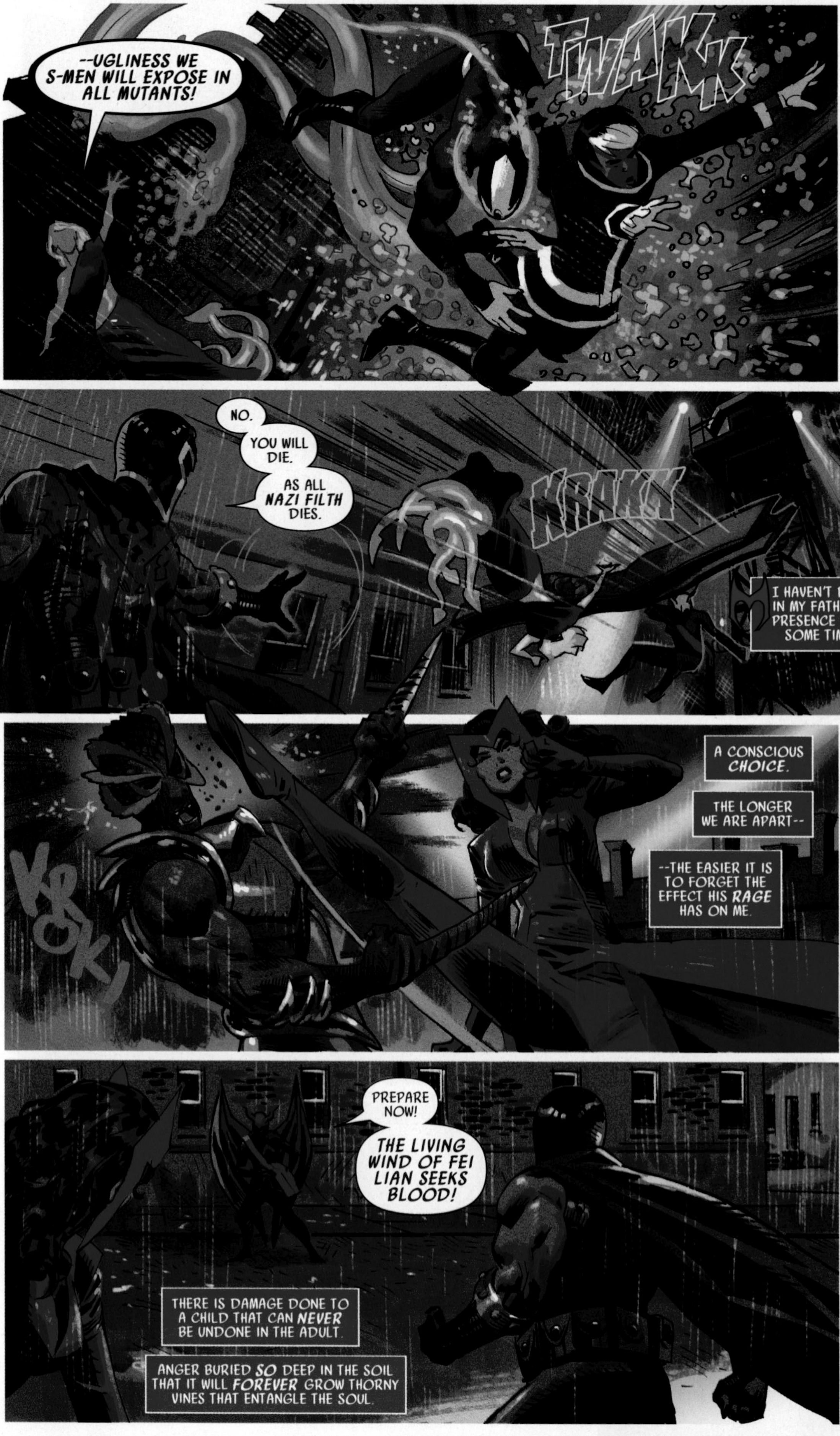
--UGLINESS WE S-MEN WILL EXPOSE IN ALL MUTANTS!
TWAKK
NO.
YOU WILL DIE.
AS ALL NAZI FILTH DIES.
KRAKK
I HAVEN'T BEEN IN MY FATHER'S PRESENCE FOR SOME TIME.
KROK
A CONSCIOUS CHOICE.
THE LONGER WE ARE APART--
--THE EASIER IT IS TO FORGET THE EFFECT HIS RAGE HAS ON ME.
PREPARE NOW!
THE LIVING WIND OF FEI LIAN SEEKS BLOOD!
THERE IS DAMAGE DONE TO A CHILD THAT CAN NEVER BE UNDONE IN THE ADULT.
ANGER BURIED SO DEEP IN THE SOIL THAT IT WILL FOREVER GROW THORNY VINES THAT ENTANGLE THE SOUL.

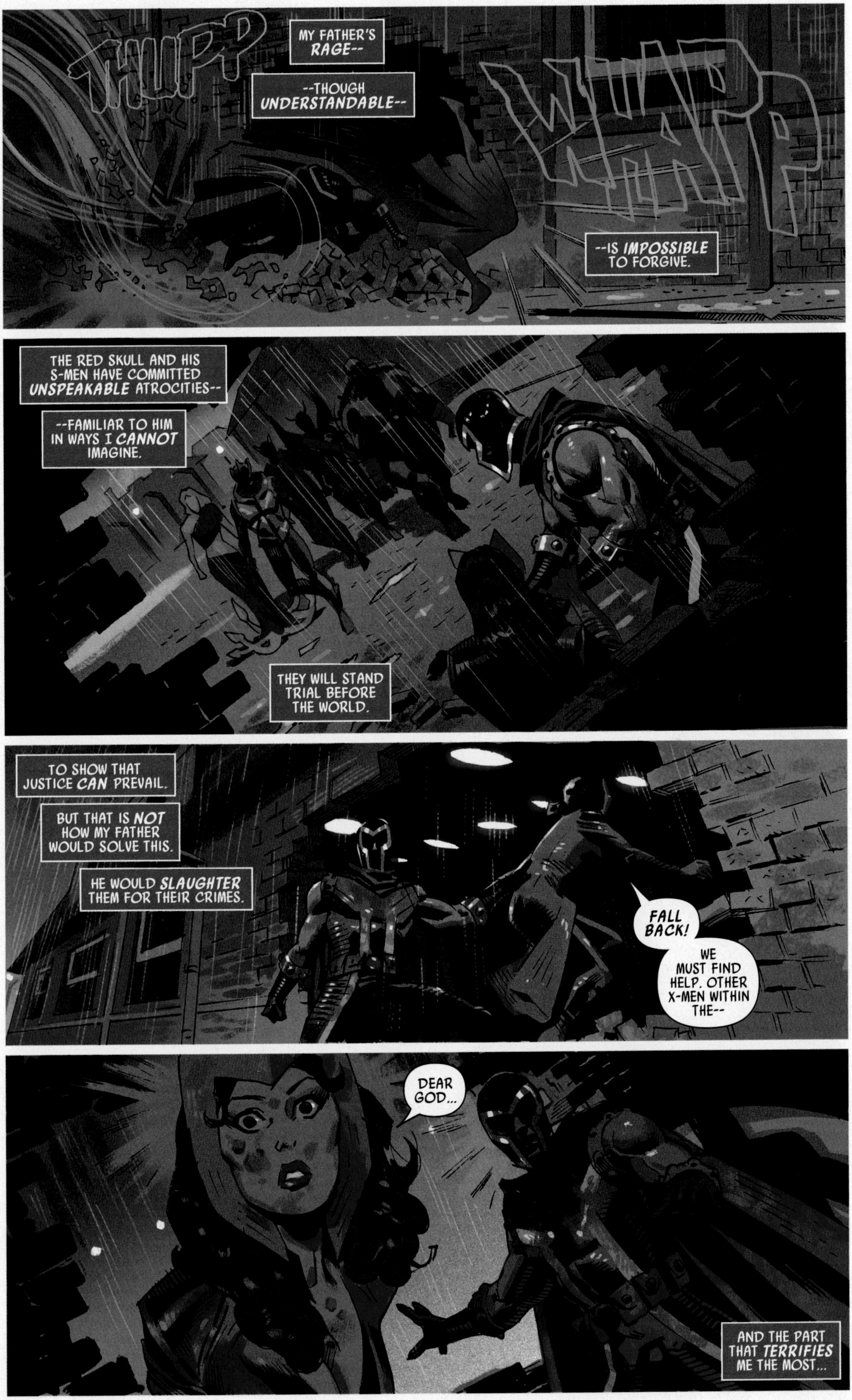
THUPP
MY FATHER'S RAGE--
--THOUGH UNDERSTANDABLE--
WHAPP
--IS IMPOSSIBLE TO FORGIVE.
THE RED SKULL AND HIS S-MEN HAVE COMMITTED UNSPEAKABLE ATROCITIES--
--FAMILIAR TO HIM IN WAYS I CANNOT IMAGINE.
THEY WILL STAND TRIAL BEFORE THE WORLD.
TO SHOW THAT JUSTICE CAN PREVAIL.
BUT THAT IS NOT HOW MY FATHER WOULD SOLVE THIS.
HE WOULD SLAUGHTER THEM FOR THEIR CRIMES.
FALL BACK!
WE MUST FIND HELP. OTHER X-MEN WITHIN THE--
DEAR GOD...
AND THE PART THAT TERRIFIES ME THE MOST...

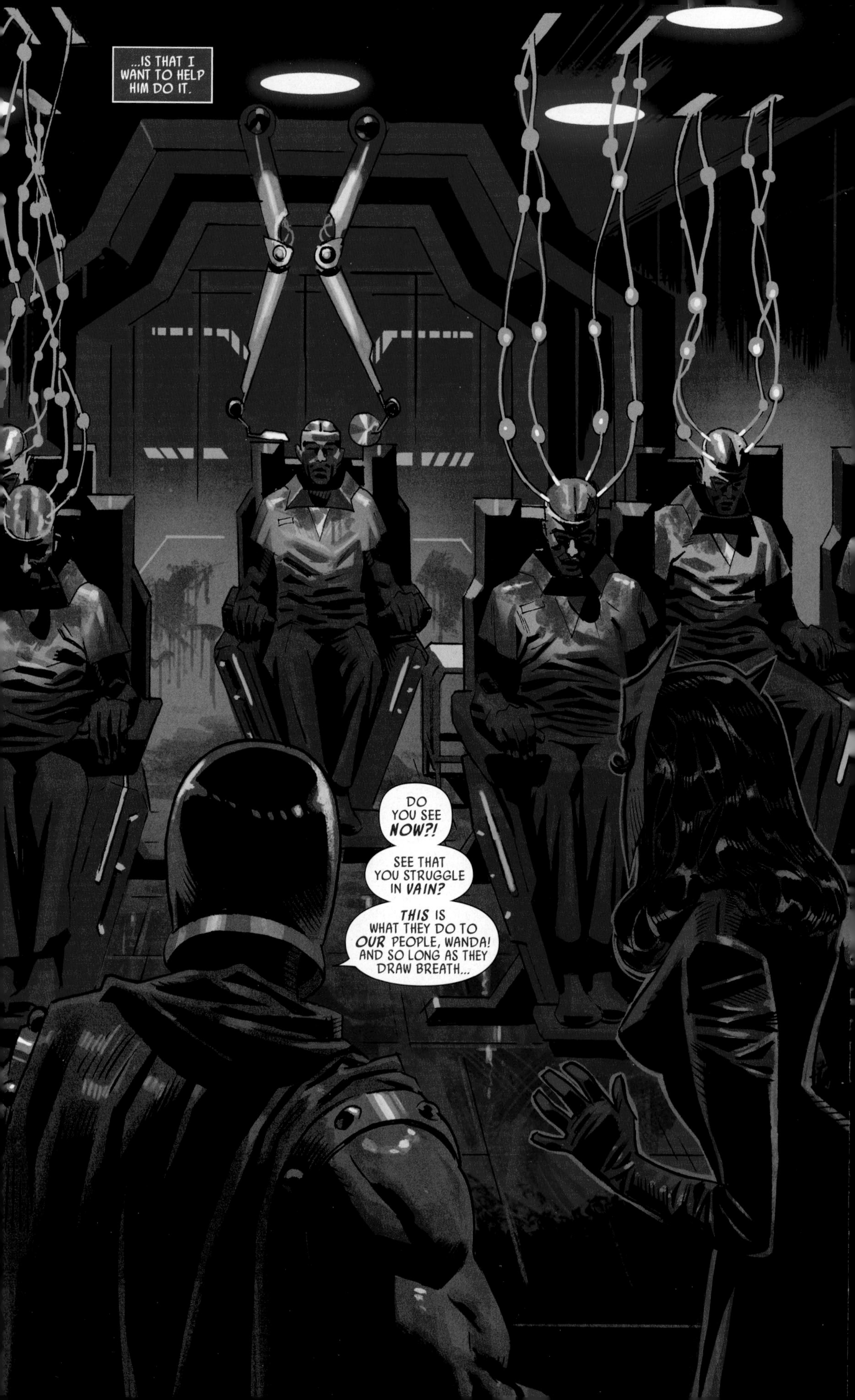
...IS THAT I WANT TO HELP HIM DO IT.
DO YOU SEE NOW?!
SEE THAT YOU STRUGGLE IN VAIN?
THIS IS WHAT THEY DO TO OUR PEOPLE, WANDA! AND SO LONG AS THEY DRAW BREATH...

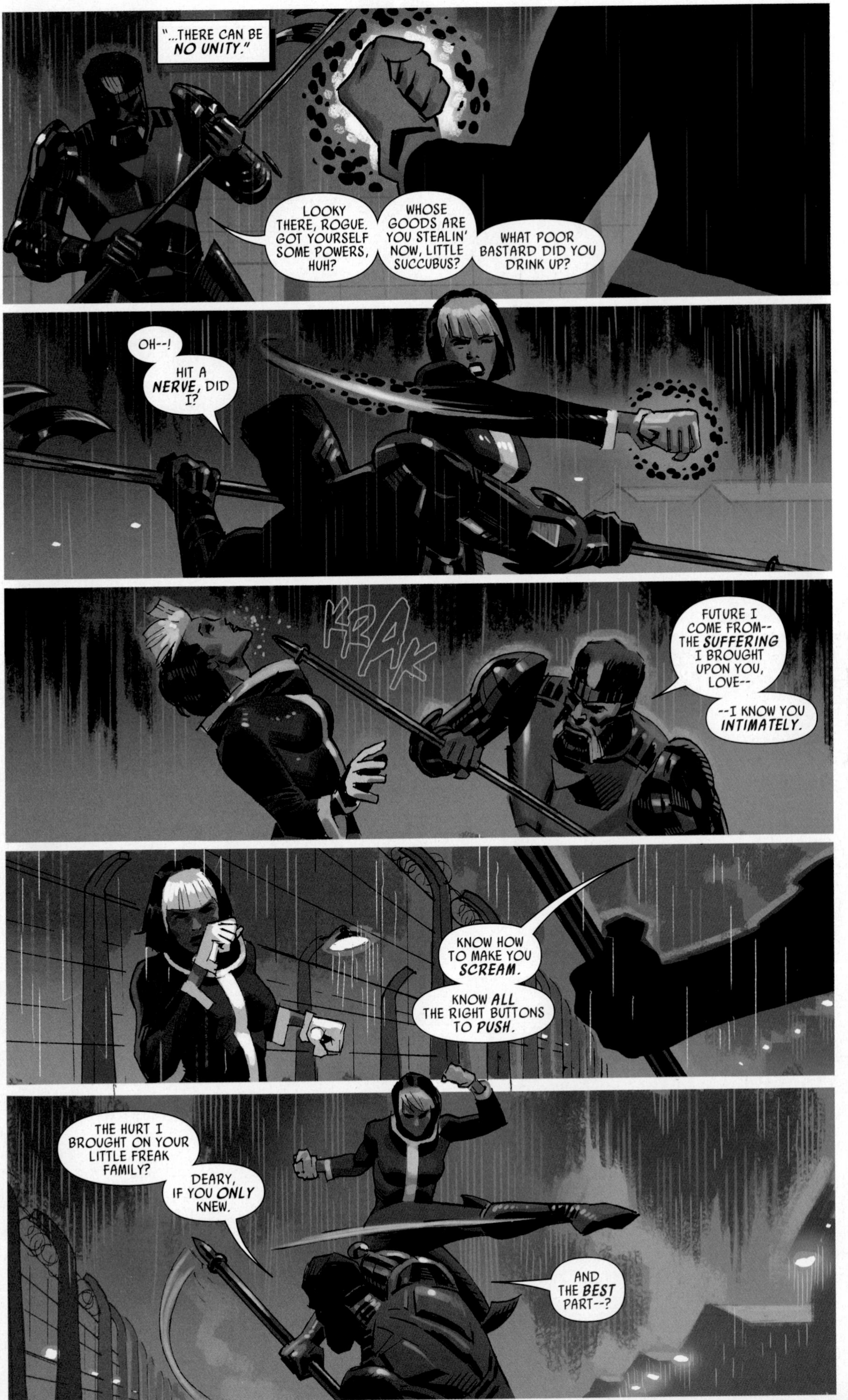
"...THERE CAN BE NO UNITY."
LOOKY THERE, ROGUE. GOT YOURSELF SOME POWERS, HUH?
WHOSE GOODS ARE YOU STEALIN' NOW, LITTLE SUCCUBUS?
WHAT POOR BASTARD DID YOU DRINK UP?
OH--!
HIT A NERVE, DID I?
KRAK
FUTURE I COME FROM-- THE SUFFERING I BROUGHT UPON YOU, LOVE--
--I KNOW YOU INTIMATELY.
KNOW HOW TO MAKE YOU SCREAM.
KNOW ALL THE RIGHT BUTTONS TO PUSH.
THE HURT I BROUGHT ON YOUR LITTLE FREAK FAMILY?
DEARY, IF YOU ONLY KNEW.
AND THE BEST PART--?

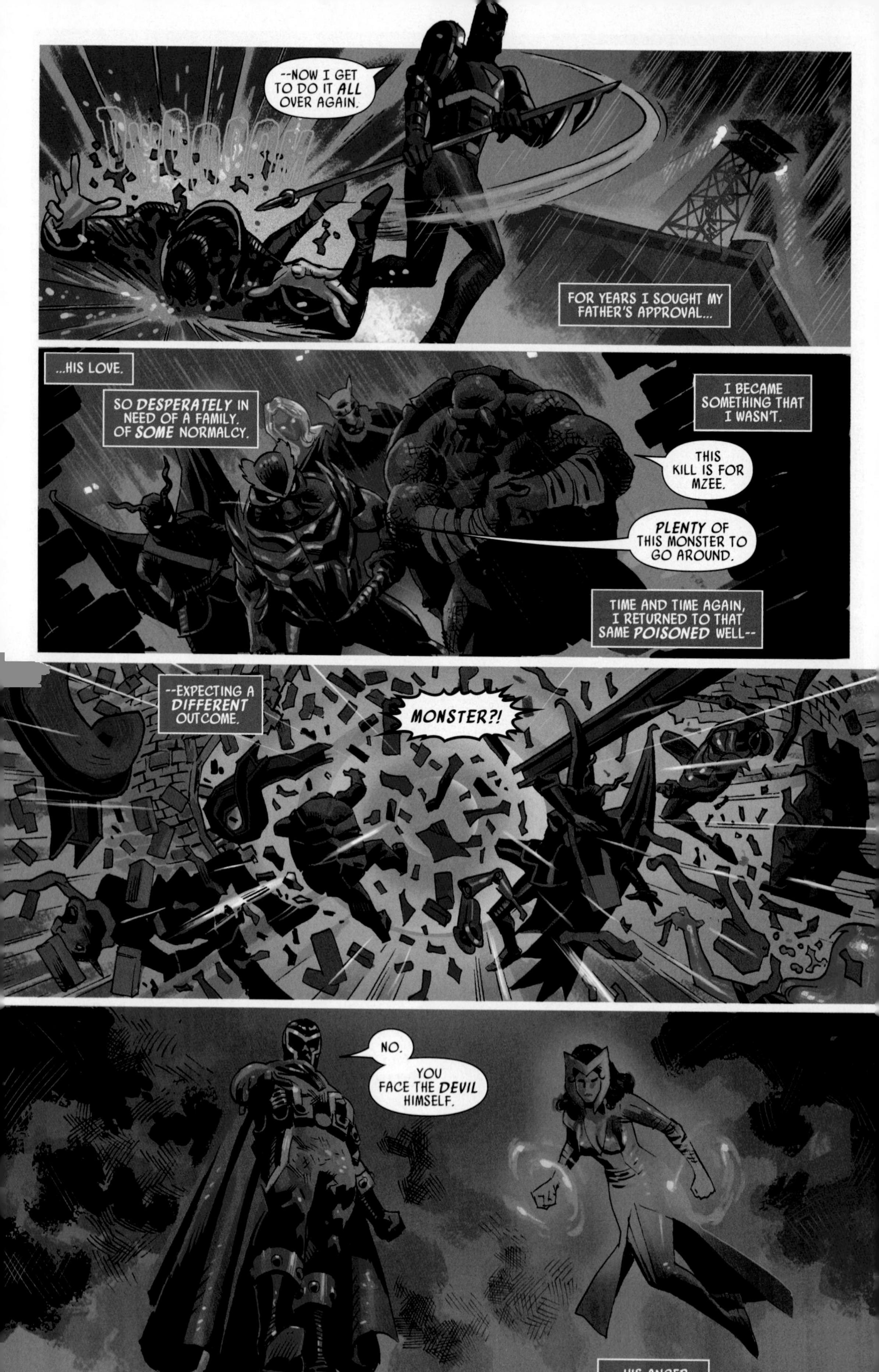
--NOW I GET TO DO IT ALL OVER AGAIN.
FOR YEARS I SOUGHT MY FATHER'S APPROVAL...
...HIS LOVE.
SO DESPERATELY IN NEED OF A FAMILY. OF SOME NORMALCY.
I BECAME SOMETHING THAT I WASN'T.
THIS KILL IS FOR MZEE.
PLENTY OF THIS MONSTER TO GO AROUND.
TIME AND TIME AGAIN, I RETURNED TO THAT SAME POISONED WELL--
--EXPECTING A DIFFERENT OUTCOME.
MONSTER?!
NO.
YOU FACE THE DEVIL HIMSELF.
HIS ANGER TERRIFIES ME.

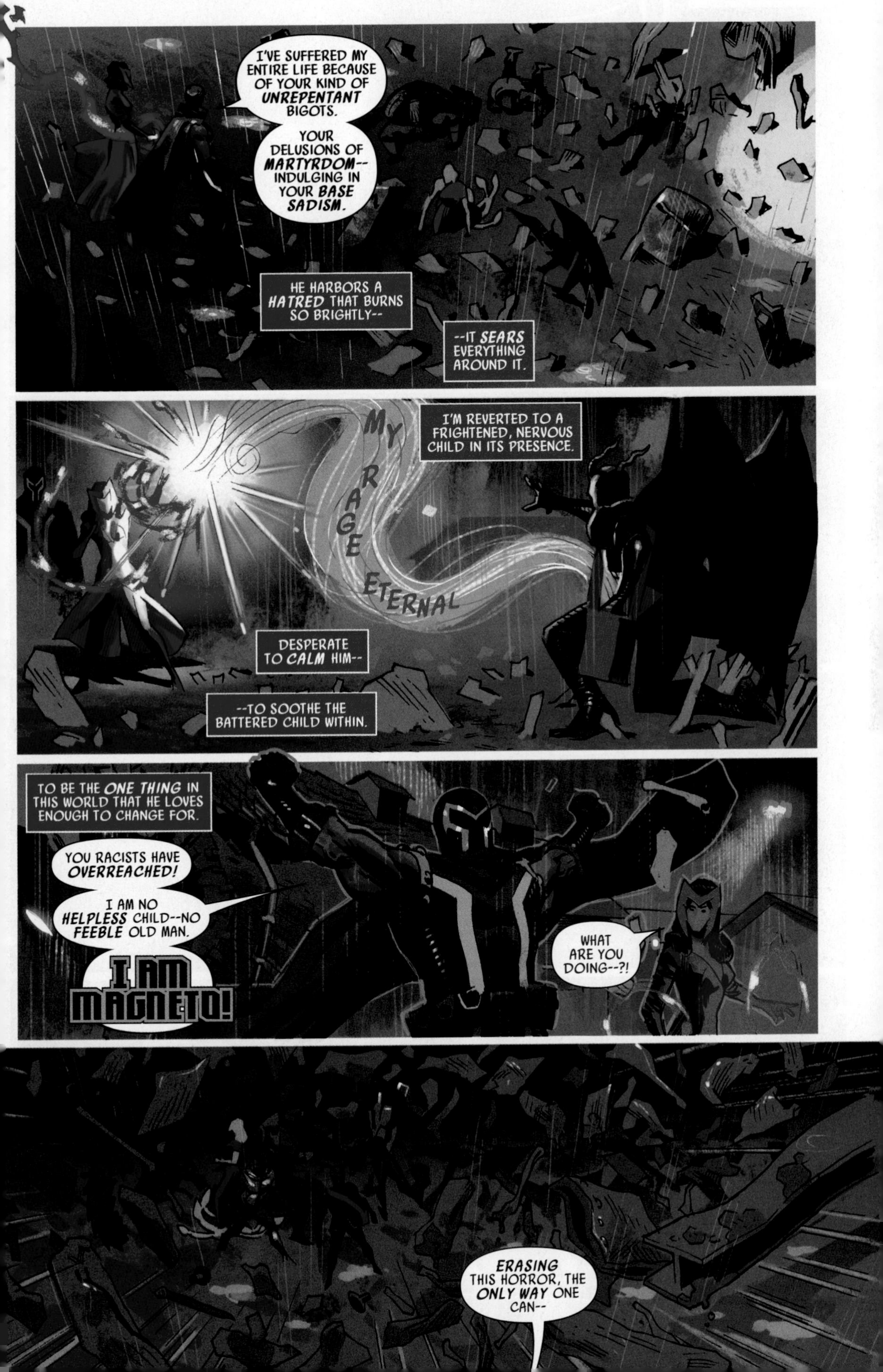

I'VE SUFFERED MY ENTIRE LIFE BECAUSE OF YOUR KIND OF UNREPENTANT BIGOTS.
YOUR DELUSIONS OF MARTYRDOM--INDULGING IN YOUR BASE SADISM.
HE HARBORS A HATRED THAT BURNS SO BRIGHTLY--
--IT SEARS EVERYTHING AROUND IT.
I'M REVERTED TO A FRIGHTENED, NERVOUS CHILD IN ITS PRESENCE.
MY RAGE ETERNAL
DESPERATE TO CALM HIM--
--TO SOOTHE THE BATTERED CHILD WITHIN.
TO BE THE ONE THING IN THIS WORLD THAT HE LOVES ENOUGH TO CHANGE FOR.
YOU RACISTS HAVE OVERREACHED!
I AM NO HELPLESS CHILD--NO FEEBLE OLD MAN.
I AM MAGNETO!
WHAT ARE YOU DOING--?!
ERASING THIS HORROR, THE ONLY WAY ONE CAN--

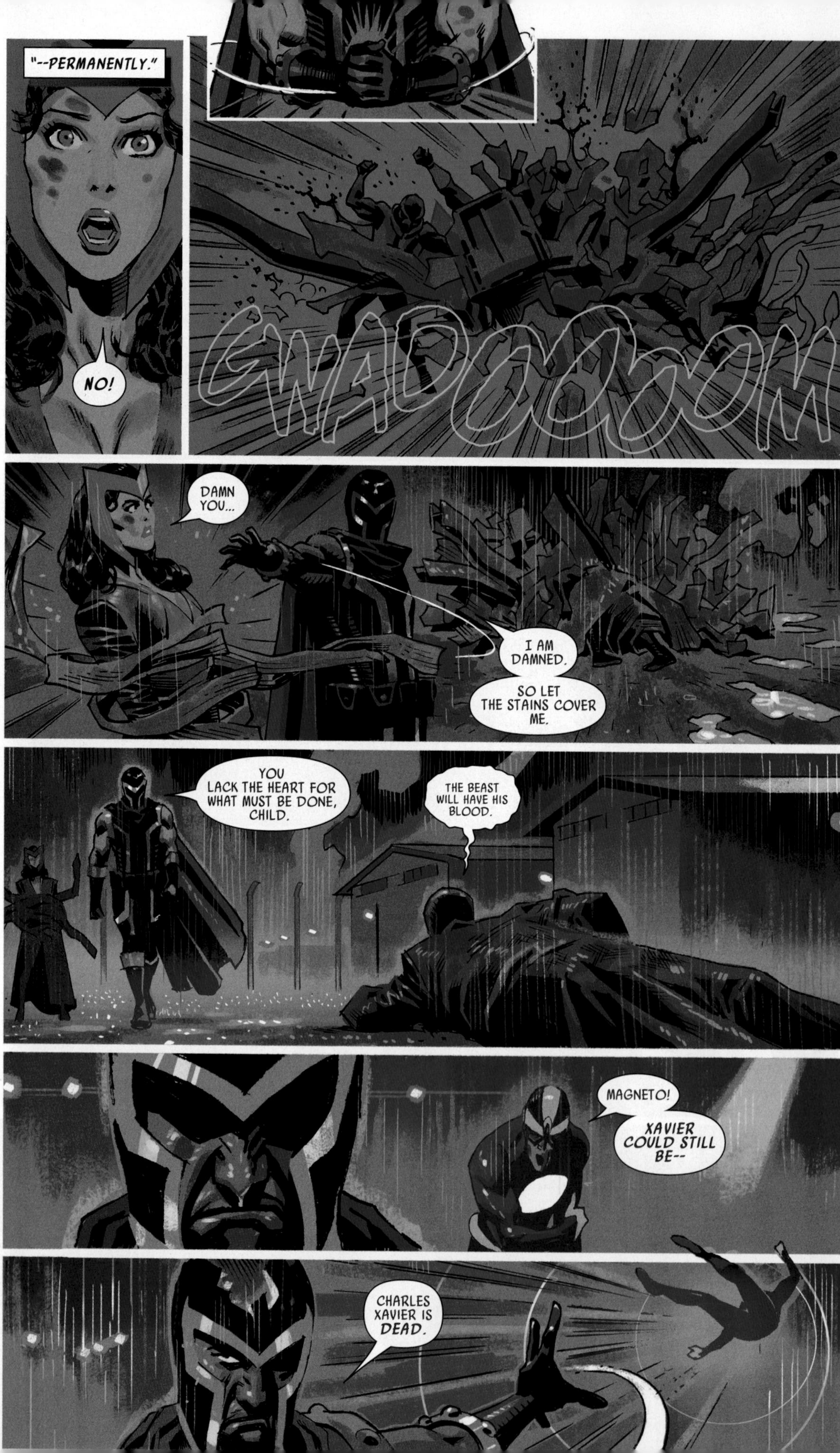
"--PERMANENTLY."
NO!
GWADOOOOOM
DAMN YOU...
I AM DAMNED.
SO LET THE STAINS COVER ME.
YOU LACK THE HEART FOR WHAT MUST BE DONE, CHILD.
THE BEAST WILL HAVE HIS BLOOD.
MAGNETO!
XAVIER COULD STILL BE--
CHARLES XAVIER IS DEAD.

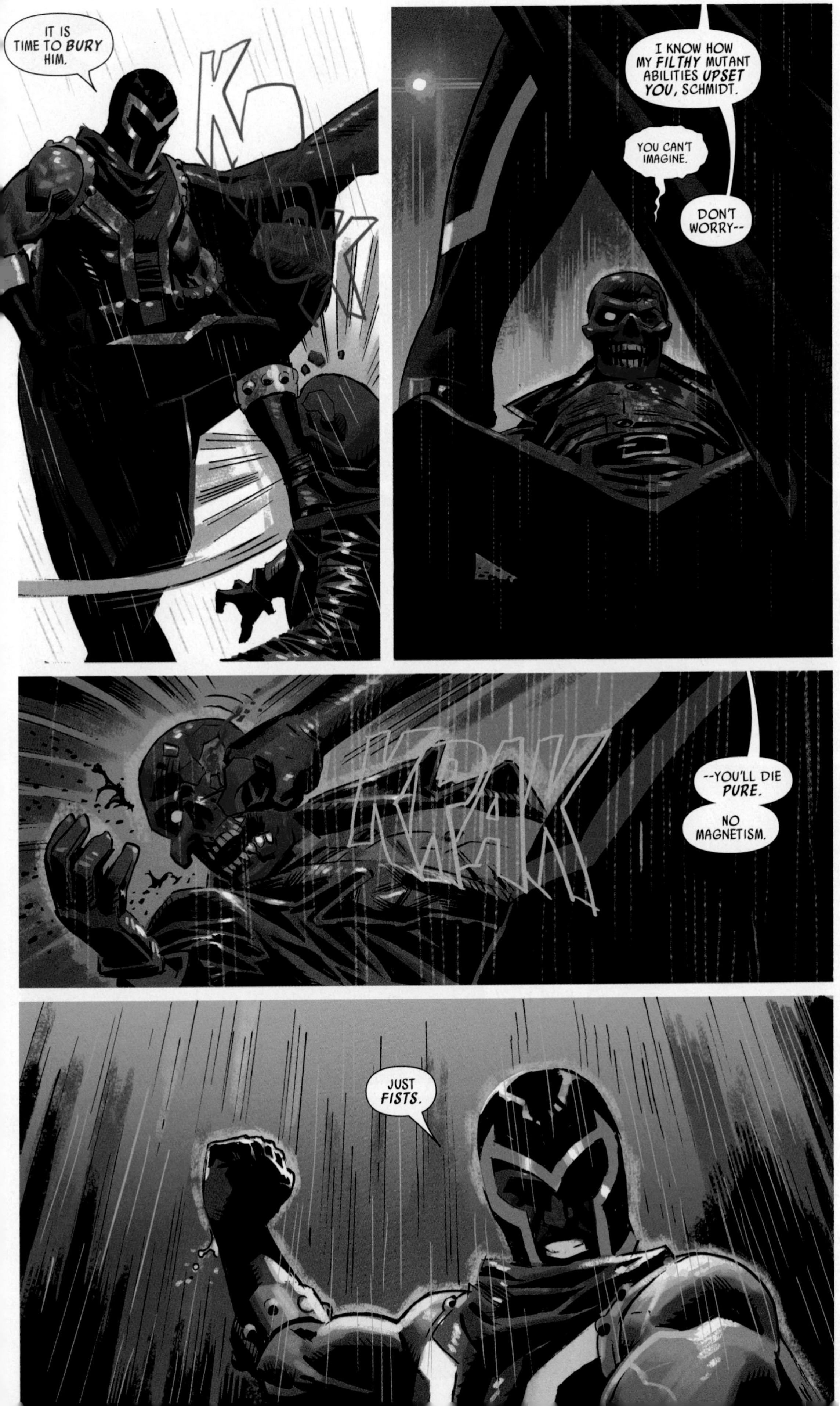
IT IS TIME TO BURY HIM.
KRAK
I KNOW HOW MY FILTHY MUTANT ABILITIES UPSET YOU, SCHMIDT.
YOU CAN'T IMAGINE.
DON'T WORRY--
KRAK
--YOU'LL DIE PURE.
NO MAGNETISM.
JUST FISTS.

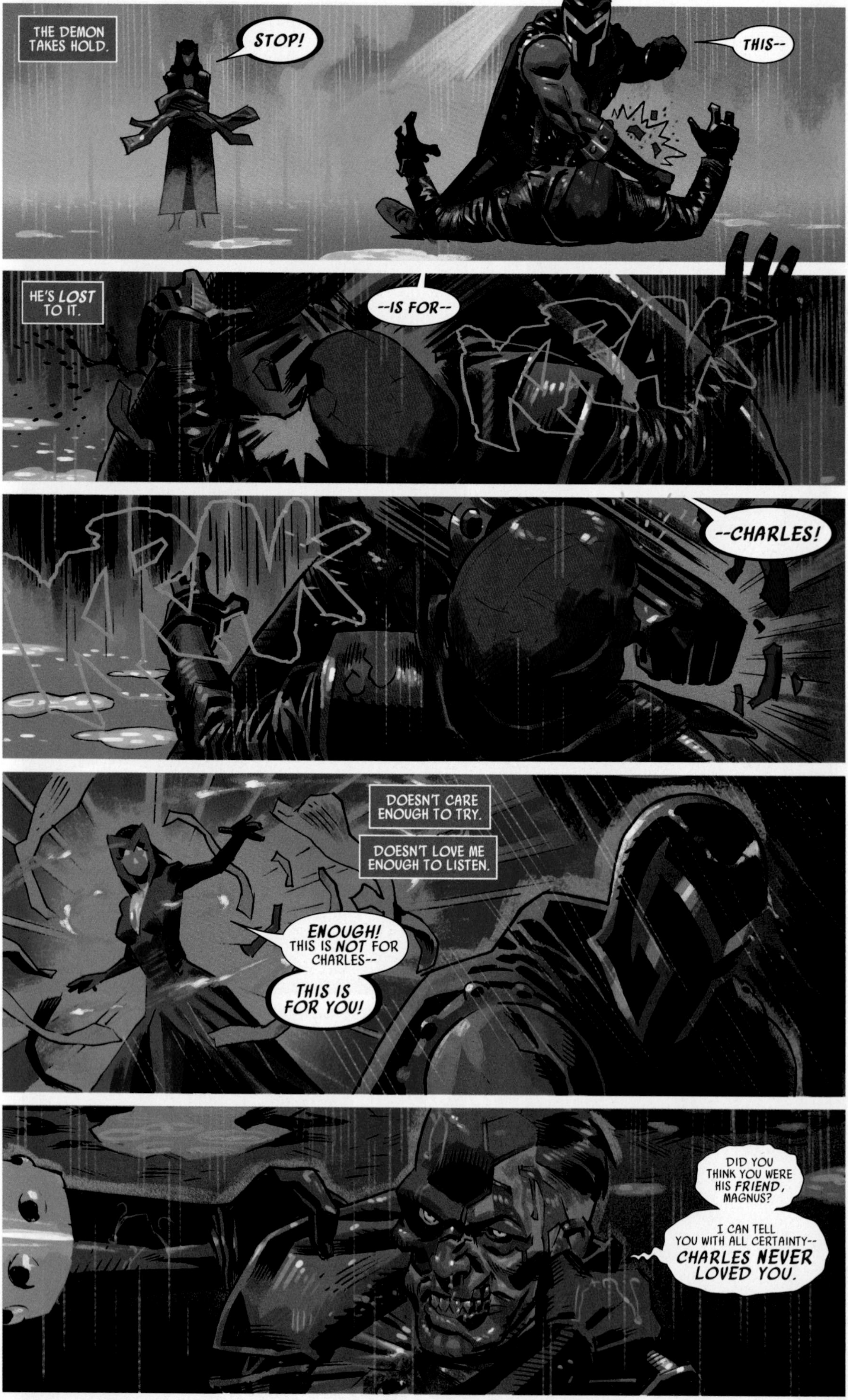
THE DEMON TAKES HOLD.
STOP!
THIS--
HE'S LOST TO IT.
--IS FOR--
--CHARLES!
DOESN'T CARE ENOUGH TO TRY.
DOESN'T LOVE ME ENOUGH TO LISTEN.
ENOUGH! THIS IS NOT FOR CHARLES--
THIS IS FOR YOU!
DID YOU THINK YOU WERE HIS FRIEND, MAGNUS?
I CAN TELL YOU WITH ALL CERTAINTY-- CHARLES NEVER LOVED YOU.

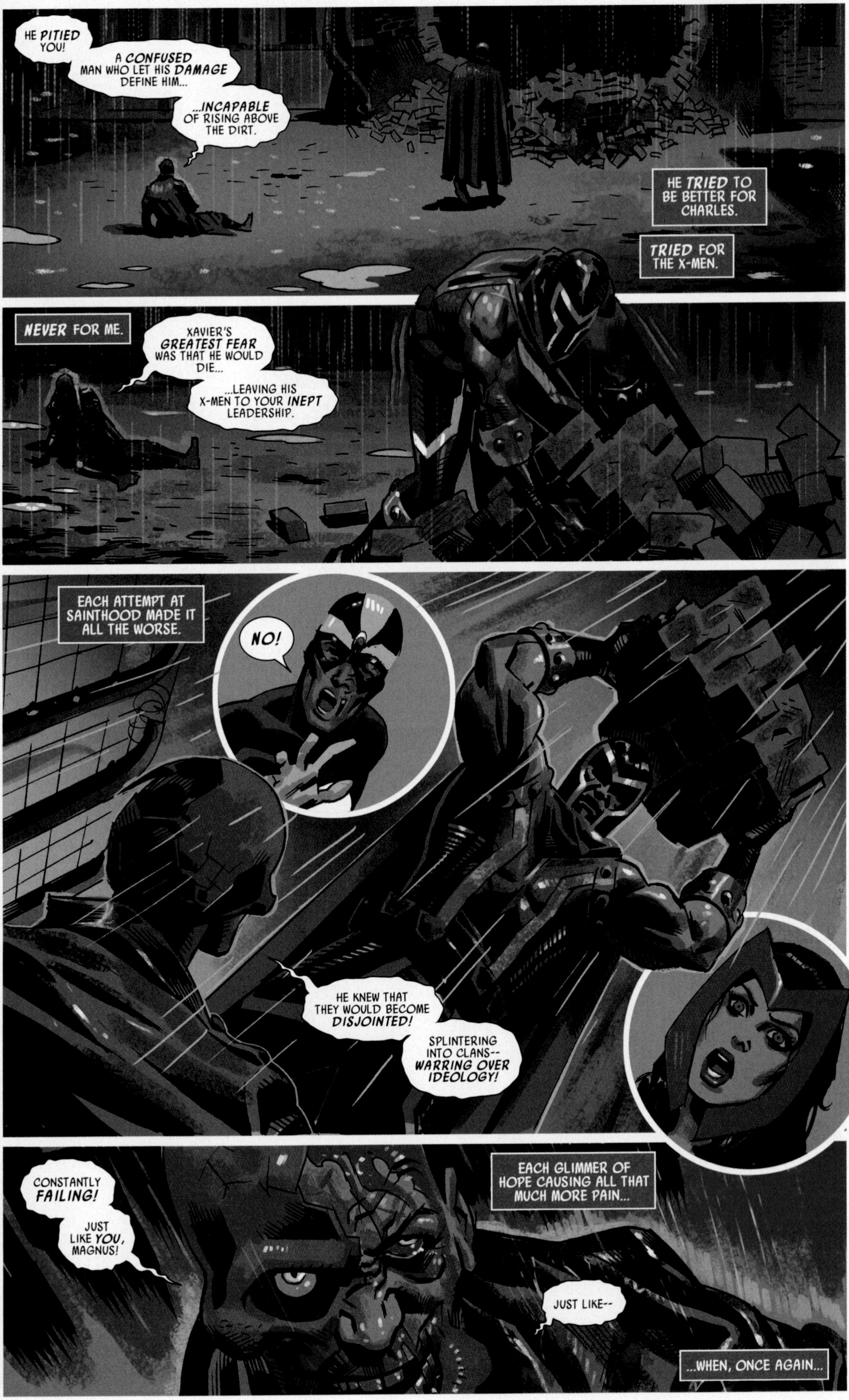
HE PITIED YOU!
A CONFUSED MAN WHO LET HIS DAMAGE DEFINE HIM...
...INCAPABLE OF RISING ABOVE THE DIRT.
HE TRIED TO BE BETTER FOR CHARLES.
TRIED FOR THE X-MEN.
NEVER FOR ME.
XAVIER'S GREATEST FEAR WAS THAT HE WOULD DIE...
...LEAVING HIS X-MEN TO YOUR INEPT LEADERSHIP.
EACH ATTEMPT AT SAINTHOOD MADE IT ALL THE WORSE.
NO!
HE KNEW THAT THEY WOULD BECOME DISJOINTED!
SPLINTERING INTO CLANS-- WARRING OVER IDEOLOGY!
CONSTANTLY FAILING!
JUST LIKE YOU, MAGNUS!
EACH GLIMMER OF HOPE CAUSING ALL THAT MUCH MORE PAIN...
JUST LIKE--
...WHEN, ONCE AGAIN...

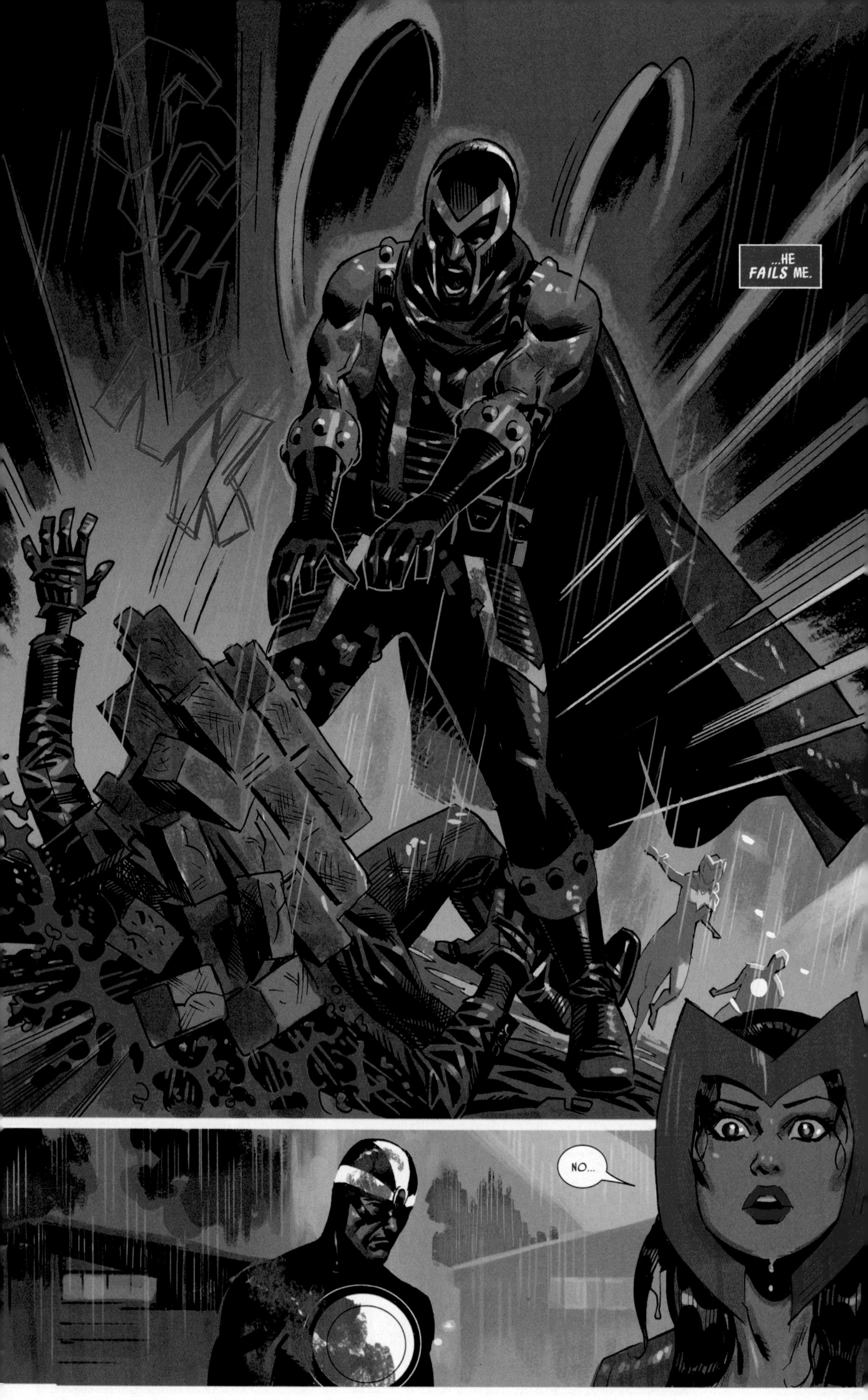
...HE FAILS ME.
NO...

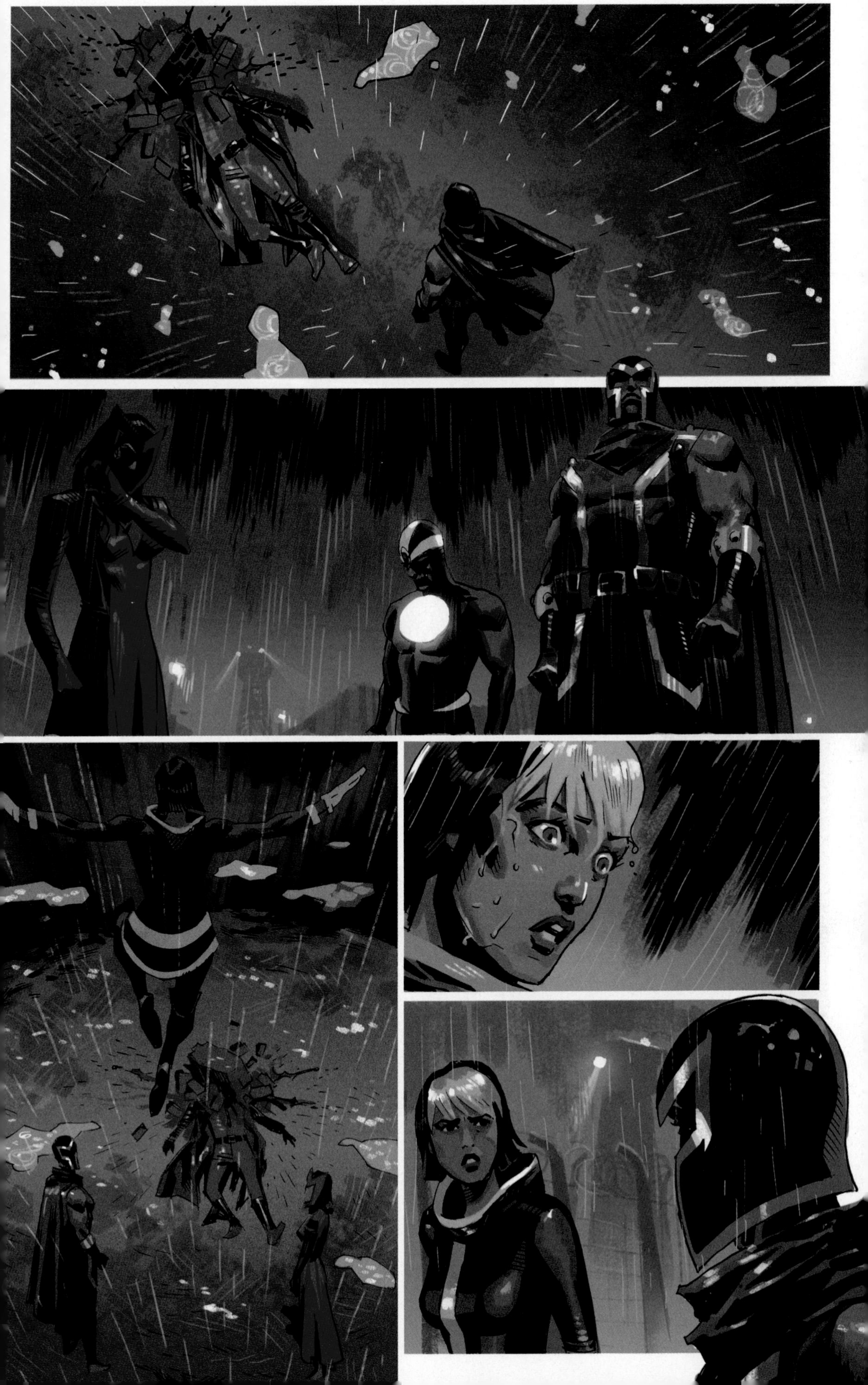

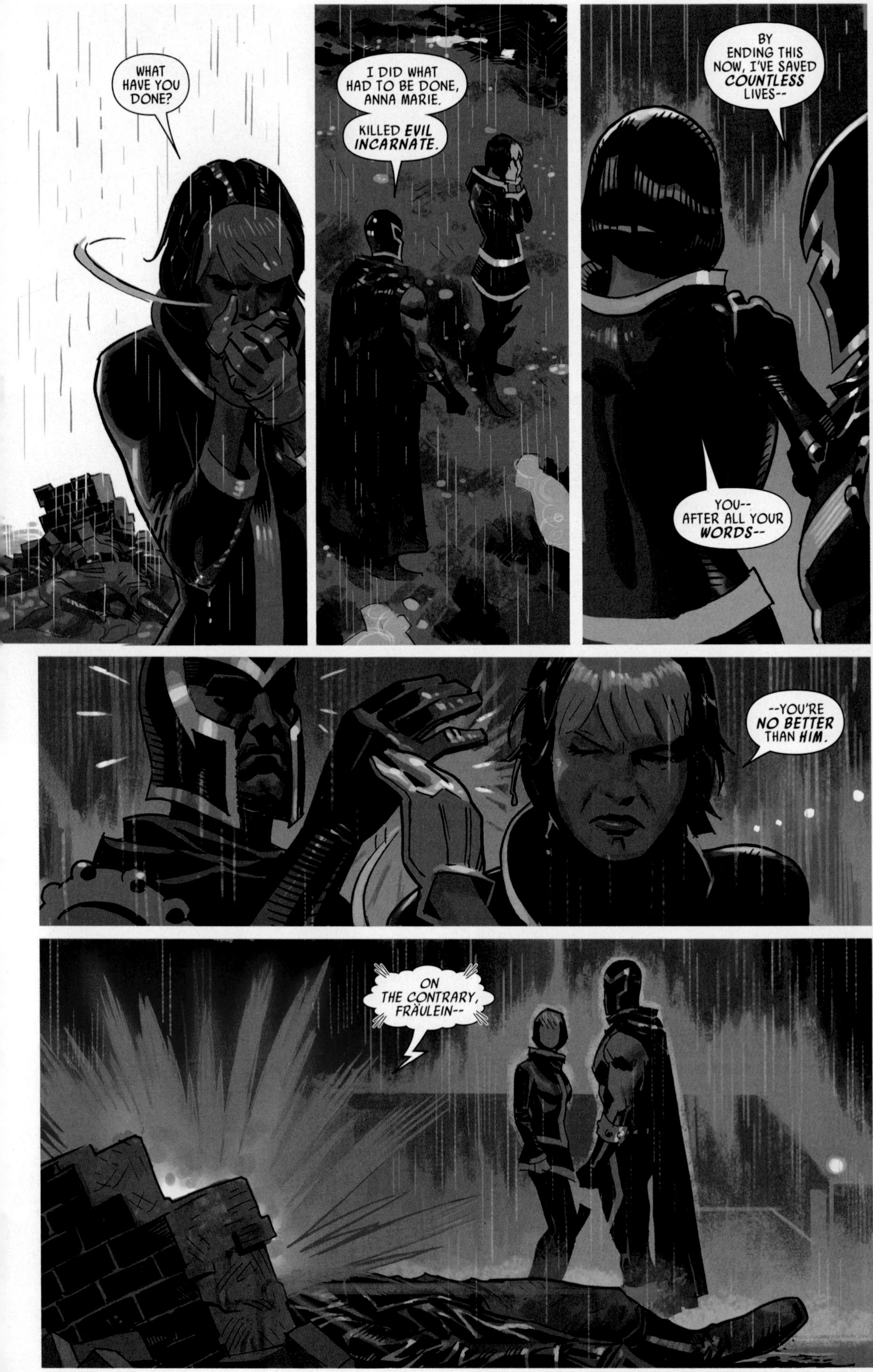
WHAT HAVE YOU DONE?
I DID WHAT HAD TO BE DONE, ANNA MARIE.
KILLED EVIL INCARNATE.
BY ENDING THIS NOW, I'VE SAVED COUNTLESS LIVES--
YOU-- AFTER ALL YOUR WORDS--
--YOU'RE NO BETTER THAN HIM.
ON THE CONTRARY, FRÄULEIN--

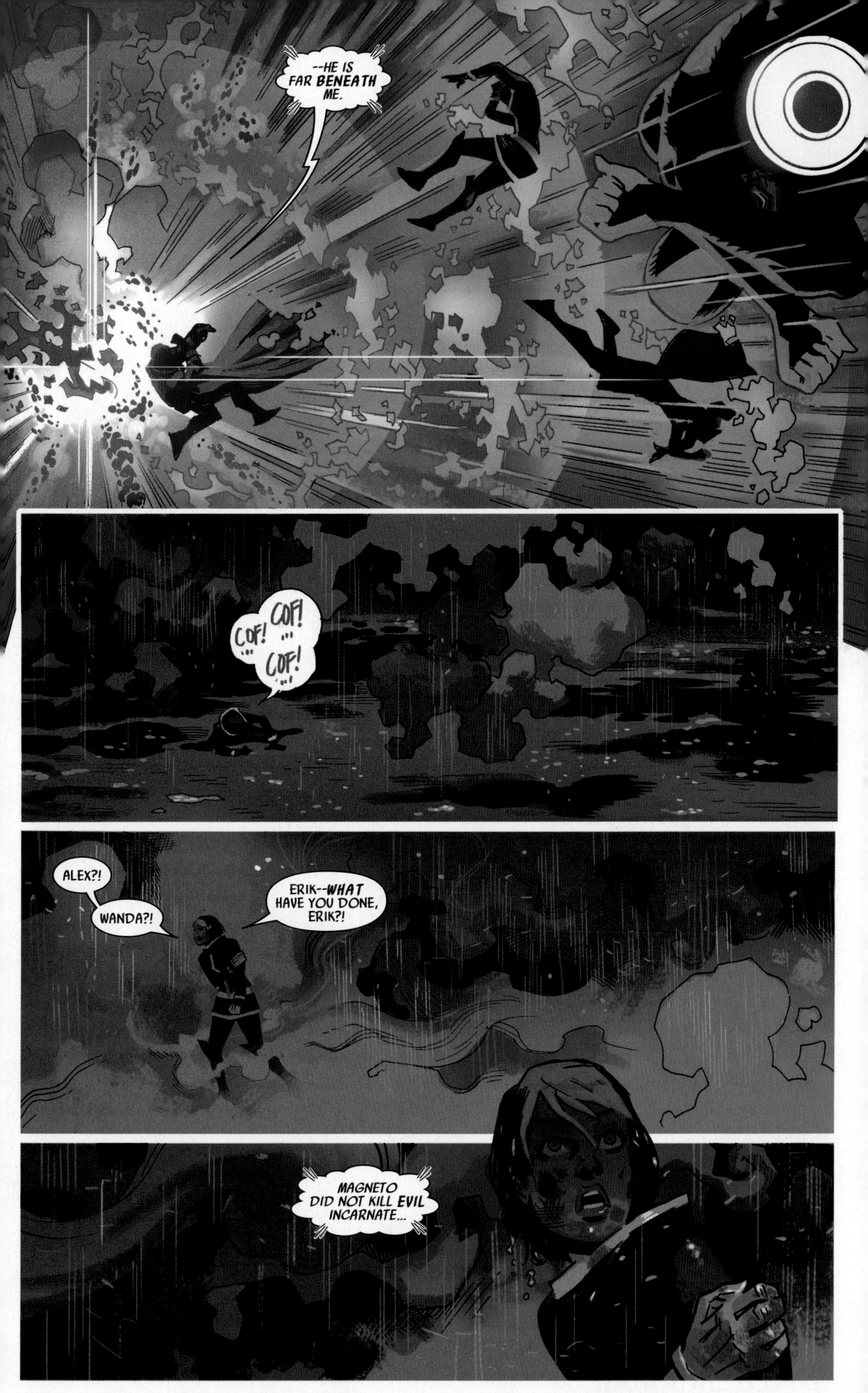
--HE IS FAR BENEATH ME.
COF! ... COF! ... COF! ...
ALEX?!
WANDA?!
ERIK--WHAT HAVE YOU DONE, ERIK?!
MAGNETO DID NOT KILL EVIL INCARNATE...

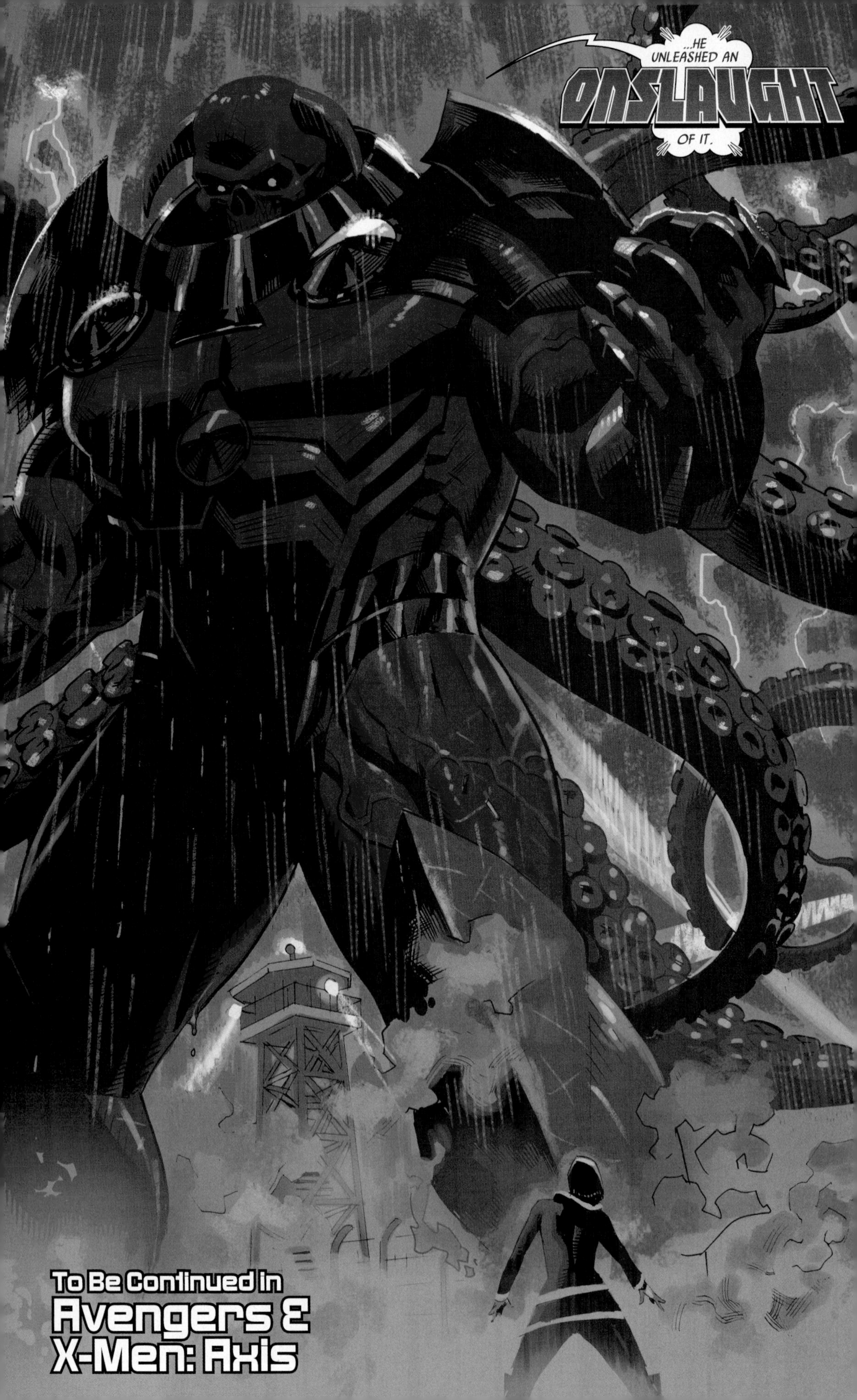
...HE UNLEASHED AN ONSLAUGHT OF IT.
To Be Continued in Avengers & X-Men: Axis

UNCANNY AVENGERS ANNUAL #1

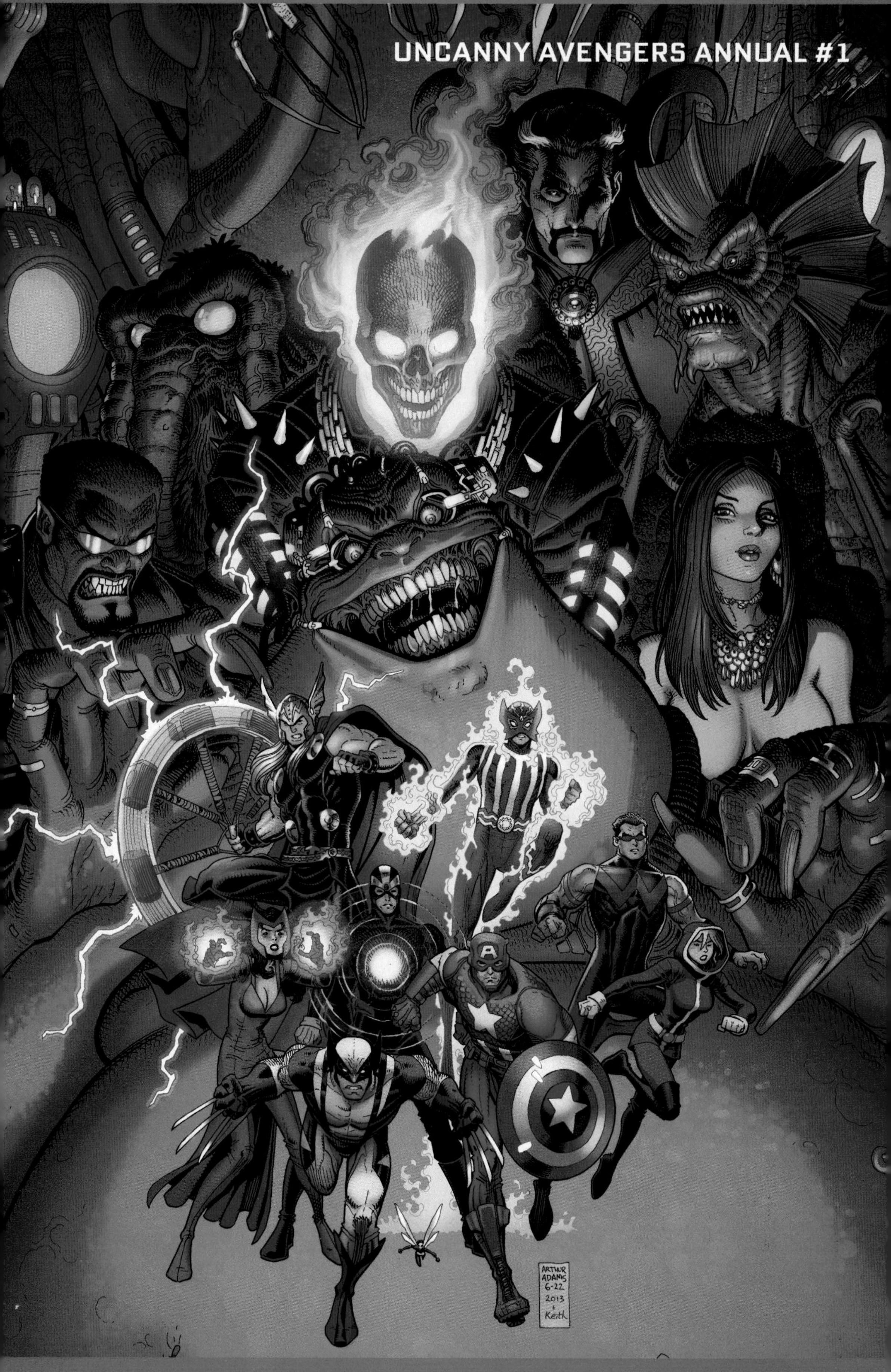
ARTHUR ADAMS 6-22 2013 + Keith

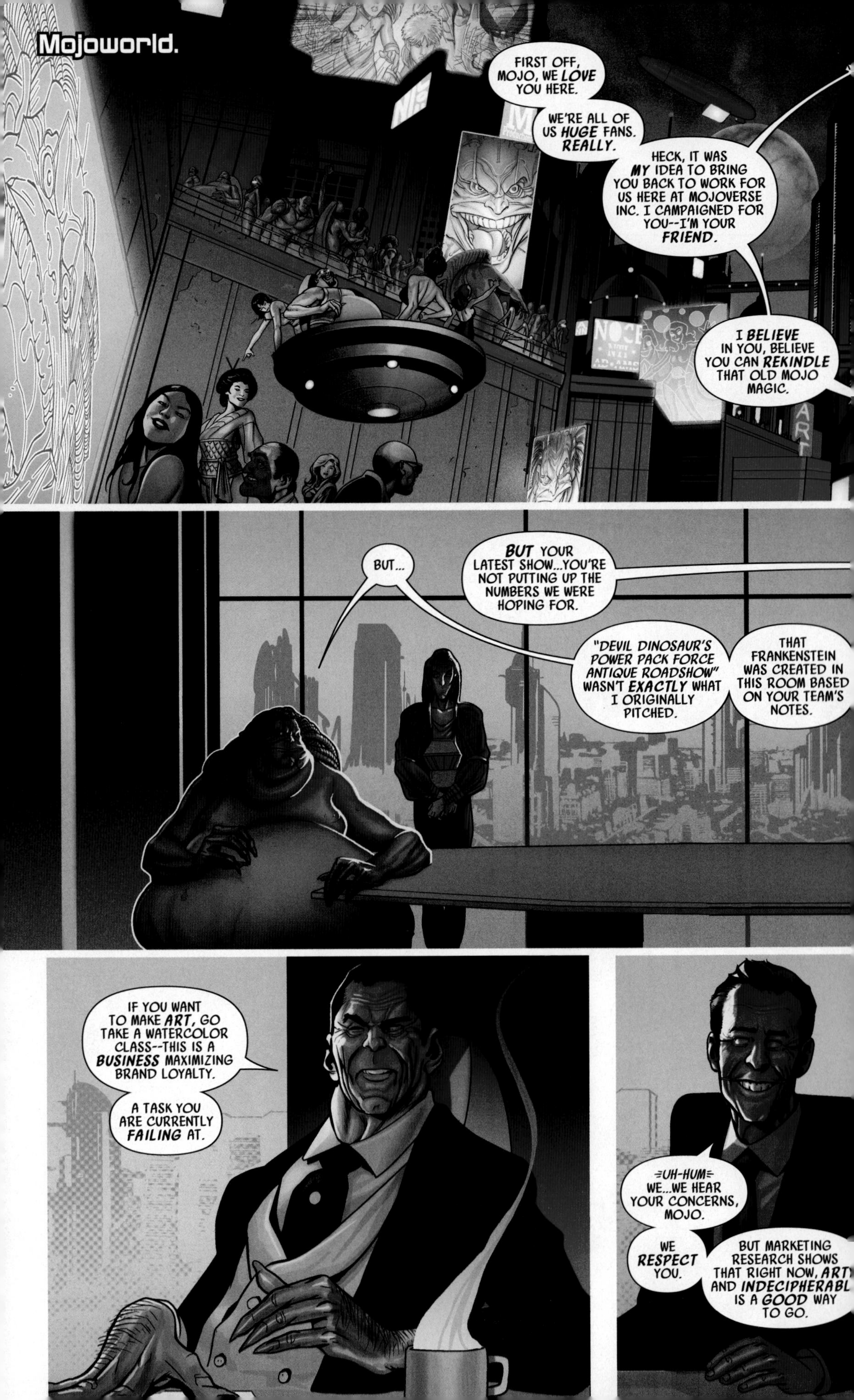
Mojoworld.
FIRST OFF, MOJO, WE LOVE YOU HERE.
WE'RE ALL OF US HUGE FANS. REALLY.
HECK, IT WAS MY IDEA TO BRING YOU BACK TO WORK FOR US HERE AT MOJOVERSE INC. I CAMPAIGNED FOR YOU--I'M YOUR FRIEND.
I BELIEVE IN YOU, BELIEVE YOU CAN REKINDLE THAT OLD MOJO MAGIC.
ART
BUT...
BUT YOUR LATEST SHOW...YOU'RE NOT PUTTING UP THE NUMBERS WE WERE HOPING FOR.
"DEVIL DINOSAUR'S POWER PACK FORCE ANTIQUE ROADSHOW" WASN'T EXACTLY WHAT I ORIGINALLY PITCHED.
THAT FRANKENSTEIN WAS CREATED IN THIS ROOM BASED ON YOUR TEAM'S NOTES.
IF YOU WANT TO MAKE ART, GO TAKE A WATERCOLOR CLASS--THIS IS A BUSINESS MAXIMIZING BRAND LOYALTY.
A TASK YOU ARE CURRENTLY FAILING AT.
=UH-HUM= WE...WE HEAR YOUR CONCERNS, MOJO.
WE RESPECT YOU.
BUT MARKETING RESEARCH SHOWS THAT RIGHT NOW, ARTY AND INDECIPHERABL IS A GOOD WAY TO GO.

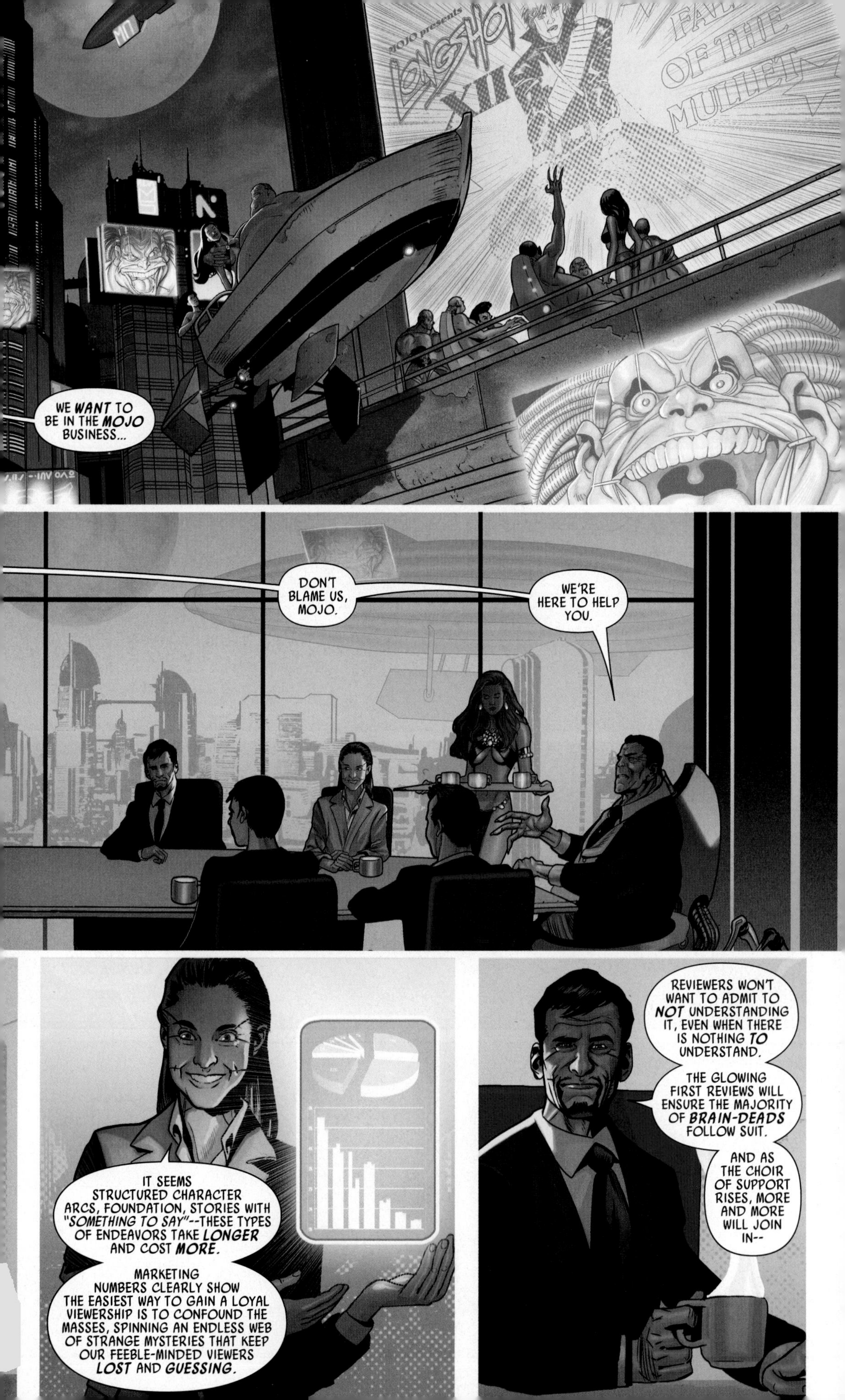
MOJO presents
LONGSHOT XII
OF THE MULLET
WE WANT TO BE IN THE MOJO BUSINESS...
DON'T BLAME US, MOJO.
WE'RE HERE TO HELP YOU.
IT SEEMS STRUCTURED CHARACTER ARCS, FOUNDATION, STORIES WITH "SOMETHING TO SAY"--THESE TYPES OF ENDEAVORS TAKE LONGER AND COST MORE.
MARKETING NUMBERS CLEARLY SHOW THE EASIEST WAY TO GAIN A LOYAL VIEWERSHIP IS TO CONFOUND THE MASSES, SPINNING AN ENDLESS WEB OF STRANGE MYSTERIES THAT KEEP OUR FEEBLE-MINDED VIEWERS LOST AND GUESSING.
REVIEWERS WON'T WANT TO ADMIT TO NOT UNDERSTANDING IT, EVEN WHEN THERE IS NOTHING TO UNDERSTAND.
THE GLOWING FIRST REVIEWS WILL ENSURE THE MAJORITY OF BRAIN-DEADS FOLLOW SUIT.
AND AS THE CHOIR OF SUPPORT RISES, MORE AND MORE WILL JOIN IN--

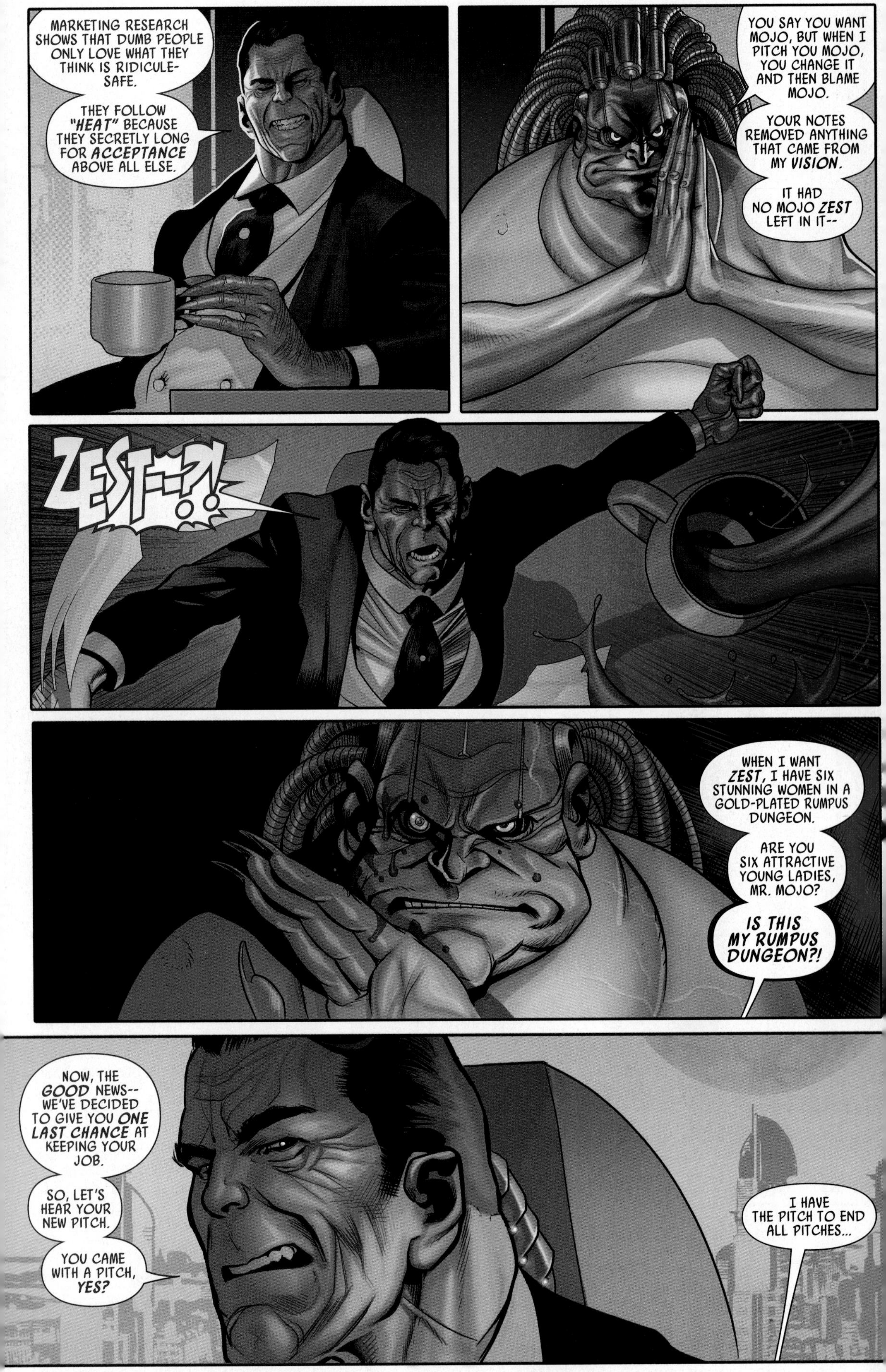
MARKETING RESEARCH SHOWS THAT DUMB PEOPLE ONLY LOVE WHAT THEY THINK IS RIDICULE-SAFE.
THEY FOLLOW "HEAT" BECAUSE THEY SECRETLY LONG FOR ACCEPTANCE ABOVE ALL ELSE.
YOU SAY YOU WANT MOJO, BUT WHEN I PITCH YOU MOJO, YOU CHANGE IT AND THEN BLAME MOJO.
YOUR NOTES REMOVED ANYTHING THAT CAME FROM MY VISION.
IT HAD NO MOJO ZEST LEFT IN IT--
ZEST--?!
WHEN I WANT ZEST, I HAVE SIX STUNNING WOMEN IN A GOLD-PLATED RUMPUS DUNGEON.
ARE YOU SIX ATTRACTIVE YOUNG LADIES, MR. MOJO?
IS THIS MY RUMPUS DUNGEON?!
NOW, THE GOOD NEWS-- WE'VE DECIDED TO GIVE YOU ONE LAST CHANCE AT KEEPING YOUR JOB.
SO, LET'S HEAR YOUR NEW PITCH.
YOU CAME WITH A PITCH, YES?
I HAVE THE PITCH TO END ALL PITCHES...

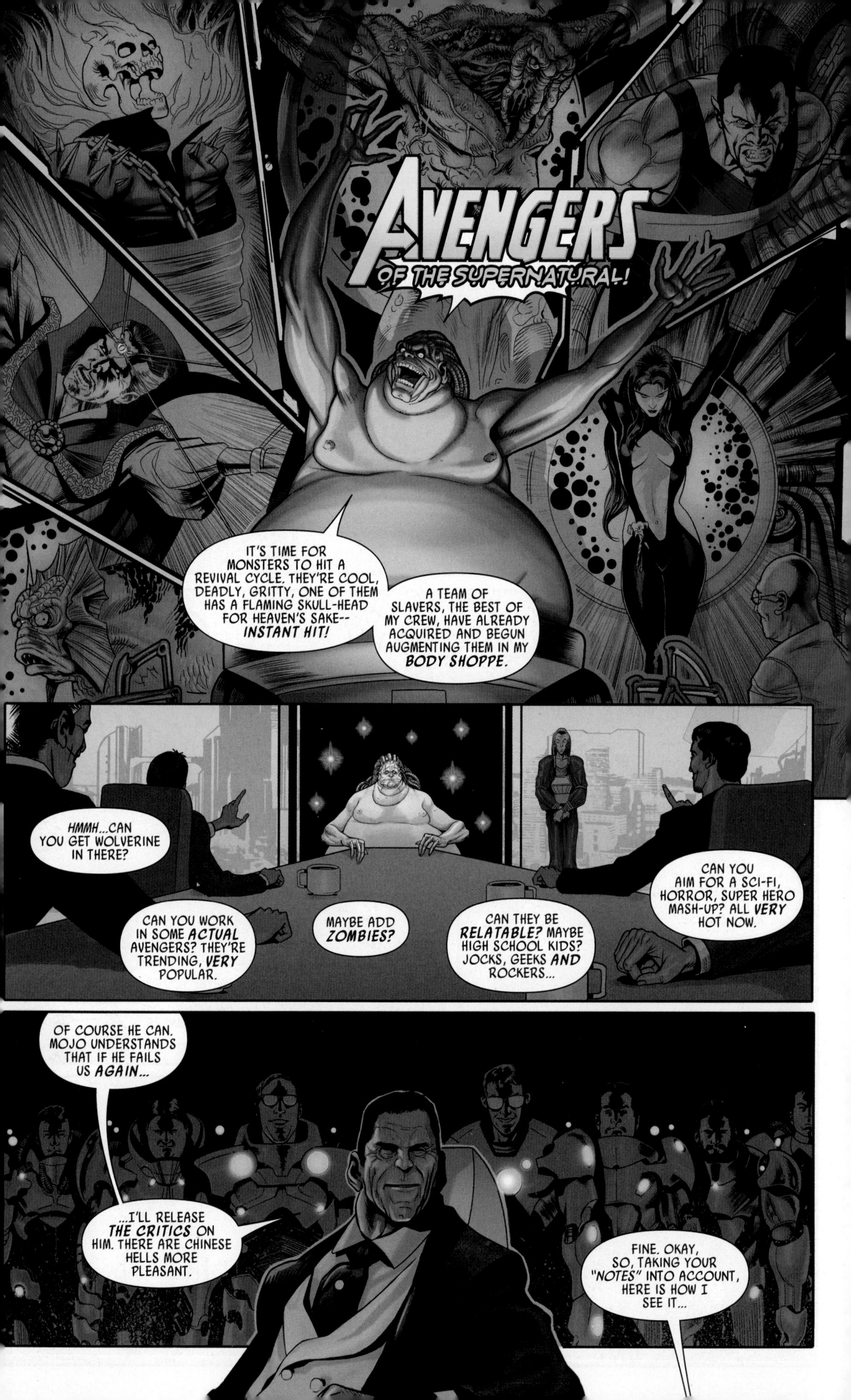
AVENGERS OF THE SUPERNATURAL!
IT'S TIME FOR MONSTERS TO HIT A REVIVAL CYCLE. THEY'RE COOL, DEADLY, GRITTY, ONE OF THEM HAS A FLAMING SKULL-HEAD FOR HEAVEN'S SAKE-- INSTANT HIT!
A TEAM OF SLAVERS, THE BEST OF MY CREW, HAVE ALREADY ACQUIRED AND BEGUN AUGMENTING THEM IN MY BODY SHOPPE.
HMMH...CAN YOU GET WOLVERINE IN THERE?
CAN YOU WORK IN SOME ACTUAL AVENGERS? THEY'RE TRENDING, VERY POPULAR.
MAYBE ADD ZOMBIES?
CAN THEY BE RELATABLE? MAYBE HIGH SCHOOL KIDS? JOCKS, GEEKS AND ROCKERS...
CAN YOU AIM FOR A SCI-FI, HORROR, SUPER HERO MASH-UP? ALL VERY HOT NOW.
OF COURSE HE CAN. MOJO UNDERSTANDS THAT IF HE FAILS US AGAIN...
...I'LL RELEASE THE CRITICS ON HIM. THERE ARE CHINESE HELLS MORE PLEASANT.
FINE. OKAY, SO, TAKING YOUR "NOTES" INTO ACCOUNT, HERE IS HOW I SEE IT...

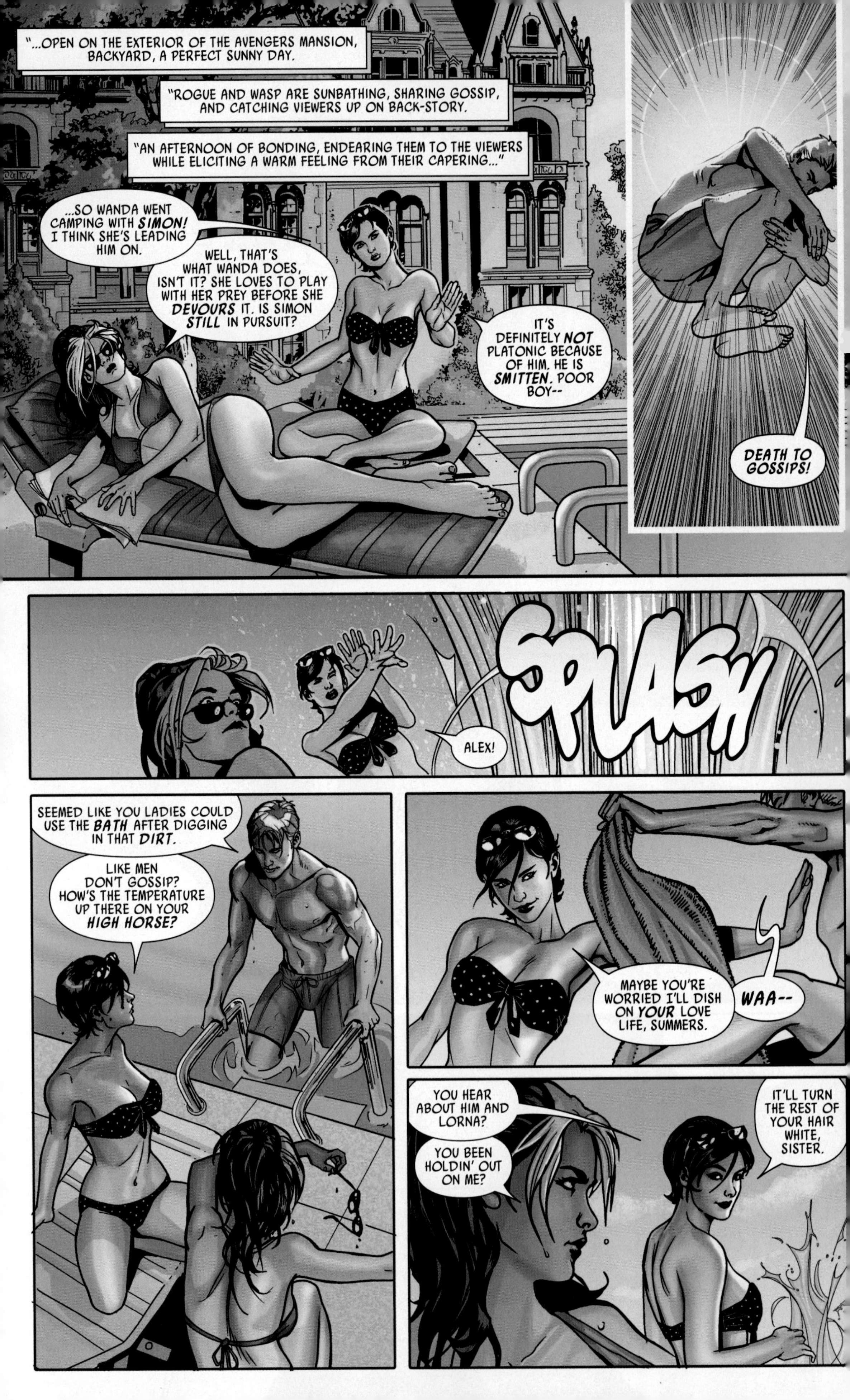
"...OPEN ON THE EXTERIOR OF THE AVENGERS MANSION, BACKYARD, A PERFECT SUNNY DAY.
"ROGUE AND WASP ARE SUNBATHING, SHARING GOSSIP, AND CATCHING VIEWERS UP ON BACK-STORY.
"AN AFTERNOON OF BONDING, ENDEARING THEM TO THE VIEWERS WHILE ELICITING A WARM FEELING FROM THEIR CAPERING..."
...SO WANDA WENT CAMPING WITH SIMON! I THINK SHE'S LEADING HIM ON.
WELL, THAT'S WHAT WANDA DOES, ISN'T IT? SHE LOVES TO PLAY WITH HER PREY BEFORE SHE DEVOURS IT. IS SIMON STILL IN PURSUIT?
IT'S DEFINITELY NOT PLATONIC BECAUSE OF HIM. HE IS SMITTEN. POOR BOY--
DEATH TO GOSSIPS!
SPLASH
ALEX!
SEEMED LIKE YOU LADIES COULD USE THE BATH AFTER DIGGING IN THAT DIRT.
LIKE MEN DON'T GOSSIP? HOW'S THE TEMPERATURE UP THERE ON YOUR HIGH HORSE?
MAYBE YOU'RE WORRIED I'LL DISH ON YOUR LOVE LIFE, SUMMERS.
WAA--
YOU HEAR ABOUT HIM AND LORNA?
YOU BEEN HOLDIN' OUT ON ME?
IT'LL TURN THE REST OF YOUR HAIR WHITE, SISTER.

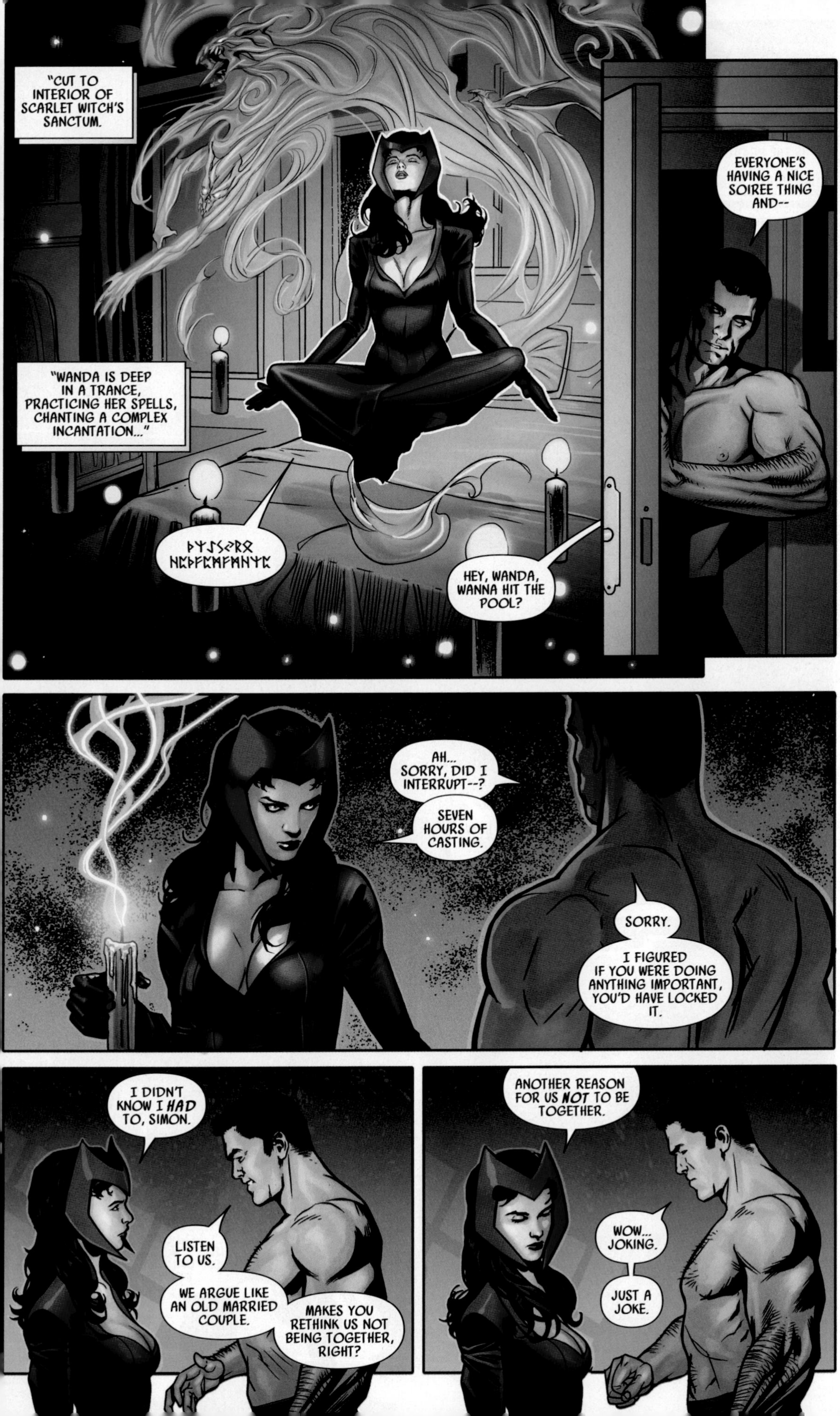
"CUT TO INTERIOR OF SCARLET WITCH'S SANCTUM.
"WANDA IS DEEP IN A TRANCE, PRACTICING HER SPELLS, CHANTING A COMPLEX INCANTATION..."
EVERYONE'S HAVING A NICE SOIREE THING AND--
HEY, WANDA, WANNA HIT THE POOL?
AH... SORRY, DID I INTERRUPT--?
SEVEN HOURS OF CASTING.
SORRY.
I FIGURED IF YOU WERE DOING ANYTHING IMPORTANT, YOU'D HAVE LOCKED IT.
I DIDN'T KNOW I *HAD* TO, SIMON.
LISTEN TO US.
WE ARGUE LIKE AN OLD MARRIED COUPLE.
MAKES YOU RETHINK US NOT BEING TOGETHER, RIGHT?
ANOTHER REASON FOR US *NOT* TO BE TOGETHER.
WOW... JOKING.
JUST A JOKE.

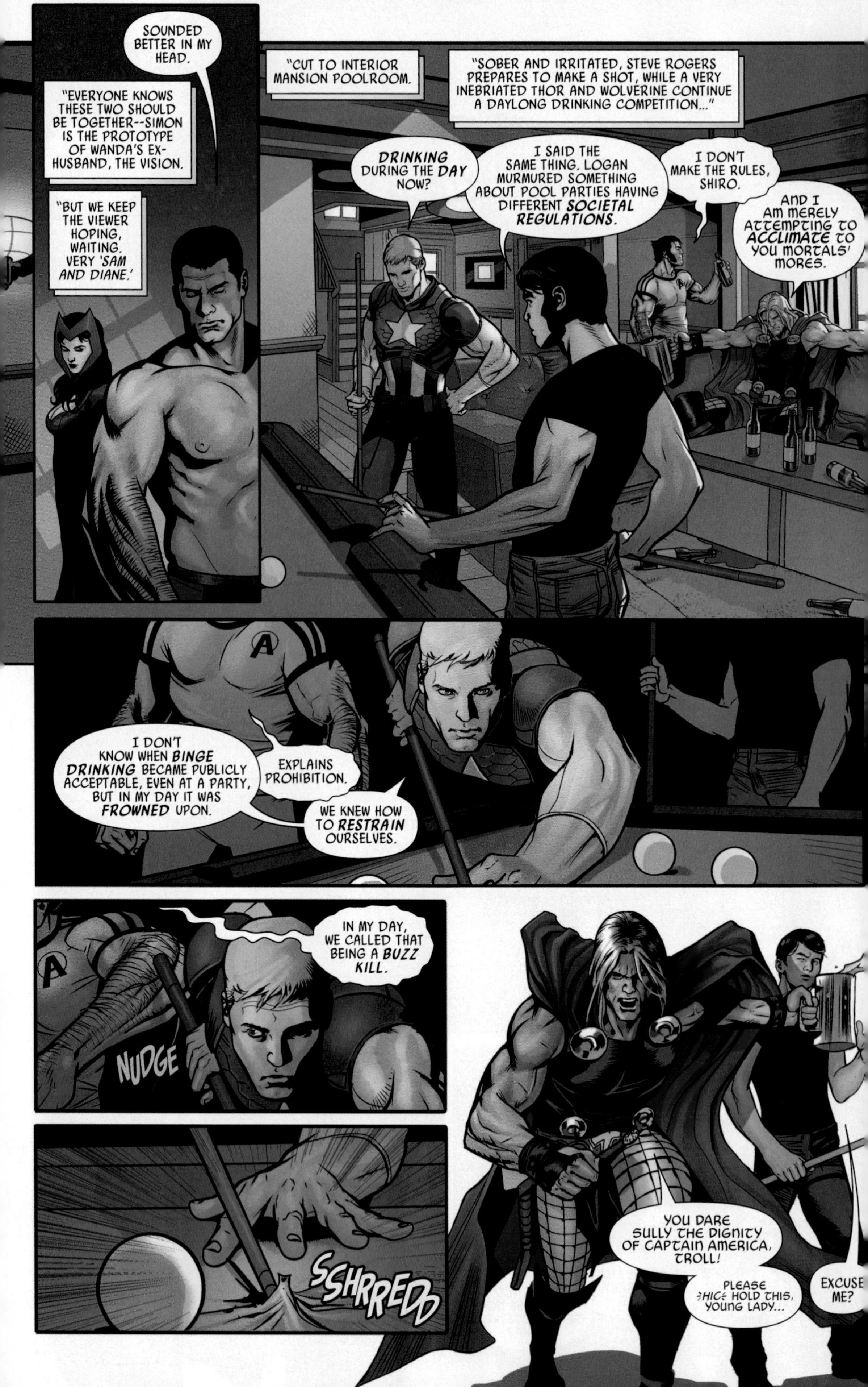
SOUNDED BETTER IN MY HEAD.
"EVERYONE KNOWS THESE TWO SHOULD BE TOGETHER--SIMON IS THE PROTOTYPE OF WANDA'S EX-HUSBAND, THE VISION.
"BUT WE KEEP THE VIEWER HOPING, WAITING. VERY 'SAM AND DIANE.'
"CUT TO INTERIOR MANSION POOLROOM.
"SOBER AND IRRITATED, STEVE ROGERS PREPARES TO MAKE A SHOT, WHILE A VERY INEBRIATED THOR AND WOLVERINE CONTINUE A DAYLONG DRINKING COMPETITION..."
DRINKING DURING THE DAY NOW?
I SAID THE SAME THING. LOGAN MURMURED SOMETHING ABOUT POOL PARTIES HAVING DIFFERENT SOCIETAL REGULATIONS.
I DON'T MAKE THE RULES, SHIRO.
AND I AM MERELY ATTEMPTING TO ACCLIMATE TO YOU MORTALS' MORES.
I DON'T KNOW WHEN BINGE DRINKING BECAME PUBLICLY ACCEPTABLE, EVEN AT A PARTY, BUT IN MY DAY IT WAS FROWNED UPON.
EXPLAINS PROHIBITION.
WE KNEW HOW TO RESTRAIN OURSELVES.
IN MY DAY, WE CALLED THAT BEING A BUZZ KILL.
NUDGE
SSHRREDD
YOU DARE SULLY THE DIGNITY OF CAPTAIN AMERICA, TROLL!
PLEASE =HIC= HOLD THIS, YOUNG LADY...
EXCUSE ME?

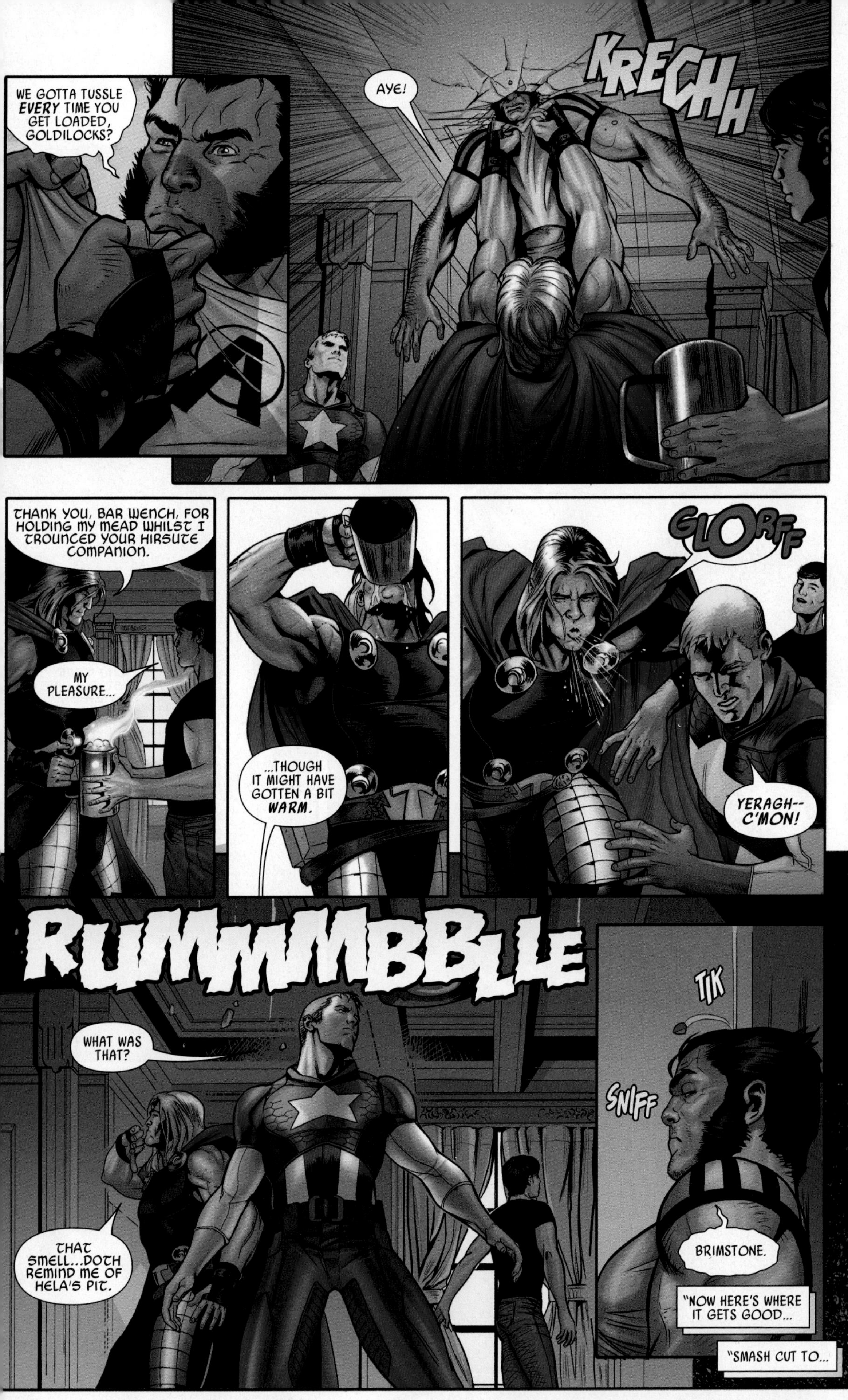
WE GOTTA TUSSLE EVERY TIME YOU GET LOADED, GOLDILOCKS?
AYE!
KRECHH
THANK YOU, BAR WENCH, FOR HOLDING MY MEAD WHILST I TROUNCED YOUR HIRSUTE COMPANION.
MY PLEASURE...
...THOUGH IT MIGHT HAVE GOTTEN A BIT WARM.
GLORFF
YERAGH--C'MON!
RUMMMBBLLE
WHAT WAS THAT?
THAT SMELL...DOTH REMIND ME OF HELA'S PIT.
TIK
SNIFF
BRIMSTONE.
"NOW HERE'S WHERE IT GETS GOOD...
"SMASH CUT TO...

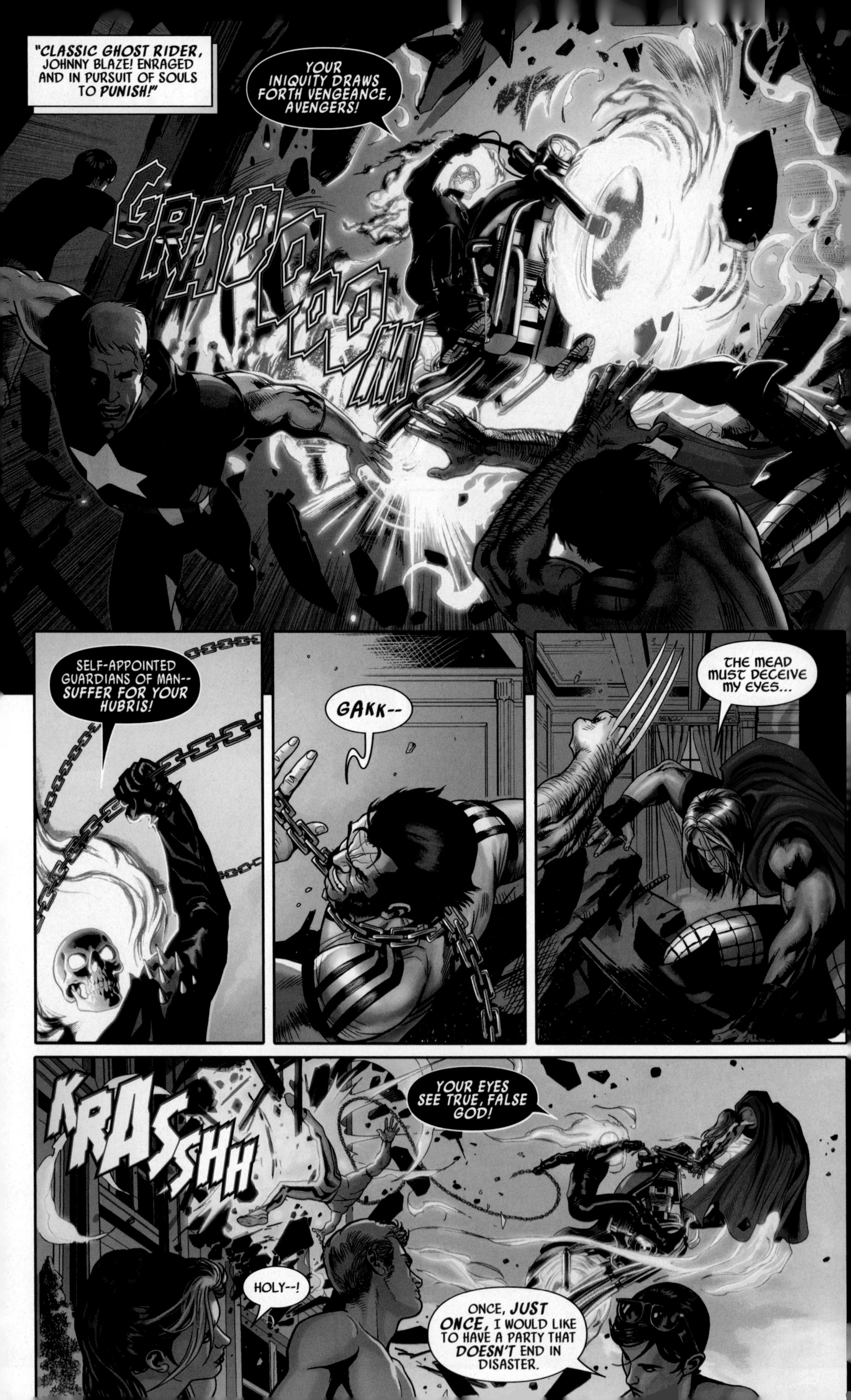
"CLASSIC GHOST RIDER, JOHNNY BLAZE! ENRAGED AND IN PURSUIT OF SOULS TO PUNISH!"
YOUR INIQUITY DRAWS FORTH VENGEANCE, AVENGERS!
GRADOOOOM
SELF-APPOINTED GUARDIANS OF MAN-- SUFFER FOR YOUR HUBRIS!
GAKK--
THE MEAD MUST DECEIVE MY EYES...
KRASSHH
YOUR EYES SEE TRUE, FALSE GOD!
HOLY--!
ONCE, JUST ONCE, I WOULD LIKE TO HAVE A PARTY THAT DOESN'T END IN DISASTER.

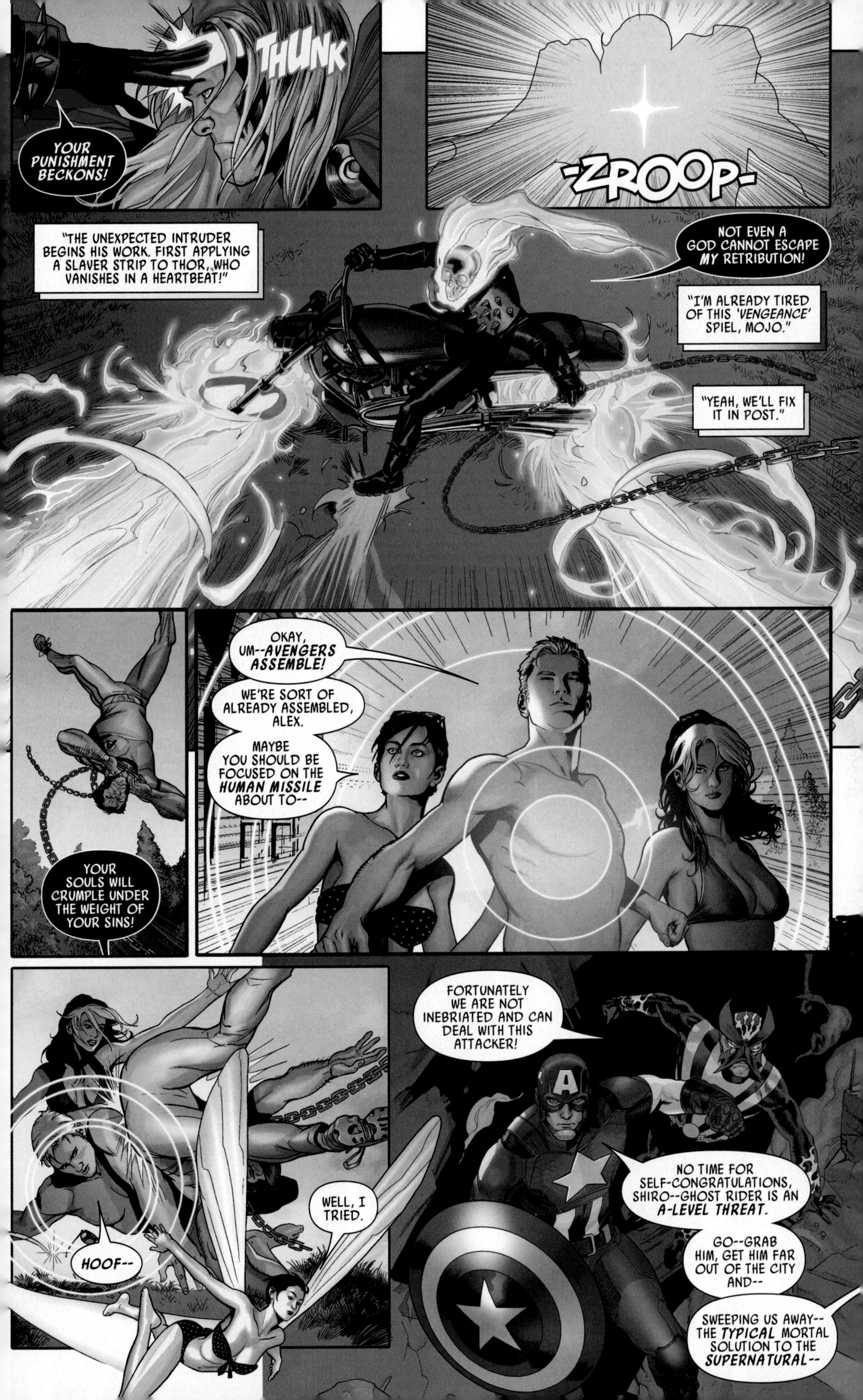
THUNK
YOUR PUNISHMENT BECKONS!
-ZROOP-
"THE UNEXPECTED INTRUDER BEGINS HIS WORK, FIRST APPLYING A SLAVER STRIP TO THOR, WHO VANISHES IN A HEARTBEAT!"
NOT EVEN A GOD CANNOT ESCAPE MY RETRIBUTION!
"I'M ALREADY TIRED OF THIS 'VENGEANCE' SPIEL, MOJO."
"YEAH, WE'LL FIX IT IN POST."
YOUR SOULS WILL CRUMPLE UNDER THE WEIGHT OF YOUR SINS!
OKAY, UM--AVENGERS ASSEMBLE!
WE'RE SORT OF ALREADY ASSEMBLED, ALEX.
MAYBE YOU SHOULD BE FOCUSED ON THE HUMAN MISSILE ABOUT TO--
HOOF--
WELL, I TRIED.
FORTUNATELY WE ARE NOT INEBRIATED AND CAN DEAL WITH THIS ATTACKER!
NO TIME FOR SELF-CONGRATULATIONS, SHIRO--GHOST RIDER IS AN A-LEVEL THREAT.
GO--GRAB HIM, GET HIM FAR OUT OF THE CITY AND--
SWEEPING US AWAY--THE TYPICAL MORTAL SOLUTION TO THE SUPERNATURAL--

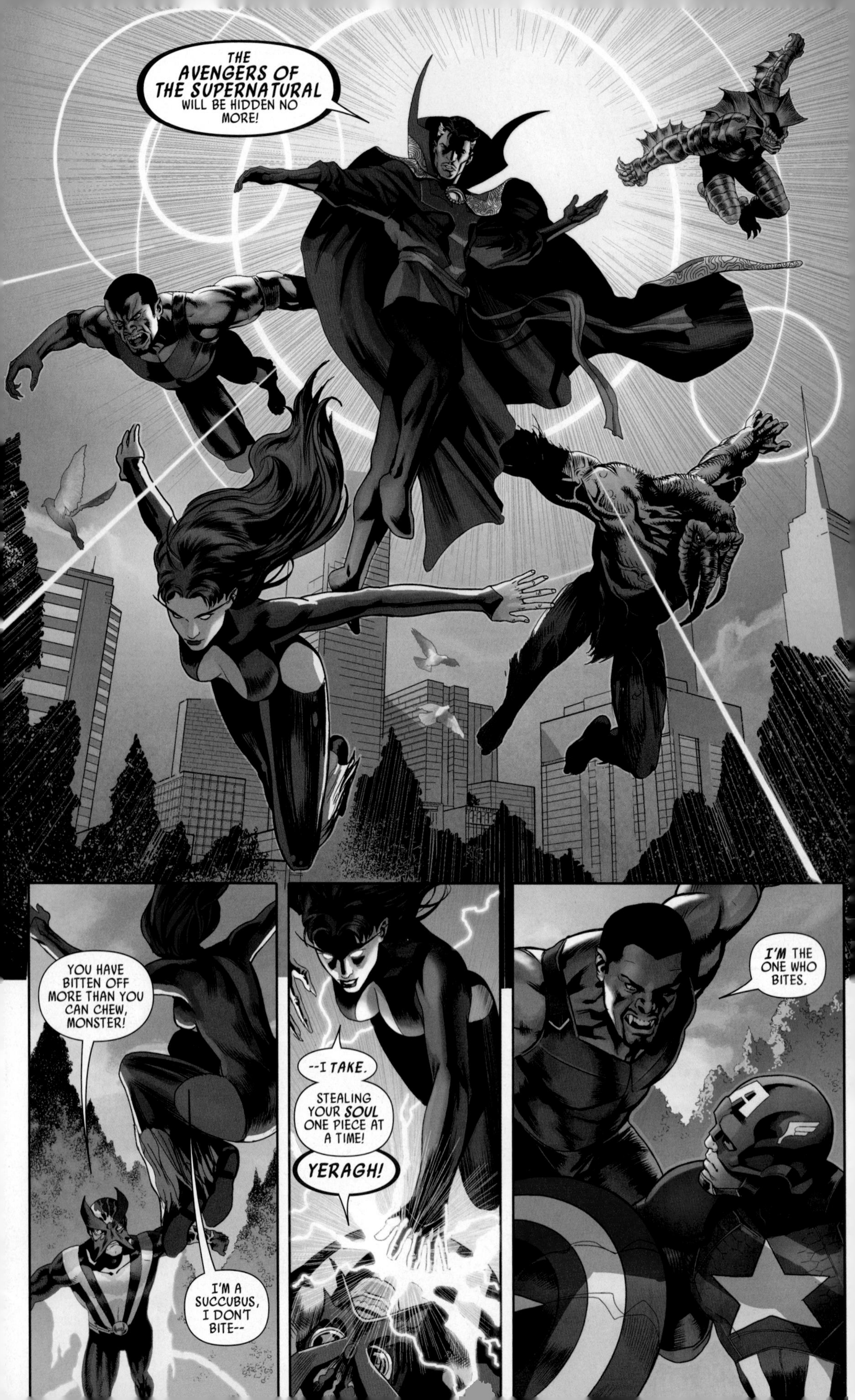
THE AVENGERS OF THE SUPERNATURAL WILL BE HIDDEN NO MORE!
YOU HAVE BITTEN OFF MORE THAN YOU CAN CHEW, MONSTER!
I'M A SUCCUBUS, I DON'T BITE--
--I TAKE.
STEALING YOUR SOUL ONE PIECE AT A TIME!
YERAGH!
I'M THE ONE WHO BITES.

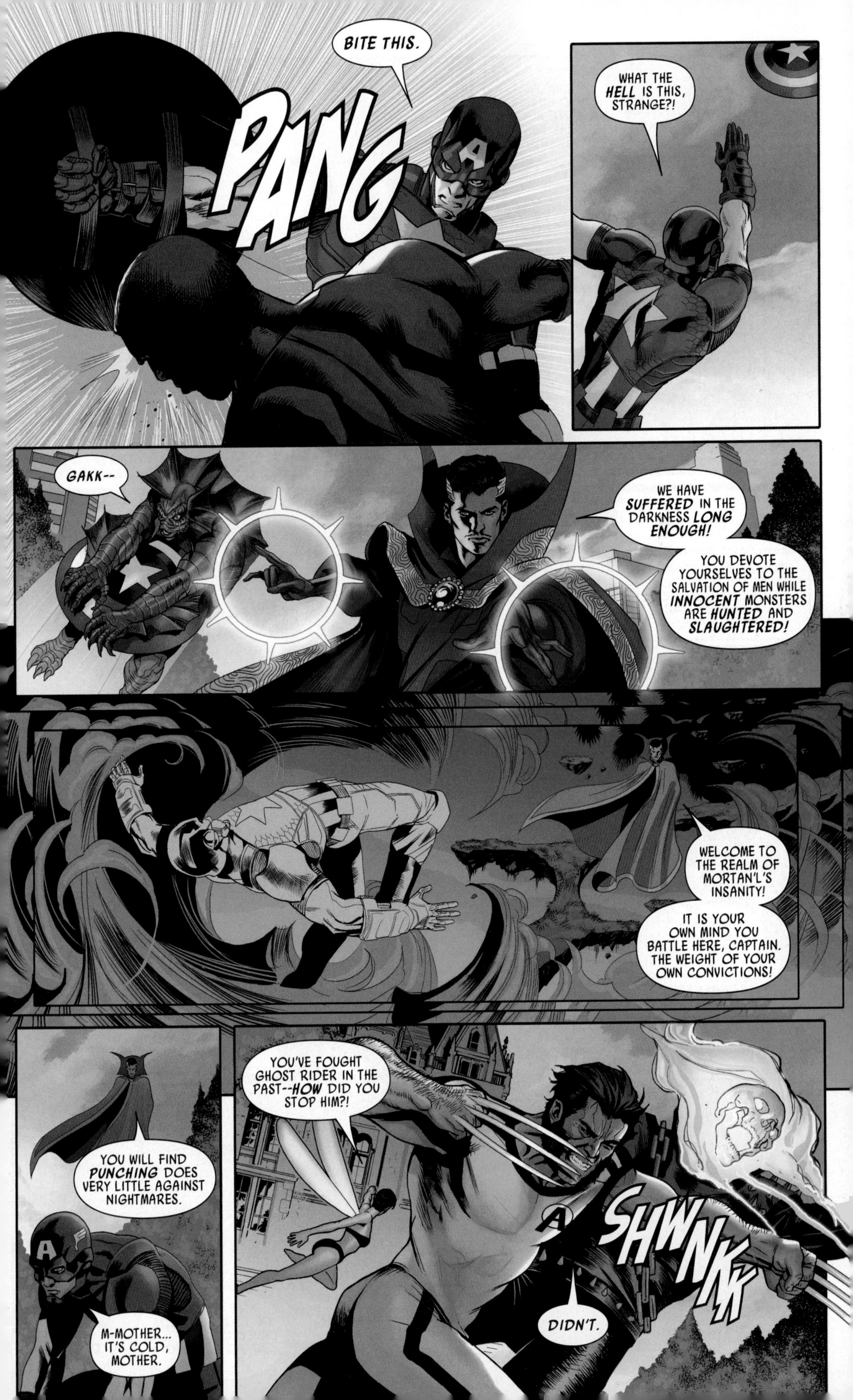
BITE THIS.
PANG
WHAT THE HELL IS THIS, STRANGE?!
GAKK--
WE HAVE SUFFERED IN THE DARKNESS LONG ENOUGH!
YOU DEVOTE YOURSELVES TO THE SALVATION OF MEN WHILE INNOCENT MONSTERS ARE HUNTED AND SLAUGHTERED!
WELCOME TO THE REALM OF MORTAN'L'S INSANITY!
IT IS YOUR OWN MIND YOU BATTLE HERE, CAPTAIN. THE WEIGHT OF YOUR OWN CONVICTIONS!
YOU WILL FIND PUNCHING DOES VERY LITTLE AGAINST NIGHTMARES.
M-MOTHER... IT'S COLD, MOTHER.
YOU'VE FOUGHT GHOST RIDER IN THE PAST--HOW DID YOU STOP HIM?!
SHWNKK
DIDN'T.

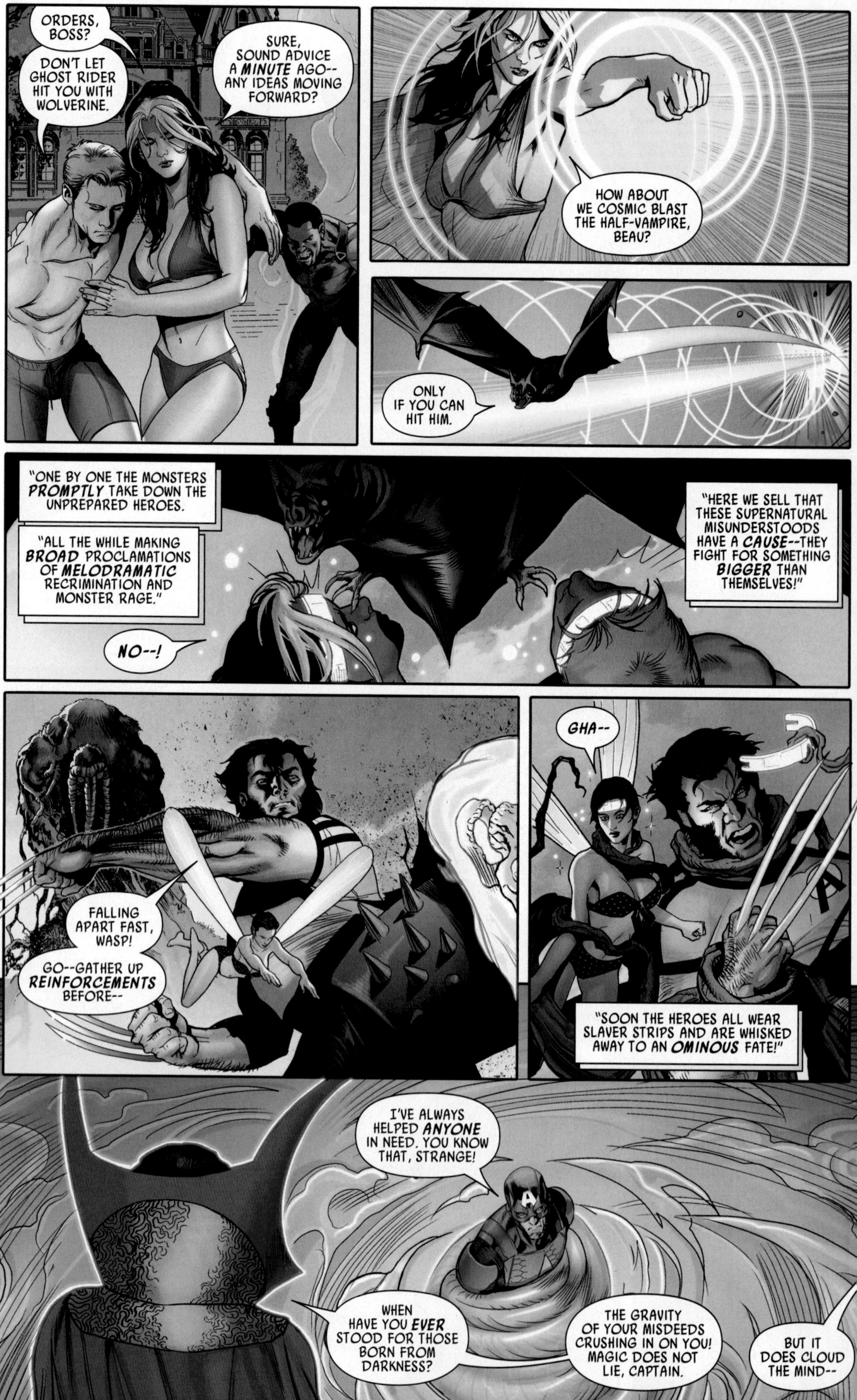
ORDERS, BOSS?
DON'T LET GHOST RIDER HIT YOU WITH WOLVERINE.
SURE, SOUND ADVICE A MINUTE AGO-- ANY IDEAS MOVING FORWARD?
HOW ABOUT WE COSMIC BLAST THE HALF-VAMPIRE, BEAU?
ONLY IF YOU CAN HIT HIM.
"ONE BY ONE THE MONSTERS PROMPTLY TAKE DOWN THE UNPREPARED HEROES.
"ALL THE WHILE MAKING BROAD PROCLAMATIONS OF MELODRAMATIC RECRIMINATION AND MONSTER RAGE."
NO--!
"HERE WE SELL THAT THESE SUPERNATURAL MISUNDERSTOODS HAVE A CAUSE--THEY FIGHT FOR SOMETHING BIGGER THAN THEMSELVES!"
FALLING APART FAST, WASP!
GO--GATHER UP REINFORCEMENTS BEFORE--
GHA--
"SOON THE HEROES ALL WEAR SLAVER STRIPS AND ARE WHISKED AWAY TO AN OMINOUS FATE!"
I'VE ALWAYS HELPED ANYONE IN NEED. YOU KNOW THAT, STRANGE!
WHEN HAVE YOU EVER STOOD FOR THOSE BORN FROM DARKNESS?
THE GRAVITY OF YOUR MISDEEDS CRUSHING IN ON YOU! MAGIC DOES NOT LIE, CAPTAIN.
BUT IT DOES CLOUD THE MIND--

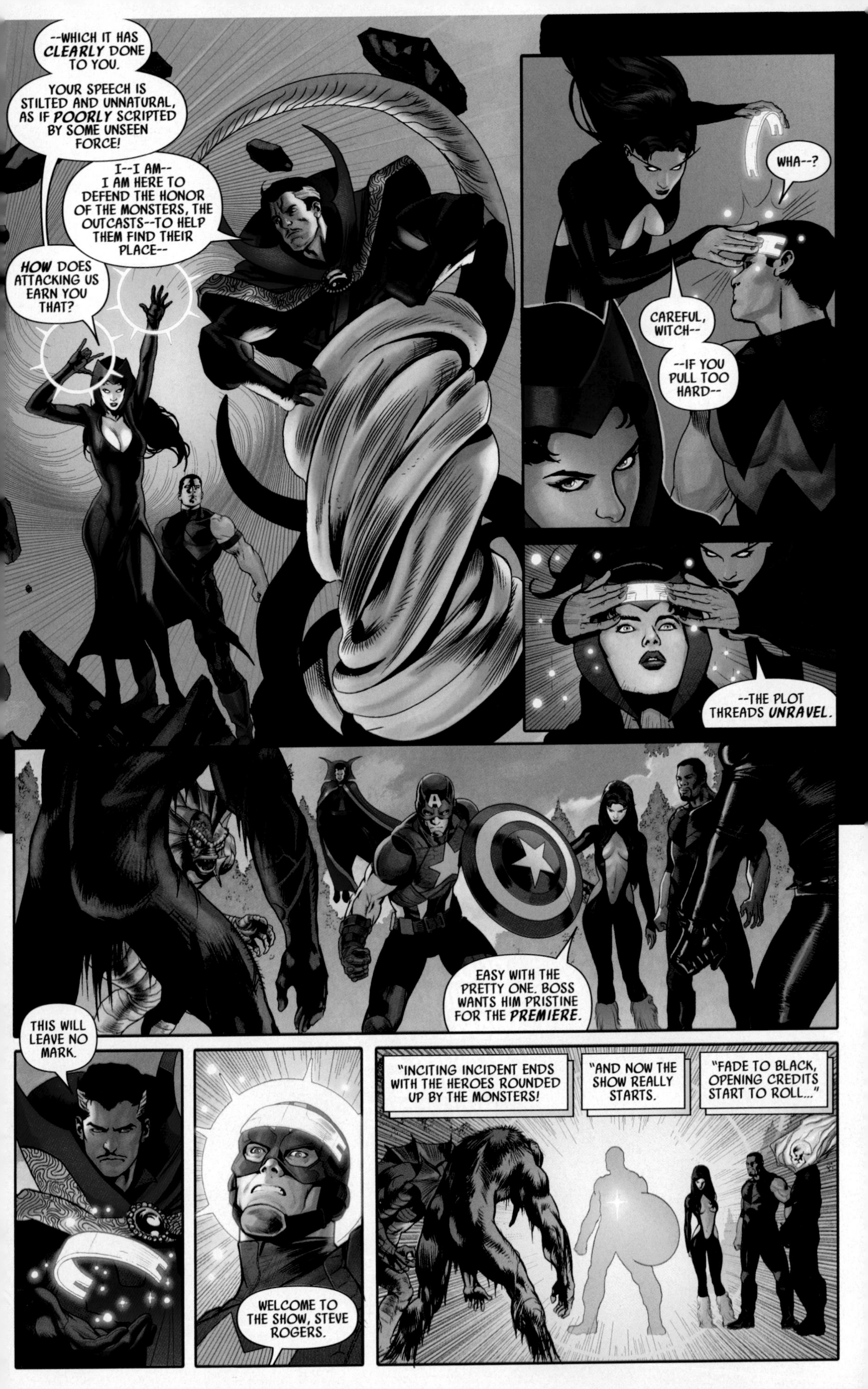
--WHICH IT HAS CLEARLY DONE TO YOU.
YOUR SPEECH IS STILTED AND UNNATURAL, AS IF POORLY SCRIPTED BY SOME UNSEEN FORCE!
I--I AM-- I AM HERE TO DEFEND THE HONOR OF THE MONSTERS, THE OUTCASTS--TO HELP THEM FIND THEIR PLACE--
HOW DOES ATTACKING US EARN YOU THAT?
WHA--?
CAREFUL, WITCH--
--IF YOU PULL TOO HARD--
--THE PLOT THREADS UNRAVEL.
EASY WITH THE PRETTY ONE. BOSS WANTS HIM PRISTINE FOR THE PREMIERE.
THIS WILL LEAVE NO MARK.
WELCOME TO THE SHOW, STEVE ROGERS.
"INCITING INCIDENT ENDS WITH THE HEROES ROUNDED UP BY THE MONSTERS!
"AND NOW THE SHOW REALLY STARTS.
"FADE TO BLACK, OPENING CREDITS START TO ROLL..."

Mojo/PLAN M Productions presents:

MARTIAN TRANSYLVANIA SUPER HERO MUTANT MONSTER HUNTER

HIGH SCHOOL

Starring

CAPTAIN AMERICA
DR. STRANGE
ROGUE
HAVOK
SUNFIRE
MAN-THING
GHOST RIDER
MANPHIBIAN
SCARLET WITCH
WONDER MAN
BLADE
WOLVERINE
WASP
THOR

and featuring
SATANA
as "The Succubus"

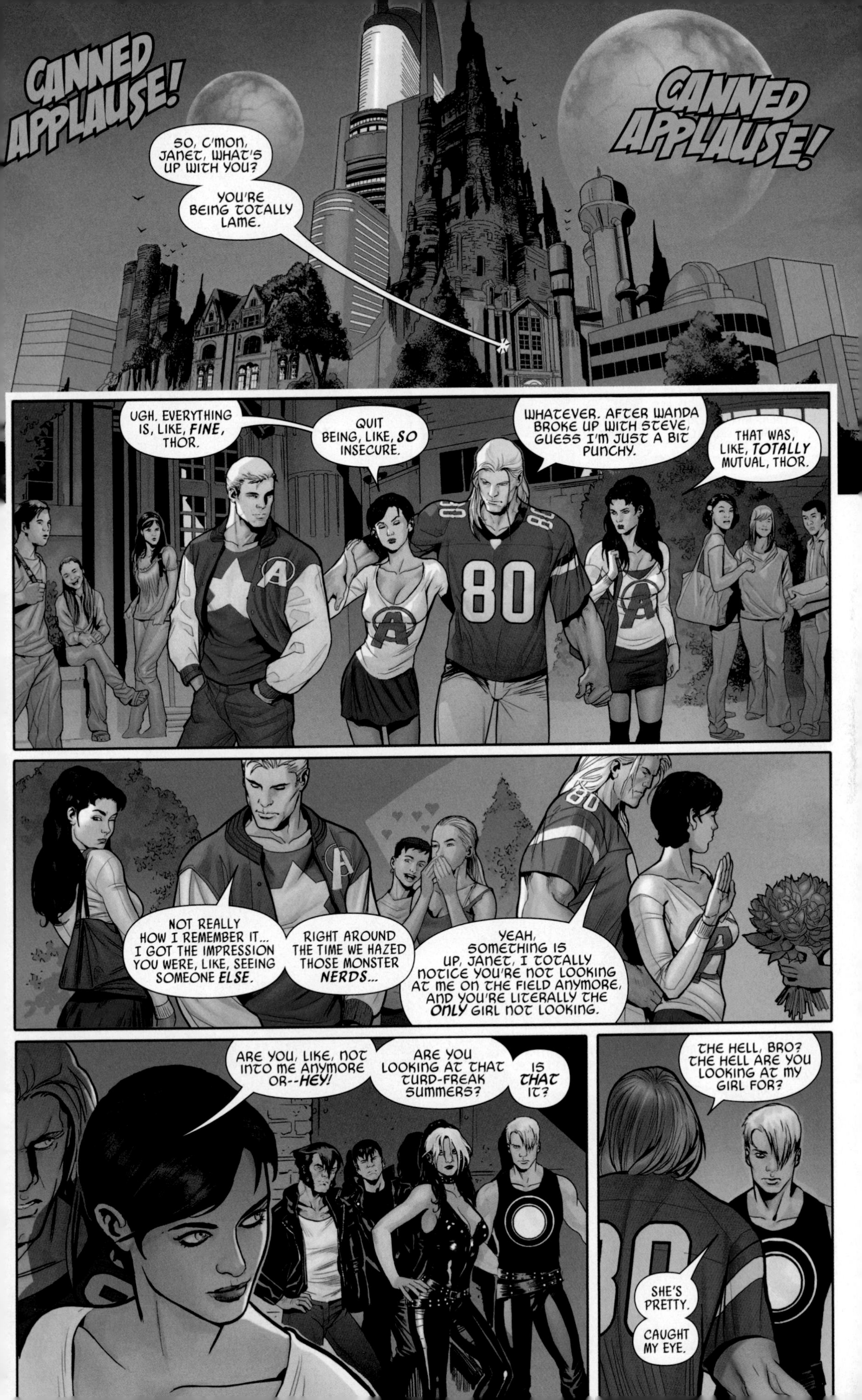
CANNED APPLAUSE!
CANNED APPLAUSE!
SO, C'MON, JANET, WHAT'S UP WITH YOU?
YOU'RE BEING TOTALLY LAME.
UGH. EVERYTHING IS, LIKE, FINE, THOR.
QUIT BEING, LIKE, SO INSECURE.
WHATEVER. AFTER WANDA BROKE UP WITH STEVE, GUESS I'M JUST A BIT PUNCHY.
THAT WAS, LIKE, TOTALLY MUTUAL, THOR.
NOT REALLY HOW I REMEMBER IT... I GOT THE IMPRESSION YOU WERE, LIKE, SEEING SOMEONE ELSE.
RIGHT AROUND THE TIME WE HAZED THOSE MONSTER NERDS...
YEAH, SOMETHING IS UP, JANET, I TOTALLY NOTICE YOU'RE NOT LOOKING AT ME ON THE FIELD ANYMORE, AND YOU'RE LITERALLY THE ONLY GIRL NOT LOOKING.
ARE YOU, LIKE, NOT INTO ME ANYMORE OR--HEY!
ARE YOU LOOKING AT THAT TURD-FREAK SUMMERS?
IS THAT IT?
THE HELL, BRO? THE HELL ARE YOU LOOKING AT MY GIRL FOR?
SHE'S PRETTY.
CAUGHT MY EYE.

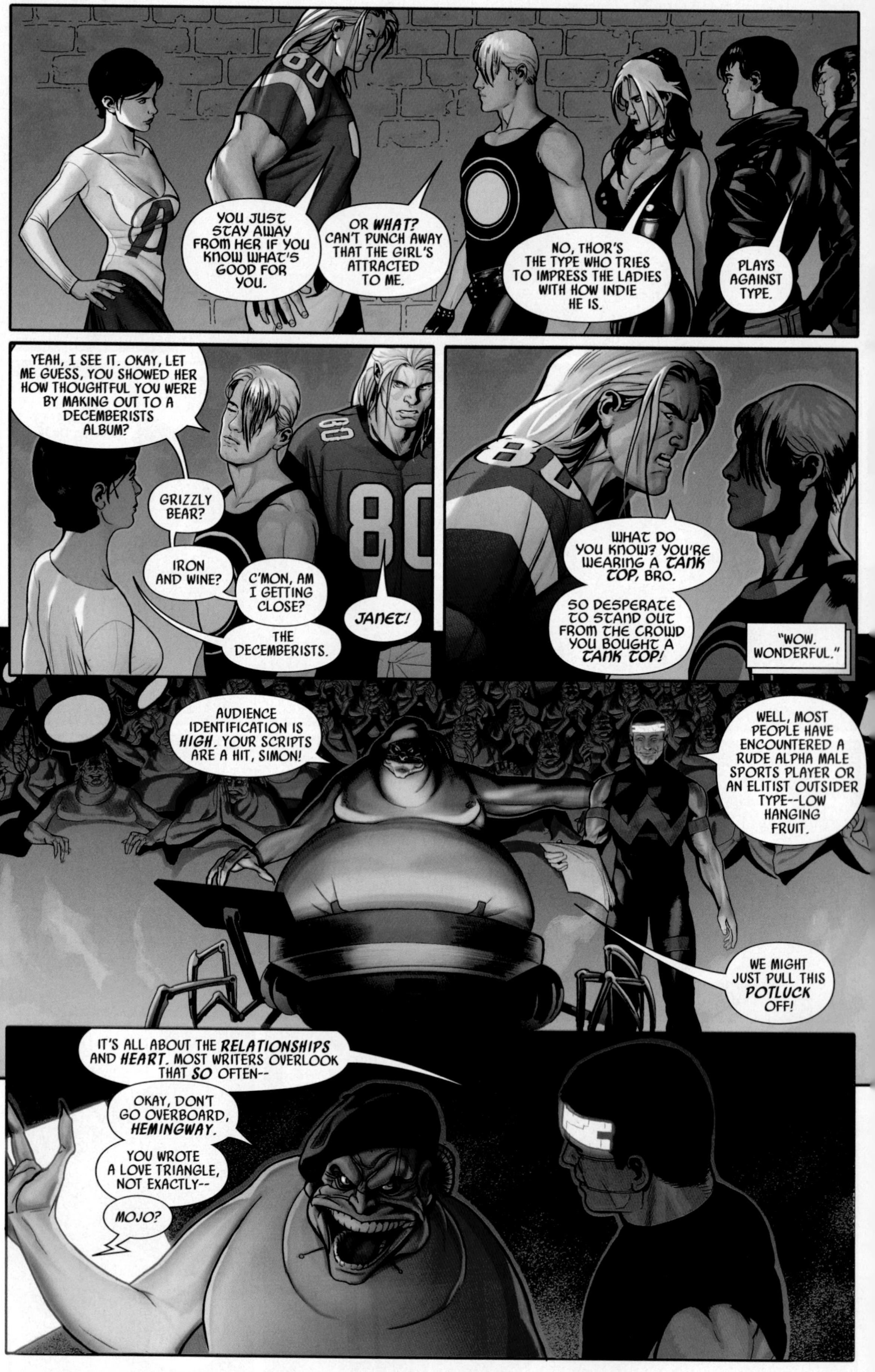

YOU JUST STAY AWAY FROM HER IF YOU KNOW WHAT'S GOOD FOR YOU.
OR WHAT? CAN'T PUNCH AWAY THAT THE GIRL'S ATTRACTED TO ME.
NO, THOR'S THE TYPE WHO TRIES TO IMPRESS THE LADIES WITH HOW INDIE HE IS.
PLAYS AGAINST TYPE.
YEAH, I SEE IT. OKAY, LET ME GUESS, YOU SHOWED HER HOW THOUGHTFUL YOU WERE BY MAKING OUT TO A DECEMBERISTS ALBUM?
GRIZZLY BEAR?
IRON AND WINE?
C'MON, AM I GETTING CLOSE?
THE DECEMBERISTS.
JANET!
WHAT DO YOU KNOW? YOU'RE WEARING A TANK TOP, BRO.
SO DESPERATE TO STAND OUT FROM THE CROWD YOU BOUGHT A TANK TOP!
"WOW. WONDERFUL."
AUDIENCE IDENTIFICATION IS HIGH. YOUR SCRIPTS ARE A HIT, SIMON!
WELL, MOST PEOPLE HAVE ENCOUNTERED A RUDE ALPHA MALE SPORTS PLAYER OR AN ELITIST OUTSIDER TYPE--LOW HANGING FRUIT.
WE MIGHT JUST PULL THIS POTLUCK OFF!
IT'S ALL ABOUT THE RELATIONSHIPS AND HEART. MOST WRITERS OVERLOOK THAT SO OFTEN--
OKAY, DON'T GO OVERBOARD, HEMINGWAY.
YOU WROTE A LOVE TRIANGLE, NOT EXACTLY--
MOJO?

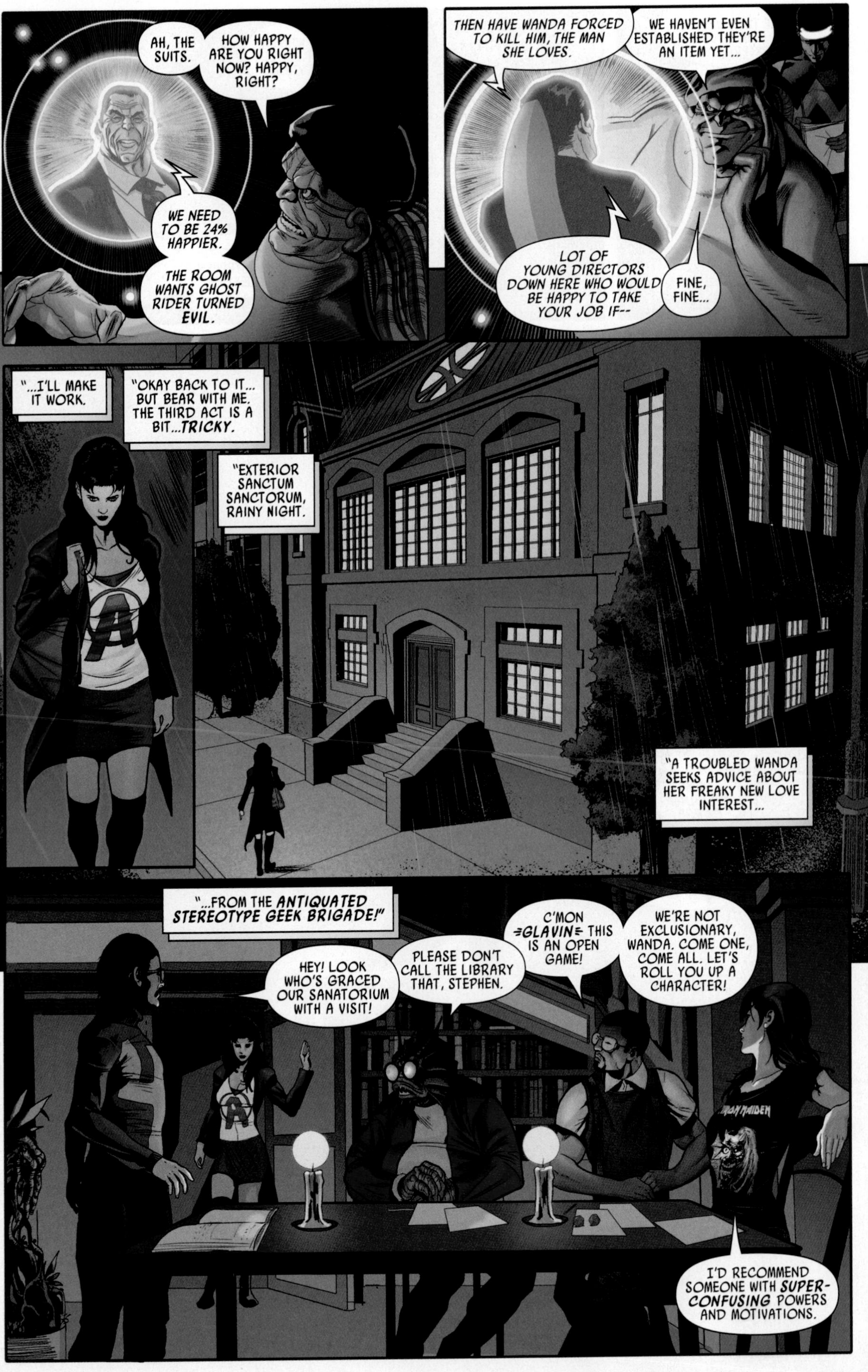
AH, THE SUITS.
HOW HAPPY ARE YOU RIGHT NOW? HAPPY, RIGHT?
WE NEED TO BE 24% HAPPIER.
THE ROOM WANTS GHOST RIDER TURNED EVIL.
THEN HAVE WANDA FORCED TO KILL HIM, THE MAN SHE LOVES.
WE HAVEN'T EVEN ESTABLISHED THEY'RE AN ITEM YET...
LOT OF YOUNG DIRECTORS DOWN HERE WHO WOULD BE HAPPY TO TAKE YOUR JOB IF--
FINE, FINE...
"...I'LL MAKE IT WORK.
"OKAY BACK TO IT... BUT BEAR WITH ME. THE THIRD ACT IS A BIT...TRICKY.
"EXTERIOR SANCTUM SANCTORUM, RAINY NIGHT.
"A TROUBLED WANDA SEEKS ADVICE ABOUT HER FREAKY NEW LOVE INTEREST...
"...FROM THE ANTIQUATED STEREOTYPE GEEK BRIGADE!"
HEY! LOOK WHO'S GRACED OUR SANATORIUM WITH A VISIT!
PLEASE DON'T CALL THE LIBRARY THAT, STEPHEN.
C'MON =GLAVIN= THIS IS AN OPEN GAME!
WE'RE NOT EXCLUSIONARY, WANDA. COME ONE, COME ALL. LET'S ROLL YOU UP A CHARACTER!
I'D RECOMMEND SOMEONE WITH SUPER-CONFUSING POWERS AND MOTIVATIONS.

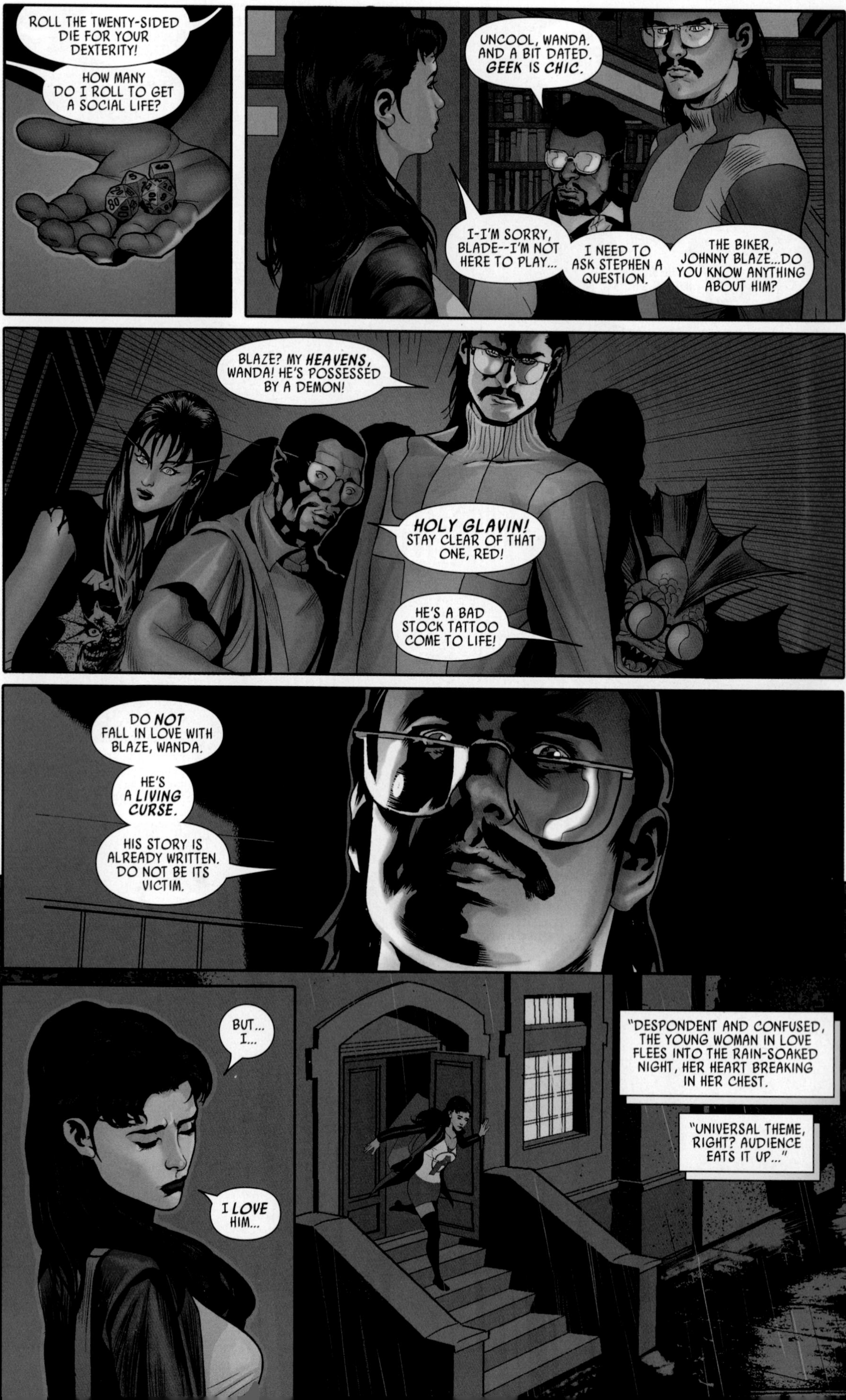

ROLL THE TWENTY-SIDED DIE FOR YOUR DEXTERITY!
HOW MANY DO I ROLL TO GET A SOCIAL LIFE?
UNCOOL, WANDA. AND A BIT DATED. GEEK IS CHIC.
I-I'M SORRY, BLADE--I'M NOT HERE TO PLAY...
I NEED TO ASK STEPHEN A QUESTION.
THE BIKER, JOHNNY BLAZE...DO YOU KNOW ANYTHING ABOUT HIM?
BLAZE? MY HEAVENS, WANDA! HE'S POSSESSED BY A DEMON!
HOLY GLAVIN! STAY CLEAR OF THAT ONE, RED!
HE'S A BAD STOCK TATTOO COME TO LIFE!
DO NOT FALL IN LOVE WITH BLAZE, WANDA.
HE'S A LIVING CURSE.
HIS STORY IS ALREADY WRITTEN. DO NOT BE ITS VICTIM.
BUT... I...
I LOVE HIM...
"DESPONDENT AND CONFUSED, THE YOUNG WOMAN IN LOVE FLEES INTO THE RAIN-SOAKED NIGHT, HER HEART BREAKING IN HER CHEST.
"UNIVERSAL THEME, RIGHT? AUDIENCE EATS IT UP..."

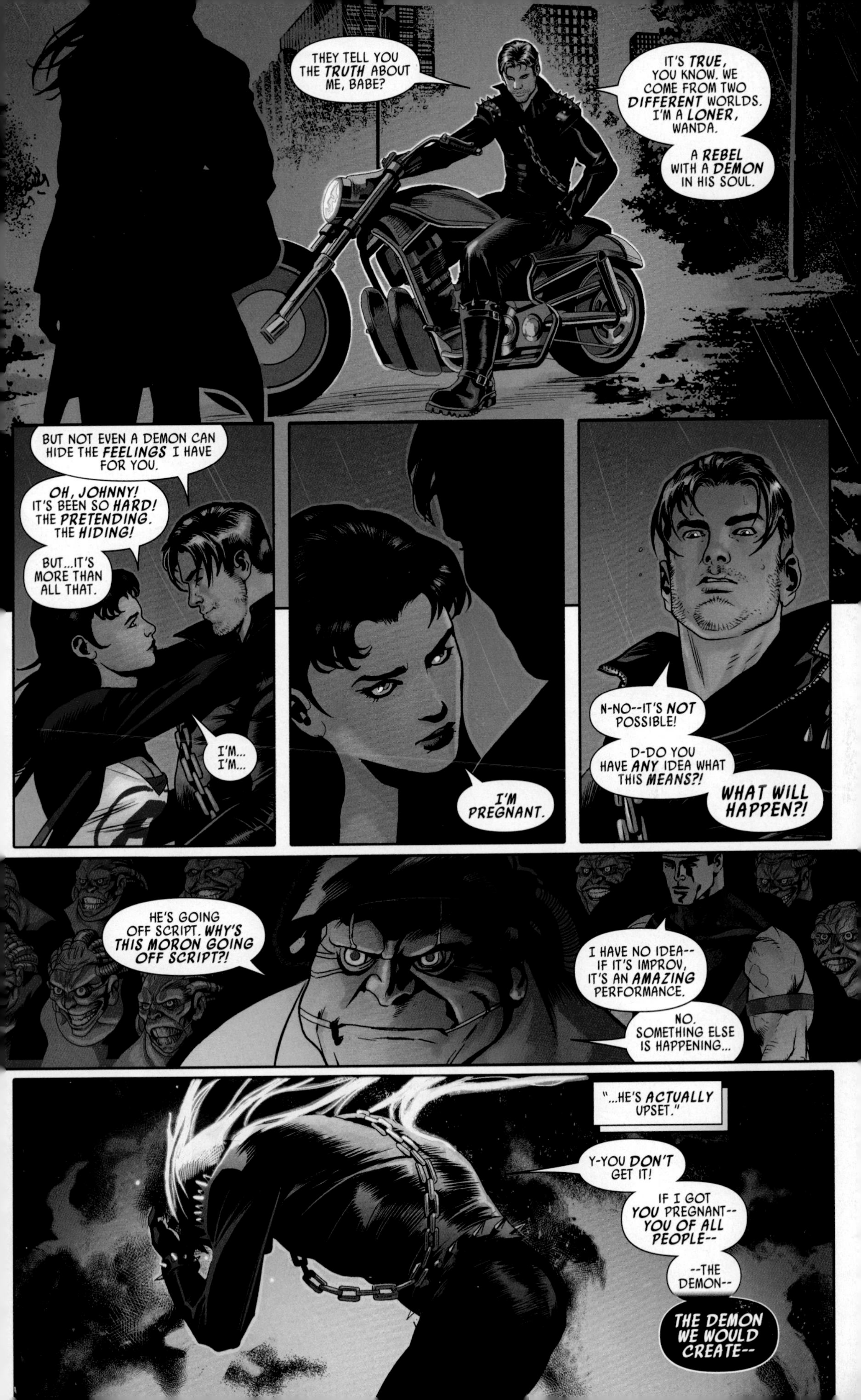
THEY TELL YOU THE TRUTH ABOUT ME, BABE?
IT'S TRUE, YOU KNOW. WE COME FROM TWO DIFFERENT WORLDS. I'M A LONER, WANDA.
A REBEL WITH A DEMON IN HIS SOUL.
BUT NOT EVEN A DEMON CAN HIDE THE FEELINGS I HAVE FOR YOU.
OH, JOHNNY! IT'S BEEN SO HARD! THE PRETENDING. THE HIDING!
BUT...IT'S MORE THAN ALL THAT.
I'M... I'M...
I'M PREGNANT.
N-NO--IT'S NOT POSSIBLE!
D-DO YOU HAVE ANY IDEA WHAT THIS MEANS?!
WHAT WILL HAPPEN?!
HE'S GOING OFF SCRIPT. WHY'S THIS MORON GOING OFF SCRIPT?!
I HAVE NO IDEA-- IF IT'S IMPROV, IT'S AN AMAZING PERFORMANCE.
NO. SOMETHING ELSE IS HAPPENING...
"...HE'S ACTUALLY UPSET."
Y-YOU DON'T GET IT!
IF I GOT YOU PREGNANT-- YOU OF ALL PEOPLE--
--THE DEMON--
THE DEMON WE WOULD CREATE--

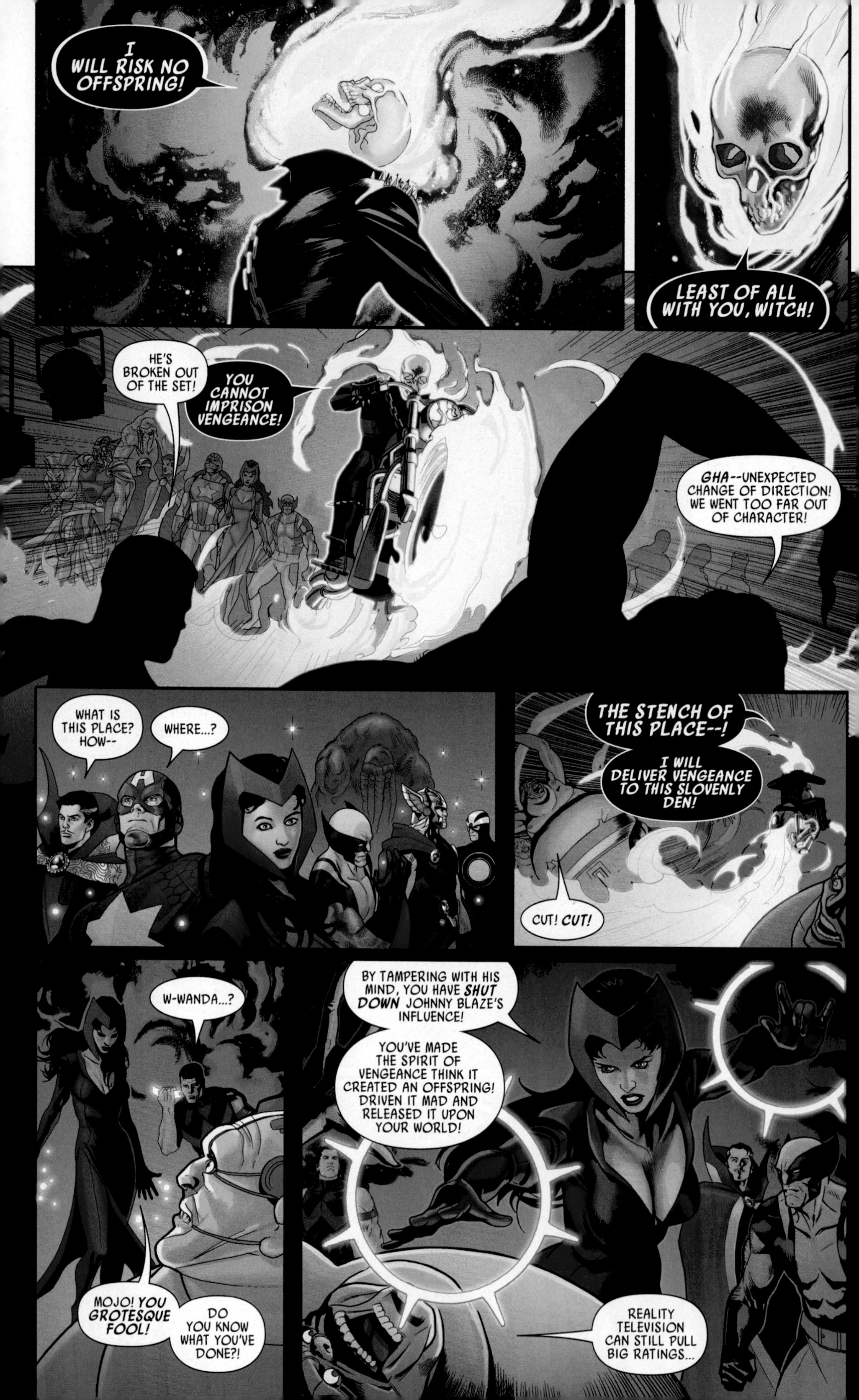

I WILL RISK NO OFFSPRING!
LEAST OF ALL WITH YOU, WITCH!
HE'S BROKEN OUT OF THE SET!
YOU CANNOT IMPRISON VENGEANCE!
GHA--UNEXPECTED CHANGE OF DIRECTION! WE WENT TOO FAR OUT OF CHARACTER!
WHAT IS THIS PLACE? HOW--
WHERE...?
THE STENCH OF THIS PLACE--!
I WILL DELIVER VENGEANCE TO THIS SLOVENLY DEN!
CUT! CUT!
W-WANDA...?
BY TAMPERING WITH HIS MIND, YOU HAVE SHUT DOWN JOHNNY BLAZE'S INFLUENCE!
YOU'VE MADE THE SPIRIT OF VENGEANCE THINK IT CREATED AN OFFSPRING! DRIVEN IT MAD AND RELEASED IT UPON YOUR WORLD!
MOJO! YOU GROTESQUE FOOL!
DO YOU KNOW WHAT YOU'VE DONE?!
REALITY TELEVISION CAN STILL PULL BIG RATINGS...

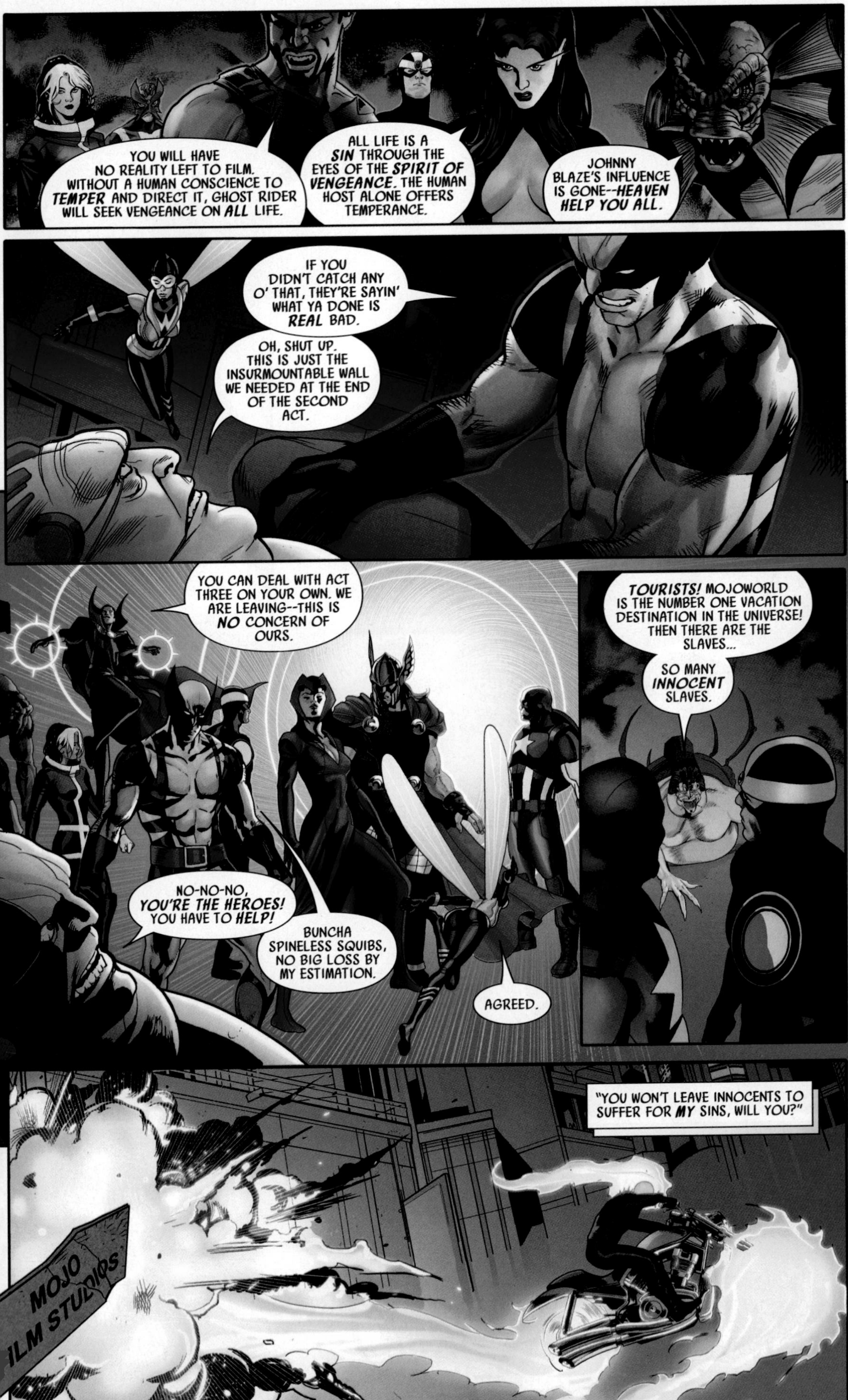
YOU WILL HAVE NO REALITY LEFT TO FILM. WITHOUT A HUMAN CONSCIENCE TO TEMPER AND DIRECT IT, GHOST RIDER WILL SEEK VENGEANCE ON ALL LIFE.
ALL LIFE IS A SIN THROUGH THE EYES OF THE SPIRIT OF VENGEANCE. THE HUMAN HOST ALONE OFFERS TEMPERANCE.
JOHNNY BLAZE'S INFLUENCE IS GONE--HEAVEN HELP YOU ALL.
IF YOU DIDN'T CATCH ANY O' THAT, THEY'RE SAYIN' WHAT YA DONE IS REAL BAD.
OH, SHUT UP. THIS IS JUST THE INSURMOUNTABLE WALL WE NEEDED AT THE END OF THE SECOND ACT.
YOU CAN DEAL WITH ACT THREE ON YOUR OWN. WE ARE LEAVING--THIS IS NO CONCERN OF OURS.
NO-NO-NO, YOU'RE THE HEROES! YOU HAVE TO HELP!
BUNCHA SPINELESS SQUIBS, NO BIG LOSS BY MY ESTIMATION.
AGREED.
TOURISTS! MOJOWORLD IS THE NUMBER ONE VACATION DESTINATION IN THE UNIVERSE! THEN THERE ARE THE SLAVES...
SO MANY INNOCENT SLAVES.
"YOU WON'T LEAVE INNOCENTS TO SUFFER FOR MY SINS, WILL YOU?"
MOJO FILM STUDIOS

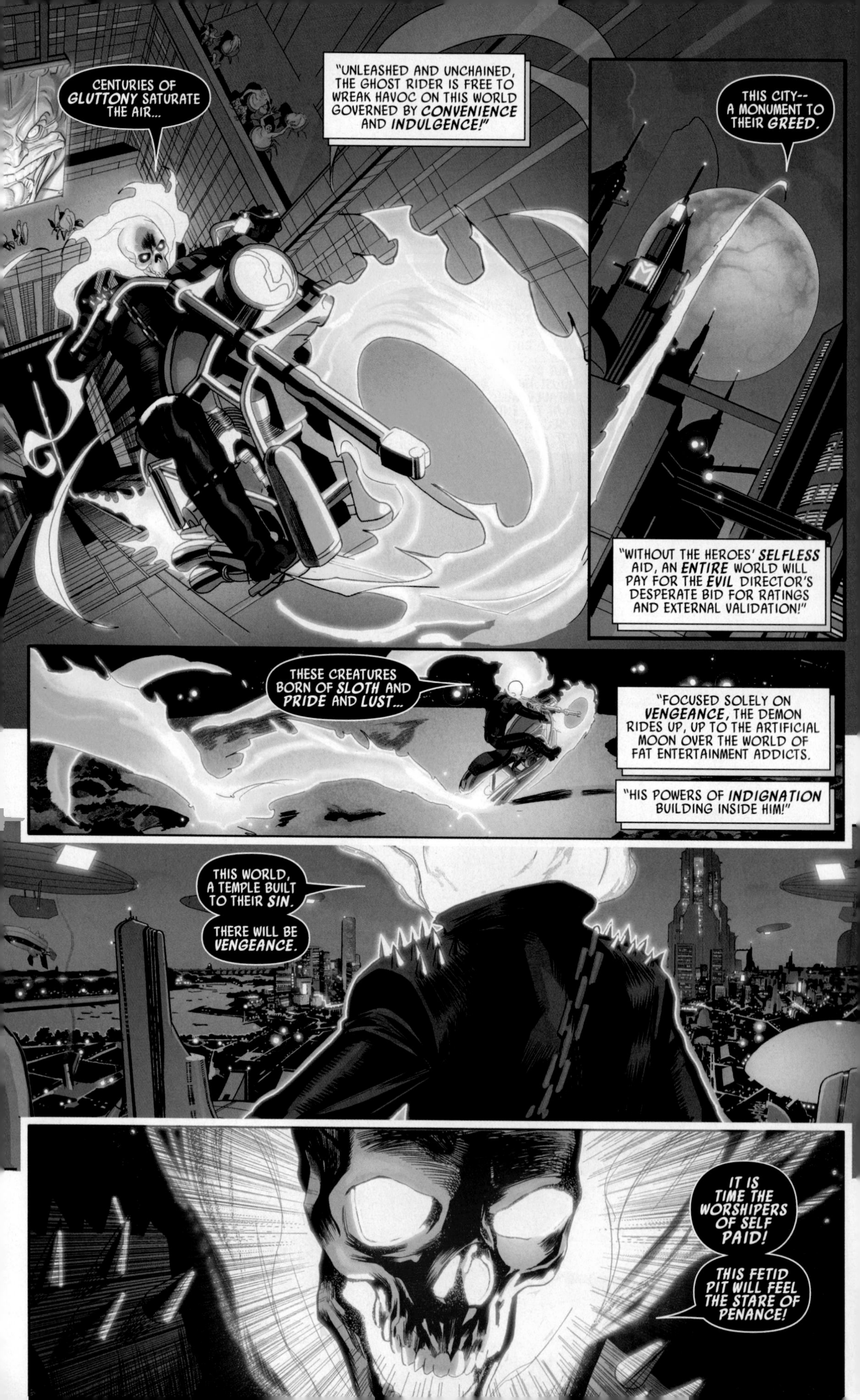
CENTURIES OF GLUTTONY SATURATE THE AIR...
"UNLEASHED AND UNCHAINED, THE GHOST RIDER IS FREE TO WREAK HAVOC ON THIS WORLD GOVERNED BY CONVENIENCE AND INDULGENCE!"
THIS CITY-- A MONUMENT TO THEIR GREED.
"WITHOUT THE HEROES' SELFLESS AID, AN ENTIRE WORLD WILL PAY FOR THE EVIL DIRECTOR'S DESPERATE BID FOR RATINGS AND EXTERNAL VALIDATION!"
THESE CREATURES BORN OF SLOTH AND PRIDE AND LUST...
"FOCUSED SOLELY ON VENGEANCE, THE DEMON RIDES UP, UP TO THE ARTIFICIAL MOON OVER THE WORLD OF FAT ENTERTAINMENT ADDICTS.
"HIS POWERS OF INDIGNATION BUILDING INSIDE HIM!"
THIS WORLD, A TEMPLE BUILT TO THEIR SIN.
THERE WILL BE VENGEANCE.
IT IS TIME THE WORSHIPERS OF SELF PAID!
THIS FETID PIT WILL FEEL THE STARE OF PENANCE!

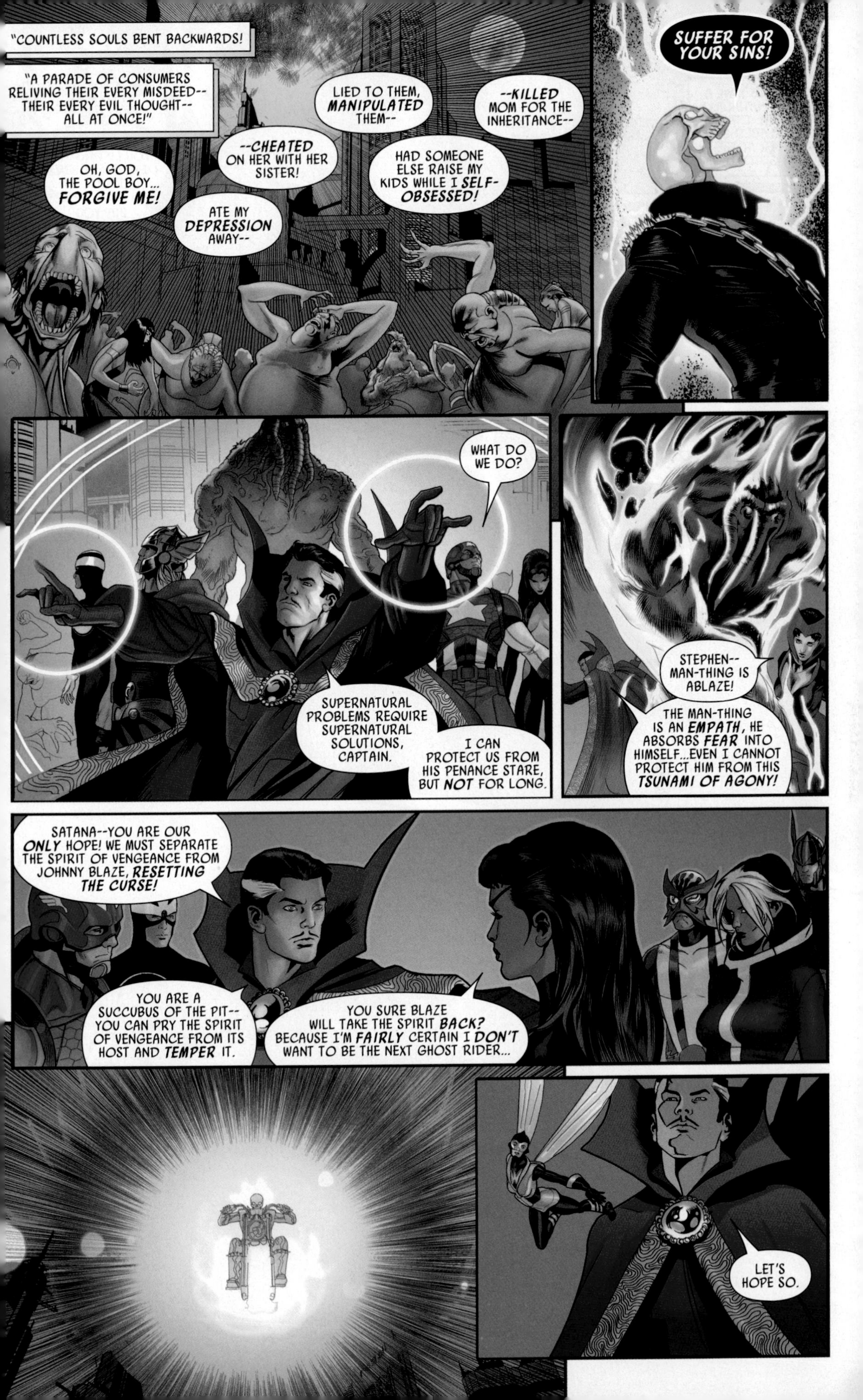
"COUNTLESS SOULS BENT BACKWARDS!
"A PARADE OF CONSUMERS RELIVING THEIR EVERY MISDEED--THEIR EVERY EVIL THOUGHT--ALL AT ONCE!"
OH, GOD, THE POOL BOY... FORGIVE ME!
--CHEATED ON HER WITH HER SISTER!
ATE MY DEPRESSION AWAY--
LIED TO THEM, MANIPULATED THEM--
HAD SOMEONE ELSE RAISE MY KIDS WHILE I SELF-OBSESSED!
--KILLED MOM FOR THE INHERITANCE--
SUFFER FOR YOUR SINS!
WHAT DO WE DO?
SUPERNATURAL PROBLEMS REQUIRE SUPERNATURAL SOLUTIONS, CAPTAIN.
I CAN PROTECT US FROM HIS PENANCE STARE, BUT NOT FOR LONG.
STEPHEN--MAN-THING IS ABLAZE!
THE MAN-THING IS AN EMPATH, HE ABSORBS FEAR INTO HIMSELF...EVEN I CANNOT PROTECT HIM FROM THIS TSUNAMI OF AGONY!
SATANA--YOU ARE OUR ONLY HOPE! WE MUST SEPARATE THE SPIRIT OF VENGEANCE FROM JOHNNY BLAZE, RESETTING THE CURSE!
YOU ARE A SUCCUBUS OF THE PIT--YOU CAN PRY THE SPIRIT OF VENGEANCE FROM ITS HOST AND TEMPER IT.
YOU SURE BLAZE WILL TAKE THE SPIRIT BACK? BECAUSE I'M FAIRLY CERTAIN I DON'T WANT TO BE THE NEXT GHOST RIDER...
LET'S HOPE SO.

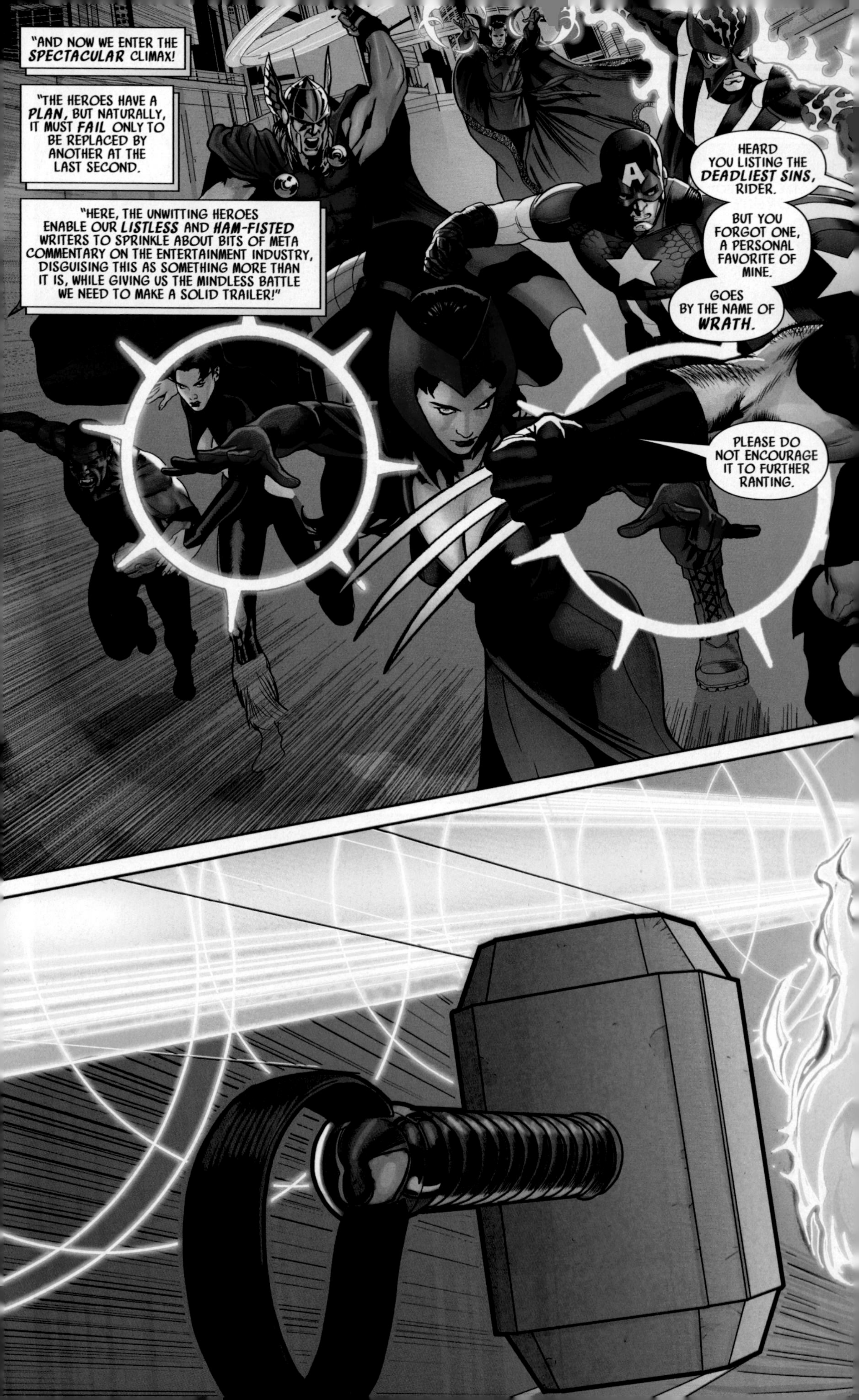
"AND NOW WE ENTER THE SPECTACULAR CLIMAX!
"THE HEROES HAVE A PLAN, BUT NATURALLY, IT MUST FAIL ONLY TO BE REPLACED BY ANOTHER AT THE LAST SECOND.
"HERE, THE UNWITTING HEROES ENABLE OUR LISTLESS AND HAM-FISTED WRITERS TO SPRINKLE ABOUT BITS OF META COMMENTARY ON THE ENTERTAINMENT INDUSTRY, DISGUISING THIS AS SOMETHING MORE THAN IT IS, WHILE GIVING US THE MINDLESS BATTLE WE NEED TO MAKE A SOLID TRAILER!"
HEARD YOU LISTING THE DEADLIEST SINS, RIDER.
BUT YOU FORGOT ONE, A PERSONAL FAVORITE OF MINE.
GOES BY THE NAME OF WRATH.
PLEASE DO NOT ENCOURAGE IT TO FURTHER RANTING.

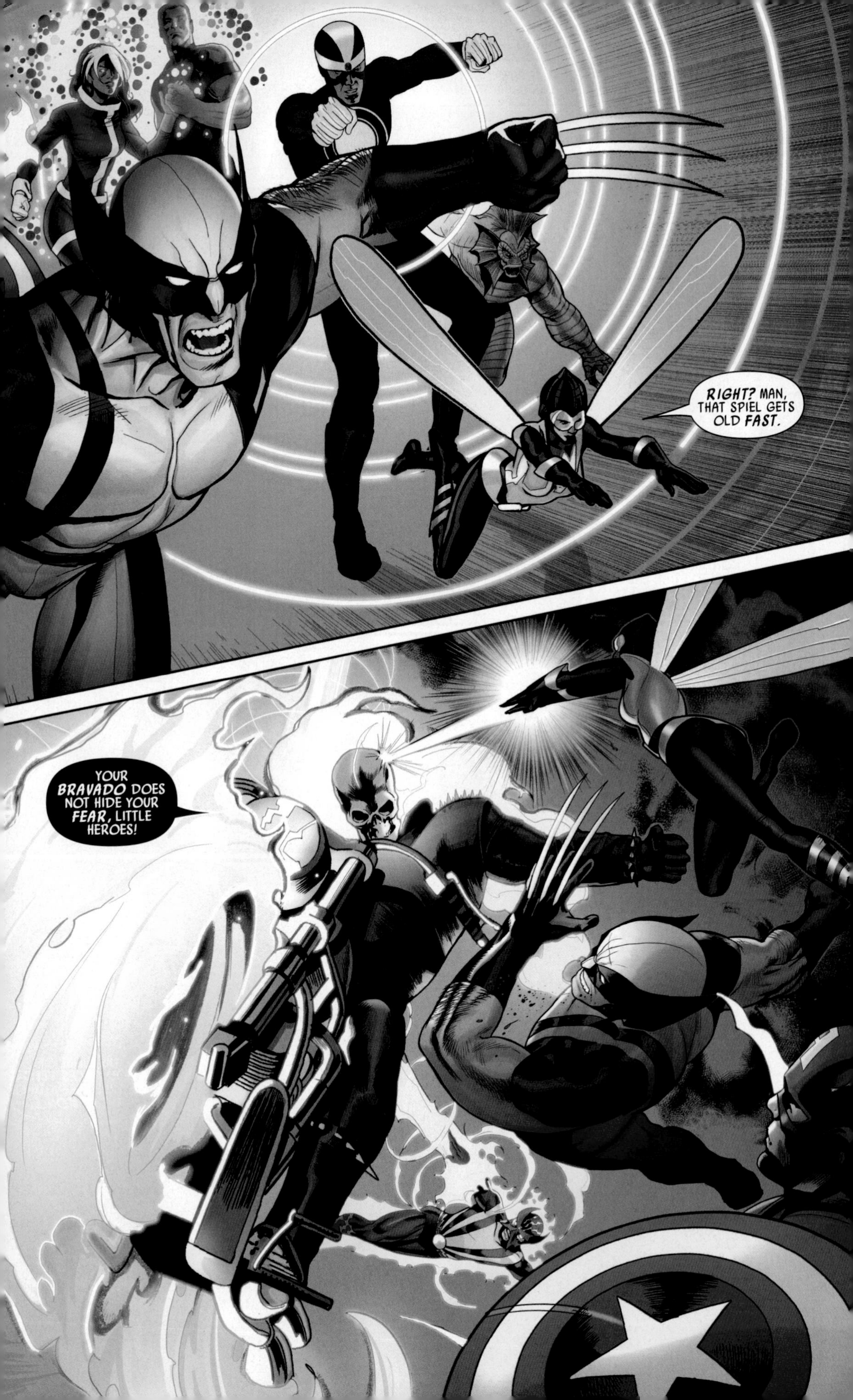
RIGHT? MAN, THAT SPIEL GETS OLD FAST.
YOUR BRAVADO DOES NOT HIDE YOUR FEAR, LITTLE HEROES!

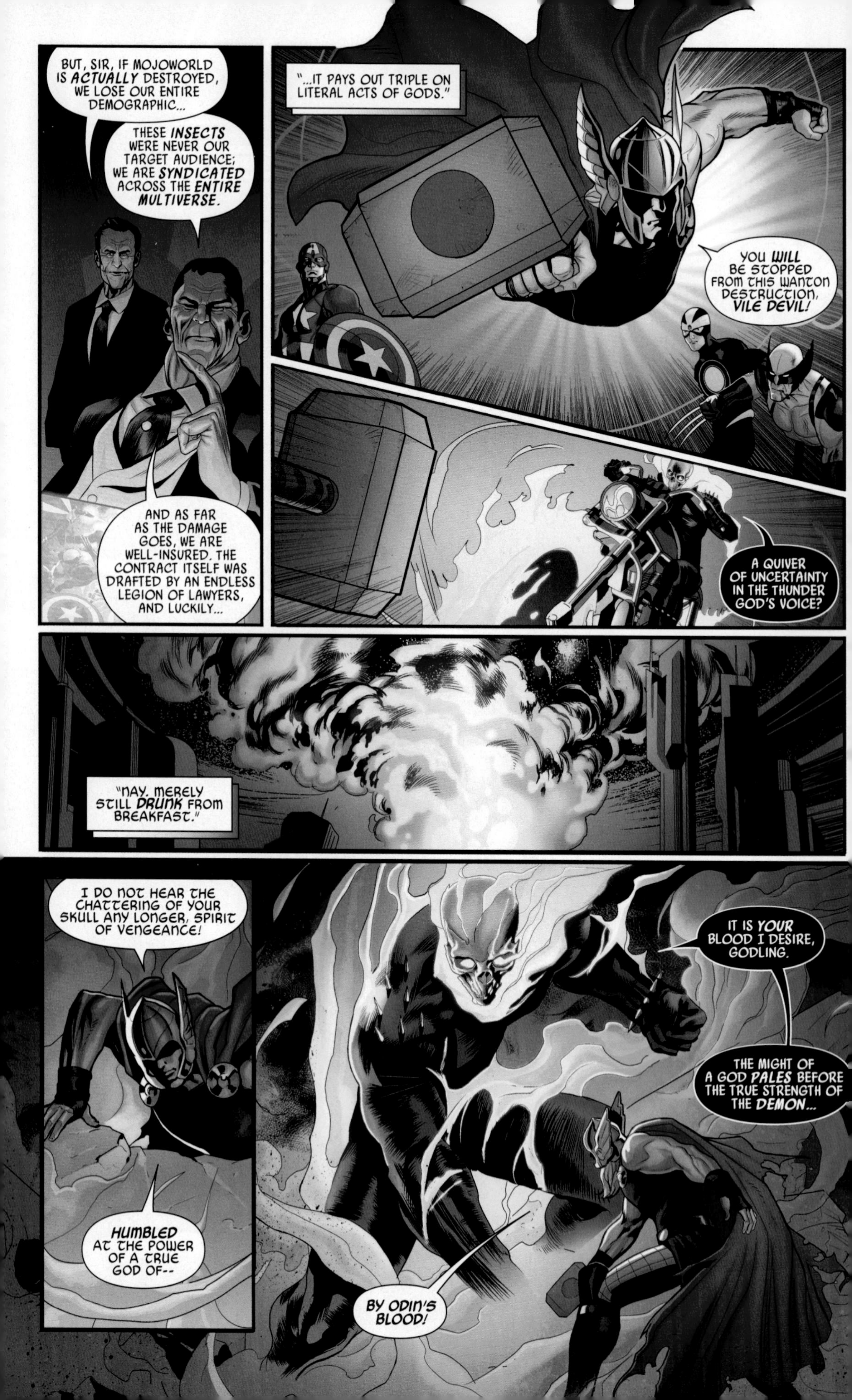

BUT, SIR, IF MOJOWORLD IS ACTUALLY DESTROYED, WE LOSE OUR ENTIRE DEMOGRAPHIC...
THESE INSECTS WERE NEVER OUR TARGET AUDIENCE; WE ARE SYNDICATED ACROSS THE ENTIRE MULTIVERSE.
AND AS FAR AS THE DAMAGE GOES, WE ARE WELL-INSURED. THE CONTRACT ITSELF WAS DRAFTED BY AN ENDLESS LEGION OF LAWYERS, AND LUCKILY...
"...IT PAYS OUT TRIPLE ON LITERAL ACTS OF GODS."
YOU WILL BE STOPPED FROM THIS WANTON DESTRUCTION, VILE DEVIL!
A QUIVER OF UNCERTAINTY IN THE THUNDER GOD'S VOICE?
"NAY. MERELY STILL DRUNK FROM BREAKFAST."
I DO NOT HEAR THE CHATTERING OF YOUR SKULL ANY LONGER, SPIRIT OF VENGEANCE!
HUMBLED AT THE POWER OF A TRUE GOD OF--
IT IS YOUR BLOOD I DESIRE, GODLING.
THE MIGHT OF A GOD PALES BEFORE THE TRUE STRENGTH OF THE DEMON...
BY ODIN'S BLOOD!

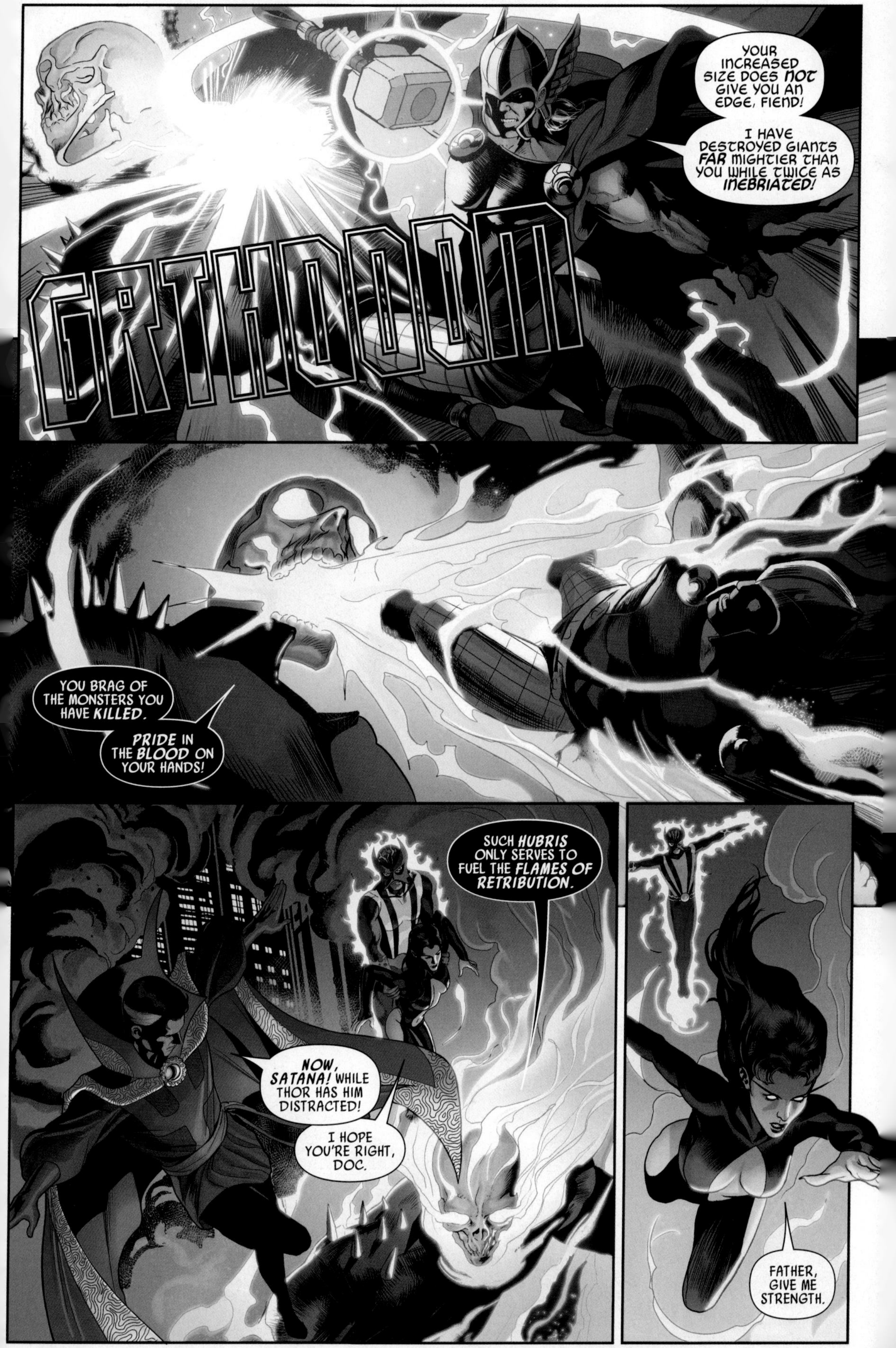
YOUR INCREASED SIZE DOES NOT GIVE YOU AN EDGE, FIEND!
I HAVE DESTROYED GIANTS FAR MIGHTIER THAN YOU WHILE TWICE AS INEBRIATED!
GRTHOOOM
YOU BRAG OF THE MONSTERS YOU HAVE KILLED.
PRIDE IN THE BLOOD ON YOUR HANDS!
SUCH HUBRIS ONLY SERVES TO FUEL THE FLAMES OF RETRIBUTION.
NOW, SATANA! WHILE THOR HAS HIM DISTRACTED!
I HOPE YOU'RE RIGHT, DOC.
FATHER, GIVE ME STRENGTH.

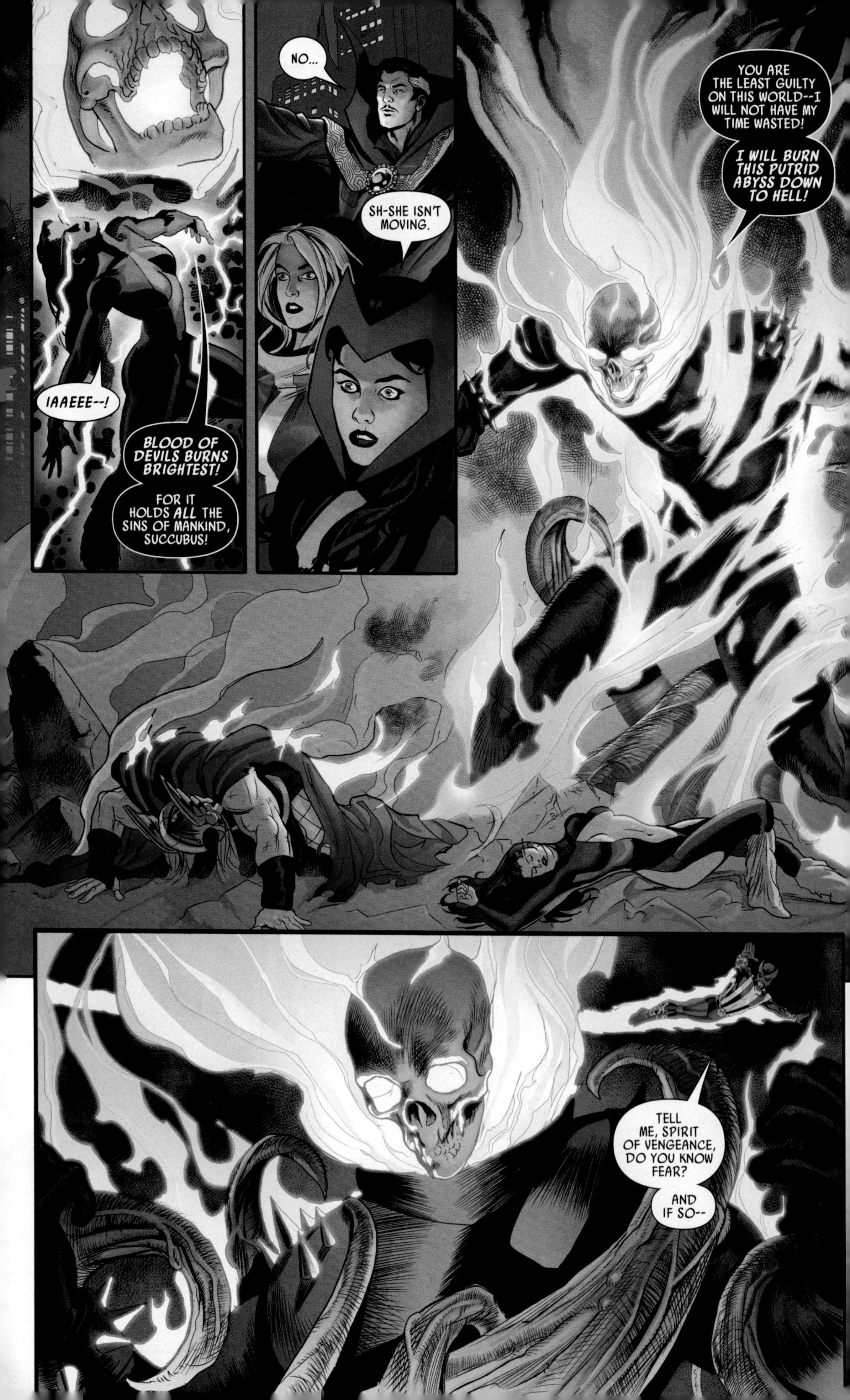
IAAEEE--!
BLOOD OF DEVILS BURNS BRIGHTEST!
FOR IT HOLDS ALL THE SINS OF MANKIND, SUCCUBUS!
NO...
SH-SHE ISN'T MOVING.
YOU ARE THE LEAST GUILTY ON THIS WORLD--I WILL NOT HAVE MY TIME WASTED!
I WILL BURN THIS PUTRID ABYSS DOWN TO HELL!
TELL ME, SPIRIT OF VENGEANCE, DO YOU KNOW FEAR?
AND IF SO--

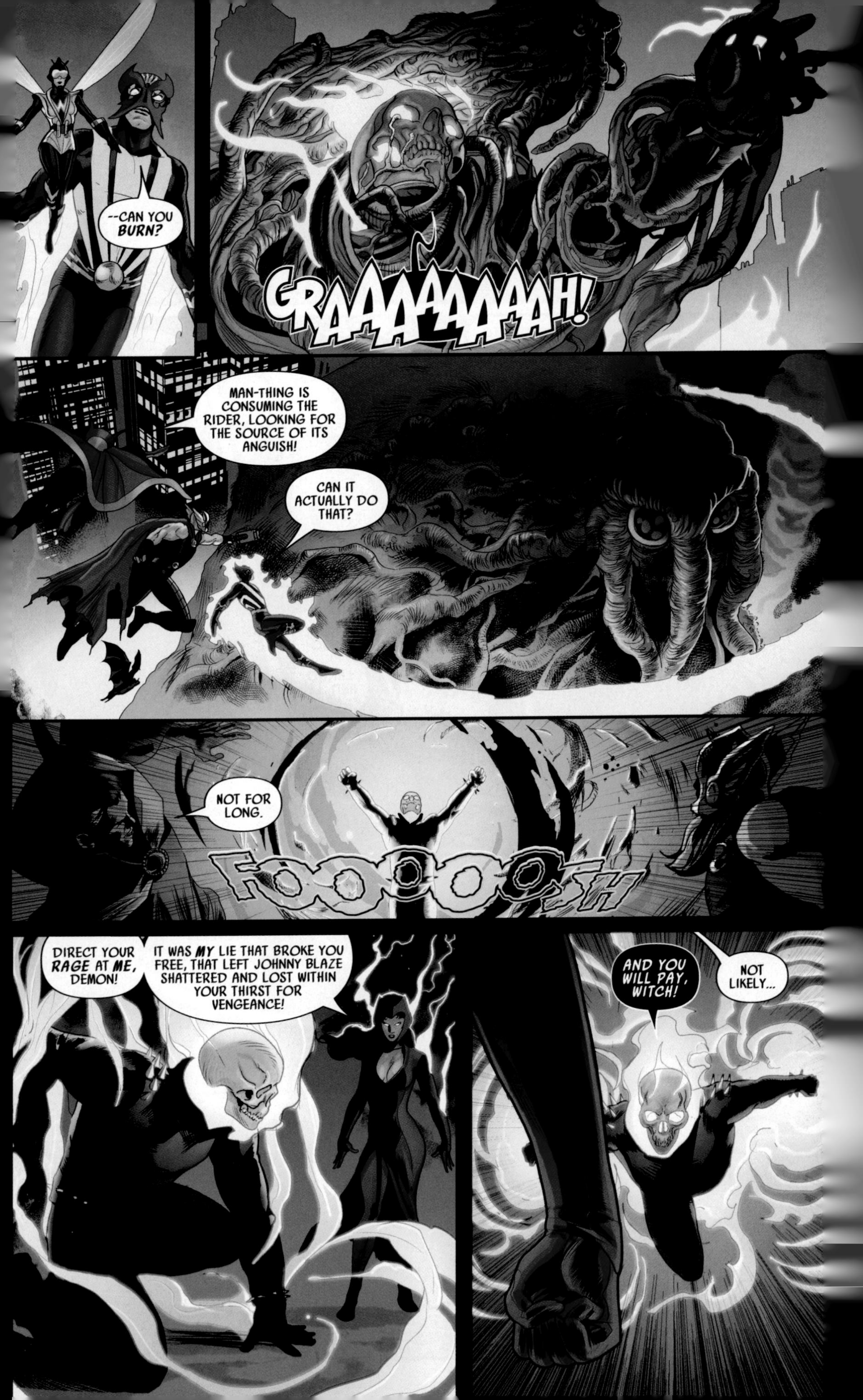
--CAN YOU BURN?
GRAAAAAAAAH!
MAN-THING IS CONSUMING THE RIDER, LOOKING FOR THE SOURCE OF ITS ANGUISH!
CAN IT ACTUALLY DO THAT?
NOT FOR LONG.
FOOOOOSH
DIRECT YOUR RAGE AT ME, DEMON!
IT WAS MY LIE THAT BROKE YOU FREE, THAT LEFT JOHNNY BLAZE SHATTERED AND LOST WITHIN YOUR THIRST FOR VENGEANCE!
AND YOU WILL PAY, WITCH!
NOT LIKELY...

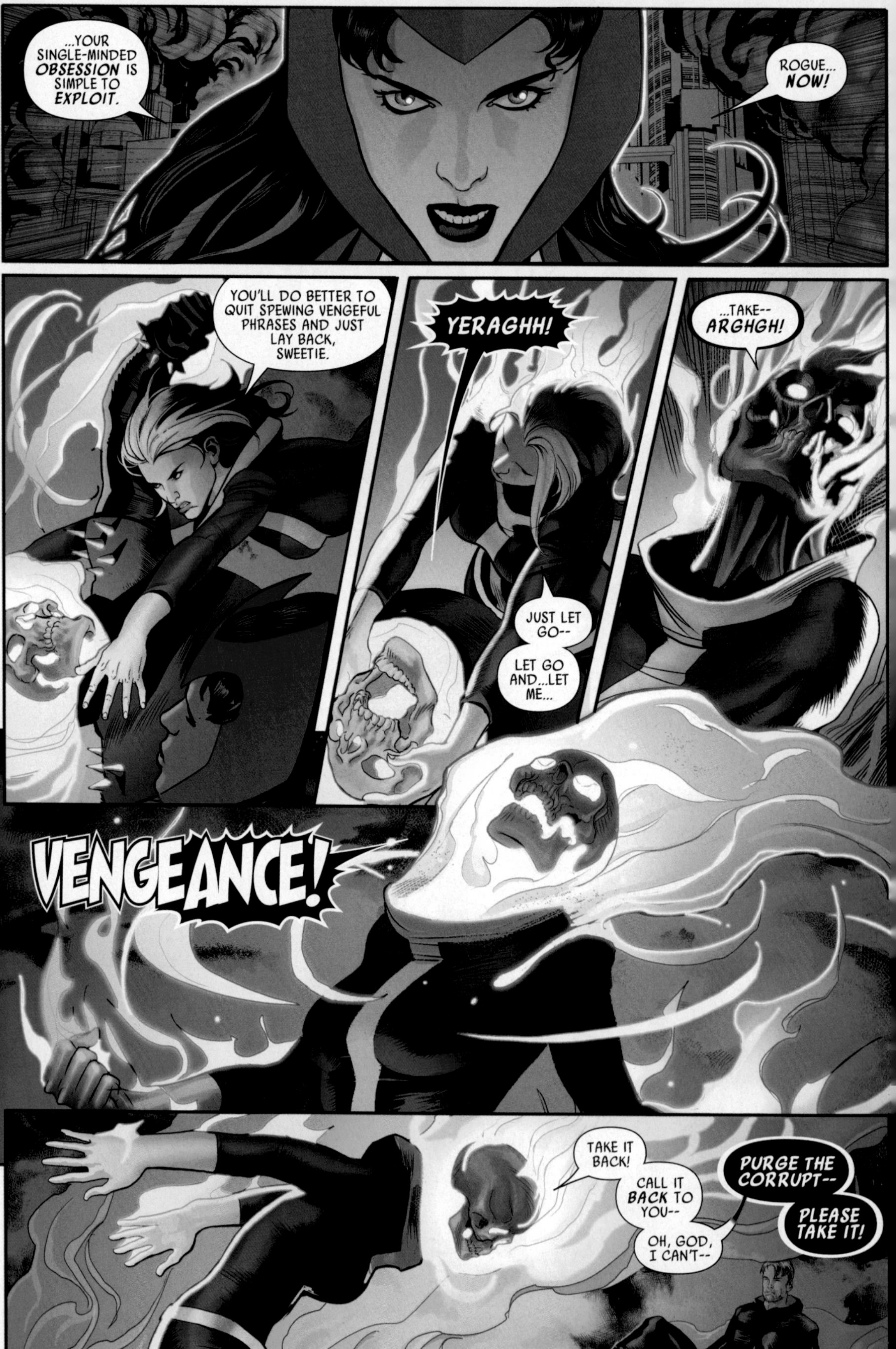
...YOUR SINGLE-MINDED OBSESSION IS SIMPLE TO EXPLOIT.
ROGUE... NOW!
YOU'LL DO BETTER TO QUIT SPEWING VENGEFUL PHRASES AND JUST LAY BACK, SWEETIE.
YERAGHH!
JUST LET GO--
LET GO AND...LET ME...
...TAKE-- ARGHGH!
VENGEANCE!
TAKE IT BACK!
CALL IT BACK TO YOU--
OH, GOD, I CAN'T--
PURGE THE CORRUPT--
PLEASE TAKE IT!

OR I COULD BE FREE OF THIS ETERNAL SACRIFICE...

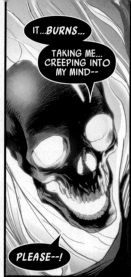

IT...BURNS...

TAKING ME... CREEPING INTO MY MIND--

PLEASE--!

...BUT THIS CURSE IS MINE.

TH-THANK... YOU...

"WAIT, SO--IS THAT IT? IS IT OVER?

"SIR, I DON'T UNDERSTAND ANY OF THIS.

"A BUNCH OF HEROES FOUGHT EACH OTHER, THEN TEAMED UP TO FIGHT A GREATER THREAT, AND THEN THEY DEFEATED THE THREAT AND..."

...IT JUST ENDS? AUDIENCES WANT A STORY THAT HAS CONSEQUENCES, THE OLD WORLD CHANGED IN A NEW, EXCITING AND LASTING WAY.

THIS SOUP MOJO COOKED UP, IT FEELS TOTALLY UNIMPORTANT.

WAS THERE ANY POINT AT ALL? IS IT A STORY ABOUT HOW A COMMITTEE CAN OVERLY COMPLICATE THINGS...?

NO, IT LEFT THAT THREAD BEHIND IN THE FIRST ACT.

IT'S MERELY SLOPPY AND DERIVATIVE.

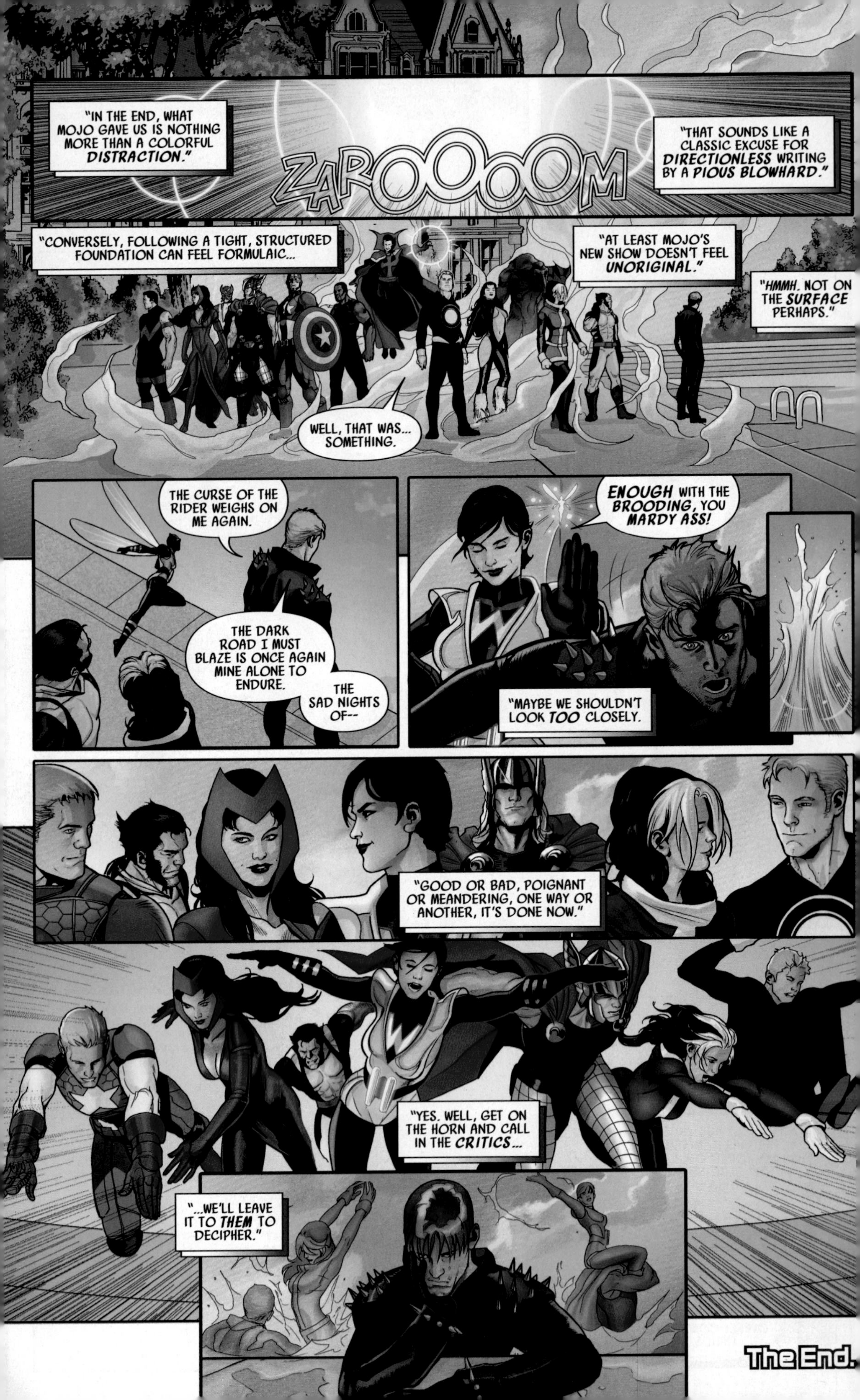
"IN THE END, WHAT MOJO GAVE US IS NOTHING MORE THAN A COLORFUL DISTRACTION."
ZAROOOoOM
"THAT SOUNDS LIKE A CLASSIC EXCUSE FOR DIRECTIONLESS WRITING BY A PIOUS BLOWHARD."
"CONVERSELY, FOLLOWING A TIGHT, STRUCTURED FOUNDATION CAN FEEL FORMULAIC...
"AT LEAST MOJO'S NEW SHOW DOESN'T FEEL UNORIGINAL."
"HMMH. NOT ON THE SURFACE PERHAPS."
WELL, THAT WAS... SOMETHING.
THE CURSE OF THE RIDER WEIGHS ON ME AGAIN.
THE DARK ROAD I MUST BLAZE IS ONCE AGAIN MINE ALONE TO ENDURE.
THE SAD NIGHTS OF--
ENOUGH WITH THE BROODING, YOU MARDY ASS!
"MAYBE WE SHOULDN'T LOOK TOO CLOSELY.
"GOOD OR BAD, POIGNANT OR MEANDERING, ONE WAY OR ANOTHER, IT'S DONE NOW."
"YES. WELL, GET ON THE HORN AND CALL IN THE CRITICS...
"...WE'LL LEAVE IT TO THEM TO DECIPHER."
The End.

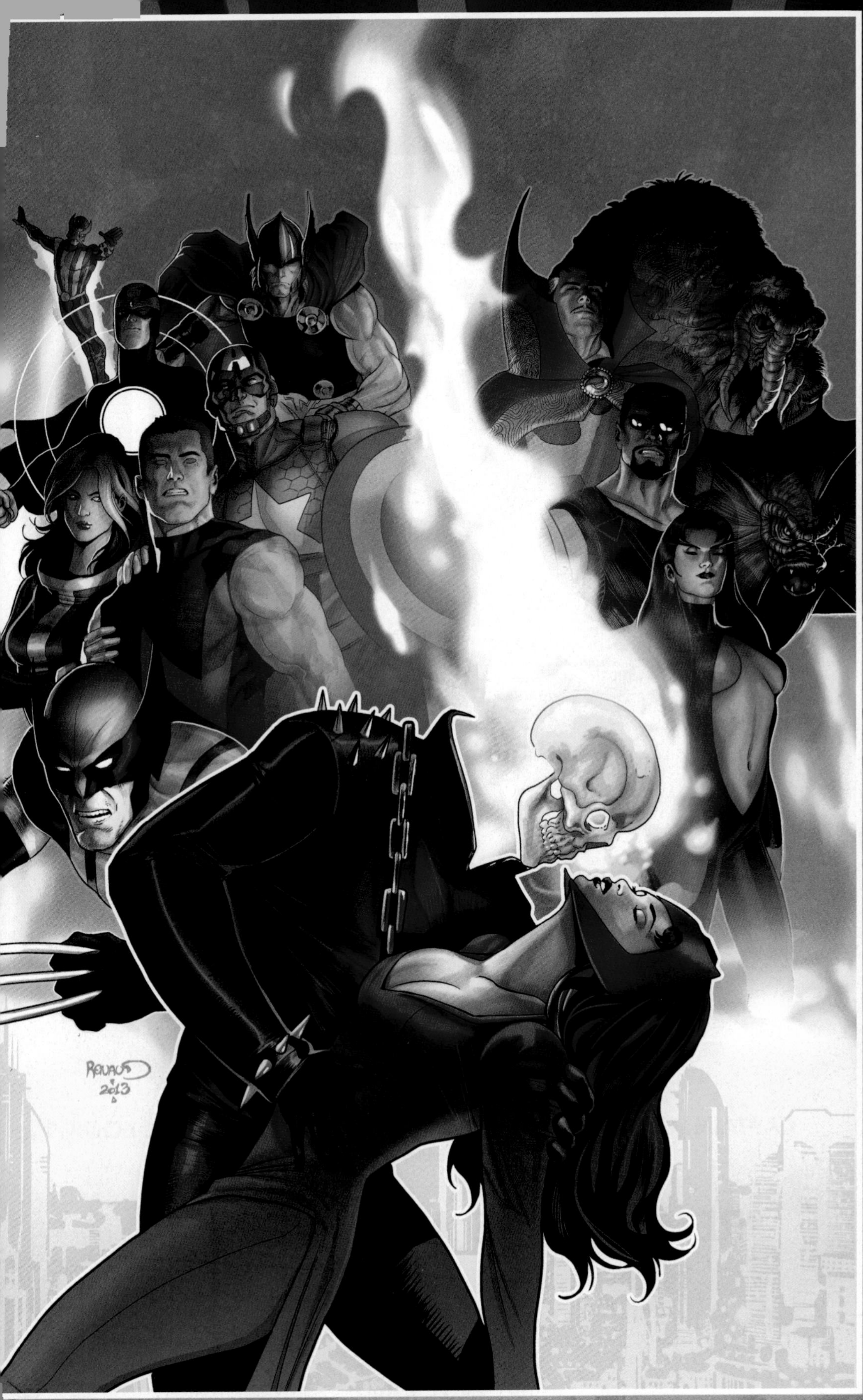

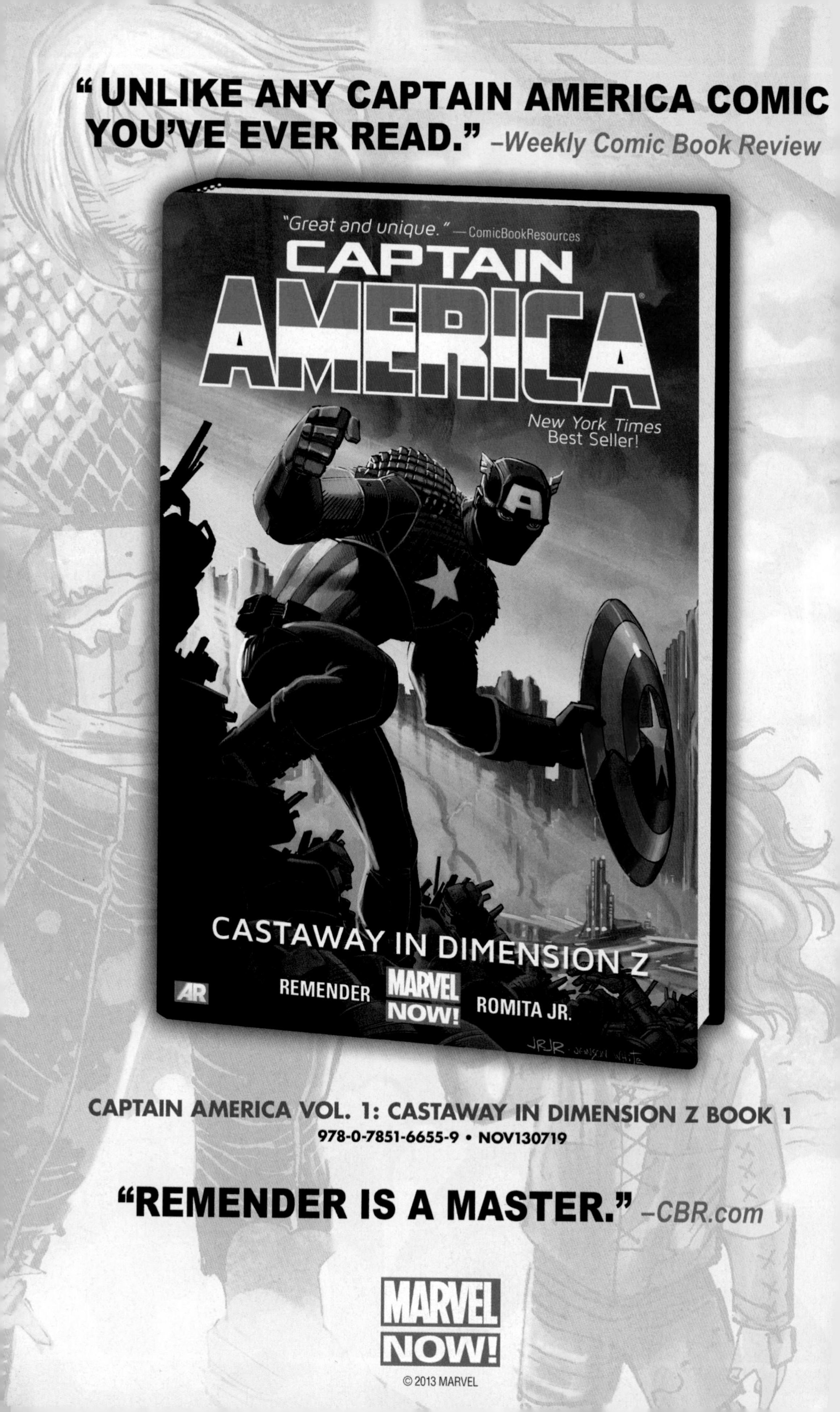

"UNLIKE ANY CAPTAIN AMERICA COMIC YOU'VE EVER READ." –Weekly Comic Book Review
"Great and unique." — ComicBookResources
CAPTAIN AMERICA
New York Times Best Seller!
CASTAWAY IN DIMENSION Z
AR
REMENDER
MARVEL NOW!
ROMITA JR.
CAPTAIN AMERICA VOL. 1: CASTAWAY IN DIMENSION Z BOOK 1
978-0-7851-6655-9 • NOV130719
"REMENDER IS A MASTER." –CBR.com
MARVEL NOW!
© 2013 MARVEL